Unstuck and On Target!

Second Edition

Unstuck and On Target!

An Executive Function Curriculum to Improve Flexibility, Planning, and Organization

Second Edition

by

Lynn Cannon, M.Ed.
The Ivymount School
The Maddux School
Rockville, Maryland

Lauren Kenworthy, Ph.D.
George Washington University School of Medicine
Children's National Health System
Washington, D.C.

Katie C. Alexander, OTD, OTR/L
The Occupational Therapy Institute
La Mesa, California

Monica Adler Werner, M.A.
The Ivymount School
Rockville, Maryland

and

Laura Gutermuth Anthony, Ph.D.
University of Colorado School of Medicine
Children's Hospital Colorado
Aurora, Colorado

PAUL·H· BROOKES PUBLISHING CO®

Baltimore • London • Sydney

·P A U L·H·
BROOKES
PUBLISHING CO.®

Paul H. Brookes Publishing Co.
Post Office Box 10624
Baltimore, Maryland 21285-0624
USA

www.brookespublishing.com

Typeset by Absolute Service, Inc., Towson, Maryland.
Manufactured in the United States of America by
Integrated Books International, Dulles, Virginia.

Cover image © iStockphoto / kali9.
Clip art © iStockphoto.

ISBN (paperback): 978-1-68125-490-6
ISBN (EPUB): 978-1-68125-491-3
ISBN (PDF): 978-1-68125-492-0

Library of Congress Control Number: 2021900473

British Library Cataloguing in Publication data are available from the British Library.

10 9 8 7 6 5 4 3 2

2025 2024 2023 2022

Contents

Unstuck Fast Facts .... inside front cover
About the Online Materials ix
About the Authors xi
Foreword *John Elder Robison* xiii
Acknowledgments xvii
Introduction 1
Reinforcement System 13
Icon Glossary 17
Script Practice Throughout the Manual 19

Topic 1 **Foundational Skills** **23**

Lesson 1 *Get to Know You* 25
- Introduction 26
- Activity 1: Code of Conduct 28
- Activity 2: Who Knows Whom? 30
- Handout: All About Me! 31
- Closing 32
- Classroom Practice 1 34
- Home Practice 1 37

Lesson 2 *Introduction to Goal, Why, Plan, Do, Check* 39
- Introduction 40
- Activity 1: Introduction to GWPDC 42
- Activity 2: Wacky GWPDC 44
- Handout: Wacky GWPDC 45
- Closing 46
- Classroom Practice 2 47
- Home Practice 2 48

Lesson 3 *Emotional Identification* 49
- Introduction 50
- Activity 1: Feelings Target 52
- Visual: Feelings Target 53
- Materials: Feelings Target Cards 54
- Activity 2: How Does It Make Me Feel? 55
- Activity 3: Feelings Chain 56
- Visual: Feelings Chain Scenarios 59
- Handout: Feelings Chain Blank 60
- Closing 62
- Classroom Practice 3 63
- Home Practice 3 64

Lesson 4 *What Can You Do to Feel Better?* 65
- Introduction 66
- Activity 1: Disappointment and Coping 68
- Handout: Disappointment and Coping 69
- Activity 2: Coping Skills Investigation 70
- Handout: How to Feel Just-Right 71
- Handout: Just-Right Strategies Investigation 72
- Handout: My Mission to Get Back to Just-Right 73
- Handout: Deep Breathing 74
- Activity 3: Strategy Cards 75
- Handout: Strategy Card Examples 76
- Additional Activity: Coping Choices 77
- Closing 79

	Classroom Practice 4	80
	Home Practice 4	81
Topic 1 Progress Report		82
Topic 2	**What Is Flexibility?**	**83**
Lesson 5	*Flexibility Investigation*	84
	Introduction	85
	Activity 1: Flexible vs. Rigid Scavenger Hunt	86
	Activity 2: Flexible Is Faster (and More Efficient)	87
	Closing	88
	Classroom Practice 5	89
	Home Practice 5	90
Lesson 6	*Flexibility*	91
	Introduction	92
	Activity 1: Mystery Word—Flexibility	93
	Handout: Mystery Word 1	94
	Educator Guide: Mystery Word 1 Key	95
	Handout: *Unstuck and On Target!* Dictionary—Flexible	96
	Activity 2: As Flexible as Putty	97
	Handout: Flexible Fun	99
	Handout: Fun Putty Recipe	100
	Closing	101
	Classroom Practice 6	102
	Home Practice 6	103
Lesson 7	*Getting Stuck*	104
	Introduction	105
	Activity 1: Mystery Word—Stuck	106
	Handout: Mystery Word 2	107
	Educator Guide: Mystery Word 2 Key	108
	Handout: *Unstuck and On Target!* Dictionary—Stuck	109
	Activity 2: Flexible/Stuck Role Play	110
	Closing	111
	Classroom Practice 7	112
	Home Practice 7	113
Topic 2 Progress Report		114
Topic 3	**How to Be Flexible**	**115**
Lesson 8	*Plan A → Plan B*	117
	Introduction	118
	Activity 1: Mystery Words—Plan A → Plan B	119
	Handout: Mystery Word 3	120
	Educator Guide: Mystery Word 3 Key	121
	Handout: *Unstuck and On Target!* Dictionary—Plan A → Plan B	122
	Activity 2: Speed B	123
	Activity 3: Build a Plan A, B, C	124
	Handout: Build a Plan A, B, C	125
	Closing	126
	Classroom Practice 8	127
	Home Practice 8	128
Lesson 9	*Compromise*	129
	Introduction	130
	Activity 1: Mystery Word—Compromise	131
	Handout: Mystery Word 4	132
	Educator Guide: Mystery Word 4 Key	133
	Handout: *Unstuck and On Target!* Dictionary—Compromise	134
	Activity 2: Compromise Game	135
	Materials: Compromise Game Cards	137
	Closing	138

	Classroom Practice 9	139
	Home Practice 9	140
Lesson 10	*Big Deal/Little Deal*	141
	Introduction	142
	Activity 1: Mystery Words—Big Deal / Little Deal	144
	Handout: Mystery Word 5	145
	Educator Guide: Mystery Word 5 Key	146
	Handout: *Unstuck and On Target!* Dictionary—Big Deal / Little Deal	147
	Activity 2: Big Deal / Little Deal Practice	148
	Materials: Big Deal / Little Deal Cards	149
	Activity 3: Converting Big Deals to Little Deals	151
	Handout: Big Deal / Little Deal Scale	152
	Closing	153
	Classroom Practice 10	154
	Home Practice 10	155
Lesson 11	*Choice/No Choice*	156
	Introduction	157
	Activity 1: Mystery Words—Choice / No Choice	158
	Handout: Mystery Word 6	159
	Educator Guide: Mystery Word 6 Key	160
	Handout: *Unstuck and On Target!* Dictionary—Choice / No Choice	161
	Activity 2: Choice / No Choice Practice	162
	Materials: Choice / No Choice Cards	163
	Closing	165
	Classroom Practice 11	166
	Home Practice 11	167
Lesson 12	*Expect the Unexpected*	168
	Introduction	169
	Activity 1: Expect the Unexpected Introduction	170
	Activity 2: Handling the Unexpected Exploration	171
	Educator Guide: Handling the Unexpected Game Rules	172
	Materials: Handling the Unexpected Game Board	173
	Materials: Handling the Unexpected Game Cards	174
	Closing	176
	Classroom Practice 12	177
	Home Practice 12	178
Topic 3 Progress Report		179
Topic 4	**Why Be Flexible?**	**181**
Lesson 13	*The Advantages of Being Flexible*	182
	Introduction	183
	Activity 1: What to Do When What I Want Is Impossible	184
	Educator Script: My Two Choices	186
	Visual: Group Flexibility Chant	187
	Activity 2: Flexibility Freeway Game	188
	Educator Guide: Flexibility Freeway Game Rules	189
	Materials: Flexibility Freeway Game Board	190
	Materials: Flexibility Freeway Game Cards	191
	Closing	197
	Classroom Practice 13	198
	Home Practice 13	199
Lesson 14	*Being Flexible Can Make Good Things Happen*	200
	Introduction	201
	Activity 1: Flexibility Powers	202
	Educator Script: Flexibility Gives You Power Scenarios	203
	Activity 2: Flexible Reputation	204
	Educator Script: Marble Jar: Flexible Reputation Scenarios	206
	Closing	208

Classroom Practice 14 ... 209
Home Practice 14 ... 210
Topic 4 Progress Report ... 211

Topic 5 Your Goals: Getting What You Want ... 213
Lesson 15 Setting and Achieving Goals Using GWPDC ... 214
Introduction ... 215
Activity 1: Think Pink—GWPDC ... 216
Handout: Think Pink—GWPDC ... 217
Closing ... 218
Classroom Practice 15 ... 219
Home Practice 15 ... 220
Lesson 16 GWPDC Application and Practice ... 221
Introduction ... 222
Activity 1: Cereal ... 223
Additional Activity: What Is a Target Goal? ... 225
Additional Activity: Target Goal Example ... 226
Closing ... 227
Classroom Practice 16 ... 228
Home Practice 16 ... 229
Lessons 17 & 18 GWPDC Stations ... 230
Introduction ... 231
Activity 1: Plan B Strategies ... 232
Activity 2: GWPDC Stations ... 234
Handout: GWPDC Station 1 ... 236
Handout: Compromise Station 2 ... 238
Handout: GWPDC Station 3 ... 240
Materials: Distractor Game Cards Station 4 ... 241
Materials: Distractor Game Cards Answer Key Station 4 ... 242
Materials: Distractor Game Tracking Sheet Station 4 ... 243
Handout: GWPDC Station 5 ... 244
Handout: GWPDC Station 5 Scenarios ... 245
Closing ... 246
Classroom Practice 17 & 18 ... 247
Home Practice 17 & 18 ... 248
Lesson 19 Event Planning ... 249
Introduction ... 250
Activity 1: Planning a Class Event ... 251
Closing ... 253
Classroom Practice 19 & 20 ... 254
Home Practice 19 & 20 ... 255
Lesson 20 Event ... 256
Topic 5 Progress Report ... 257

Topic 6 Flexible/Goal-Directed Futures ... 259
Lesson 21 Interview (& Optional Game) ... 260
Introduction ... 261
Activity 1: Talk Show ... 262
Handout: Flexible Futures ... 263
Additional Activity: Four Corners ... 265
Educator Script: Four Corners Questions & Answer Key ... 266
Closing ... 267
Handout: Graduation Certificate ... 268
Classroom Practice 21 ... 269
Home Practice 21 ... 270
Topic 6 Progress Report ... 271

Appendix ... 273

Index ... 281

About the Online Materials

Unstuck and On Target! An Executive Function Curriculum to Improve Flexibility, Planning, and Organization, Second Edition, offers online companion materials to supplement and expand the knowledge and strategies provided in this text. All purchasers of the book may access, download, and print the handouts, resource materials, posters, and gameboards for educational purposes.

The online materials include:

- Two digital, print-ready gameboards, available as one-page 11" x 17" PDFs, two-page 8.5" x 11" PDFs, and PowerPoint files
- Four digital posters, available as print-ready PDFs and PowerPoint files
- 50+ handouts—digital downloads available as fillable PDFs

To access the materials that come with this book:

1. Go to the Brookes Publishing Download Hub: http://downloads.brookespublishing.com
2. Register to create an account or log in with an existing account.
3. Redeem the code 22nnLyW90 to access any locked materials.

About the Authors

Lynn Cannon, M.Ed., is a Social Learning Specialist at The Ivymount School and The Maddux School. Ms. Cannon received her master's degree in special education from the University of Virginia. For more than 15 years, she has worked as an educator, administrator, and program director, serving students with neurodevelopmental disabilities. Ms. Cannon is also a coauthor of *Solving Executive Function Challenges: Simple Ways to Get Kids with Autism Unstuck and on Target* (Paul H. Brookes Publishing Co., 2014), a resource guide for teachers and parents, and *The Conversation Club* (Autism Asperger Publishing Company, 2018), an instructional manual for teaching conversation skills to students with neurodevelopmental disabilities. Her research and teaching interests are in developing interventions and support materials for students with neurodevelopmental disabilities, therapists, educators, and their families. She is currently working with federal grant to develop IvySCIP, an assessment, individualized education program development tool, and curricular resource for children with neurodevelopmental disabilities.

Lauren Kenworthy, Ph.D., is Professor of Neurology, Pediatrics, and Psychiatry at the George Washington University School of Medicine and Director of the Center for Autism Spectrum Disorders at Children's National Health System. Dr. Kenworthy received her bachelor of arts degree from Yale University and her doctoral degree from the University of Maryland. Her research interests are in describing and treating the neuropsychological phenotype of autism. She is the author of more than 60 peer-reviewed publications and a coauthor of the *Behavior Rating Inventory of Executive Function* (*BRIEF*; Gioia, Isquith, Guy, & Kenworthy, 2015). She is completing a trial of Unstuck and On Target! in low-income schools for children with attention-deficit/hyperactivity disorder or autism spectrum disorder.

Katie C. Alexander, OTD, OTR/L, is an Occupational Therapist, a Clinician-Researcher, and Founder of The Occupational Therapy Institute, an organization dedicated to innovation and high-quality, evidence-based practices. Dr. Alexander received her bachelor of science and postprofessional graduate degrees from the University of Kansas Medical Center. For almost two decades, she has specialized in community and school-based intervention for individuals with neurodevelopmental disabilities and served as the founding program director for the Model Asperger Program at The Ivymount School. Her research and clinical interests are in developing interventions and supports that improve the daily lives of individuals with neurodevelopmental disabilities and their families. Through her work as an author and national presenter, Dr. Alexander remains committed to enhancing evidence-based and collaborative practices across professional disciplines.

Monica Adler Werner, M.A., is a Program Director for Development, Training and Consulting at The Ivymount School and parent coach in the Washington, D.C., area. Prior to that she was the director of the Model Asperger Program (MAP) at The Ivymount School. In that capacity, she has spearheaded the development of a social learning curriculum that emphasizes problem solving, self-advocacy and self-regulation while keeping students on track academically. She is a coauthor of the first edition of *Unstuck and On Target!* (Paul H. Brookes Publishing Co., 2011) and *Solving Executive Function Challenges: Simple Ways to Get Kids with Autism Unstuck and on Target* (Paul H. Brookes Publishing Co., 2014). She is the coauthor of numerous papers and posters about working with children with Asperger syndrome/high-functioning autism. Prior to joining The Ivymount School staff, Ms. Werner co-founded of Take2 Summer Camp, a program designed to pilot the application of evidence-based social skills programs. Ms. Werner has an undergraduate degree from the University of Pennsylvania and a master's degree from Johns Hopkins University. She has completed the coursework for her Board Certified Behavior Analyst certification.

Laura Gutermuth Anthony, Ph.D., is an Associate Professor in the Division of Child and Adolescent Psychiatry, Department of Psychiatry, University of Colorado School of Medicine, Children's Hospital Colorado. Dr. Anthony completed a dual degree doctoral program in clinical and developmental psychology at the University of Illinois, Chicago, in 1997. Since then, she has focused her research and clinical work on children with neurodevelopmental disabilities and authored or coauthored more than 30 publications. She has also received funding for 11 federally funded and seven foundation research grants. Among these is an ongoing Patient Centered Outcome Research Institute (PCORI) Addressing Disparities Award to study the *Unstuck and On Target!* program with children who have autism and attention-deficit/hyperactivity disorder.

Foreword

Seven years ago I was proud to write the foreword for the original *Unstuck and On Target!* workbook. Since then, the range of *Unstuck* therapy has grown tremendously. From its start as therapy for younger kids, it's been proven effective and expanded to serve a wider range of people of all ages. Compared to the original, this release is updated and streamlined, and will be joined by companion editions in the very near future.

Unstuck is the first evidence-based therapy that helps people develop cognitive flexibility. Lack of flexibility is a problem with many autistic people, me included. We're said to love ritual and hate change. I've always struggled to see the other person's point of view, if I even realized they had one. Lack of flexibility is a disability, one that makes it harder for us to hold jobs or sustain relationships.

Flexibility is not just an autistic thing. Anyone can be rigid in his or her thinking. *Unstuck* was developed as an autism therapy, but it's really useful for anyone who wants to be more open. That's the thing about good behavioral therapies. They are developed for specific groups of people but end up broadly applicable to the whole population.

Flexibility is what allows us to accept that there may be more than one way to do things. I had terrible trouble with that, as a little boy. I watched other kids playing with trucks and dinosaurs, and they did it wrong! Sometimes the errors other kids made were so egregious, smoke would curl from my ears and it would hurt to watch.

Green blocks would be haphazardly piled on collections of red. Dump trucks would be parked upside down on piles of dirt and dinosaurs. Helicopters would be mixed with Easter bunnies. The natural order of things—so obvious to me—seemed invisible or irrelevant to most other kids.

Whenever I tried to show my playmates the error of their ways, they resisted. Even worse, they retaliated by making fun of me, calling me names, and excluding me from playgroups in the future.

It sure was hard being a kid who knew right from wrong, when it came to play. And the teachers seldom helped, telling me I was in the wrong even as I watched them play incorrectly too. Then I looked at myself, mocked and ridiculed. I never did figure out why, but that's how it was, and how it still is today.

When I look back on my childhood, I can date the beginning of my social success to the day I realized that the arrangement of blocks in the sandbox was not worth a fight. The other tykes might still be arranging their blocks wrong, but I learned to ignore them and stay reasonably calm. That was the only way I could tolerate other children playing next to me.

The authors of this book would say that's the first step in learning flexibility—putting up with other people and the things they do. It's an essential ability, if you want to have friends. However, tolerance is only the first step. Real success requires more.

I took the next step up the social skills ladder when I realized other kids might not be wrong at all. That is, their method of playing might be just as "correct" as my own, even though it was different. Of course, my way remained the best whether they knew it or not, but accepting that other techniques might also be valid opened my eyes. I realized I might learn different ways of doing things from other people.

That was a really important turning point for me, in the world of relationships. Suddenly, other people could show me how they did things, and I could watch and learn, without distress. If their methods worked better than mine, I could embrace them and make them my own. If my ideas were better, the other people learned from me.

That marked the beginning of give-and-take learning for me. I cannot overstate the importance of that skill. It's how we integrate the knowledge of those who came before us, and it's the foundation of group learning, teamwork, and much social progress. As valuable as that is, it's really hard to do. Accepting that someone else's idea may be better than ours raises the distinct possibility that other people may be as smart as us; maybe even more so. For an Aspergian kid who grew up as the center of the world, that is a bitter pill to swallow.

Unfortunately, I could only accept other ways of doing things in small doses, so my chances to grow through group interaction remained limited. I wasn't very skilled at accepting different points of view, and I didn't know how to practice, so doing so remained stressful. Where might I be if I had become really flexible and accepting as a kid? I might be a basketball coach, or the president of some big company, instead of a solitary Aspergian book writer.

Kids with Asperger's confront social challenges like I describe every single day. Helping them meet those challenges is vital, because childhood success resolving social issues predicts more general success later in life. A child's ability to emerge from disability depends in large part upon his ability to fit in and be accepted by other people.

My recognition of the power of flexibility came much later than it had to, because no one was there to teach me. In fact, when I went to school, school administrators did not even know social skills needed to be taught at all. Some kids, after all, are born with the apparatus for social skill, and they pick them up instinctively. Educators—many of whom were in that "instinctively social" group themselves—assumed everyone was like them.

Kids who did not have working social instincts were, in the thinking of the 1960s, deliberately ignoring the nonverbal signals of those around them. It was only in the 1980s that researchers realized that autism is the cause of this problem. Today we know it's a continuum and that autistic disorder includes both "not speaking" and "not understanding subtle social cues."

That realization led to the definition of what we now call the autism spectrum. We learned that some autism is obvious, when the person's spoken language and functionality are clearly impaired. Other autism, like my own, is hidden, when strong verbal skills mask the inability to read other people's unspoken messages.

Many techniques have been developed to help the more obviously impaired autistic population. Time and research have shown some of those interventions to be effective. Unfortunately, we do not yet have a comparable arsenal of well-proven tools to remediate social disability. We are just beginning to develop them. This book represents an important step in that direction.

Some folks would ask why we don't have more clinically validated methods of teaching social skills. The simple answer is that the need to teach these things is just now being recognized. The importance of reading and math has always been self-evident. If you want to prosper in our society, you need to be able to read a menu and count your money. When a kid can't walk or talk, the need to help him solve those problems is unmistakable.

Consequently, those are the areas where educators have directed most of their efforts. In choosing where to focus their teaching efforts, they have indeed been Masters of the Obvious. Today, we want and expect more. We want to help kids whose disability is real, but more subtle, and less easily defined.

What about the kids who "just don't act right?" Kids who don't do what their teachers want; kids who have no friends? Until recently, we did not understand what kind of help children like that might need. We are just now realizing the role of cognitive flexibility and how its lack can keep a person disabled. We've learned that unexpected behavior is often the result of innocent oblivion, as opposed to conscious defiance.

Now that we know unspoken social cues are clear to some people and invisible to others, can we teach the kids who miss those cues how to pick them up? I think we can, but the path to that understanding is not direct.

People who lack cognitive flexibility are more likely to adopt extreme positions in all aspects of life. As a kid my certainty that "my way was the only way to play" contributed to my isolation and consequent sadness. Later, my inability to accommodate other views made me criticize co-workers as incompetent fools, and "only I could do the job right." That cost me jobs and friendships, and in light of the teachable skills revealed in this book, it was a needless loss.

That is the vital point—*Unstuck* is a way to help people learn the flexibility to confront life's problems on our own or as part of a larger human group. My friends at The Ivymount School and Children's National Medical Center (CNMC) have spent the last decade developing and proving out the *Unstuck* curriculum you are about to meet in this book. Their writing is entirely based on real-world experience teaching social skills to autistic kids like me. Teaching staff worked with the CNMC psychologists and researchers to identify the most successful techniques for teaching flexibility, goal setting, and avoiding the trap of circular thinking—three essential abilities for success in today's world.

The techniques in *Unstuck* were developed for autistic kids, but they are actually much more broadly applicable. First of all, these techniques are obviously useful for any person who lacks cognitive flexibility, autistic or not. In addition, it's evident that the concepts translate to people of any age. In fact, the authors are working on editions of this book for older people right now.

I was very surprised to realize that I could use ideas from *Unstuck* in my own life to avoid the traps of circular negative thought that have plagued me most of my life. I am more receptive to alternate points of view, which makes me more successful on all fronts. As an autistic person and as a father of an autistic son, I can say from experience that the techniques in this book work. I therefore recommend them based on my own experience.

With all this said, there may still be time when flexibility fails. When that happens, I suggest the following wise counsel:

There is an Old Russian Proverb.
When times get hard, and the cupboards are bare,
And the kids stop working and start screaming . . .
The noisiest child is the first into the stew pot.

We ate the first kid, but the others were guided by that example and this wisdom and grew up healthy and strong. I hope you are able to put this to good use.

John Elder Robison
Author of Look Me in the Eye *(2007),* Be Different *(2011),*
Raising Cubby *(2013), and* Switched On *(2016)*
Neurodiversity Scholar, The College of William & Mary
Visiting Professor of Practice, Bay Path University

Acknowledgments

The authors thank the people with autism, attention-deficit/hyperactivity disorder, their families, and their teachers who have inspired and guided us throughout the creation of *Unstuck and On Target!*

We also thank staff from the Take2 Summer Camp, The Ivymount School Model Asperger Program, Children's National Center for Autism Spectrum Disorders, and many schools in the Washington, D.C./Virginia region, who contributed to the development of this curriculum. They tested lessons, suggested modifications, and collected data on the curriculum's efficacy. Most important, they encouraged us during the long journey that has culminated in this evidence-based second edition.

To the children and their families who have educated and inspired us and who make the world a richer place through their unique insights and perspectives

To Mark Ylvisaker, whose work on executive function intervention strategies motivated this curriculum; prior to his untimely death, Mark's generous collaboration with us guided many initial facets of this intervention

Introduction

GOAL OF THIS MANUAL

Unstuck and On Target! is a plan of action for teaching students how to be more flexible, planful, and goal directed. The goal of this intervention is twofold:

1. To increase the cognitive flexibility, organization, and planning abilities of students with executive dysfunction so that they can more easily shift from topic to topic, task to task, and person to person; consider new ideas, alternative beliefs, or another person's point of view; and work independently on multistep tasks in the classroom and beyond.
2. To provide the intervention in a way that works in the classroom and ultimately creates more time for the teacher to focus on teaching and less time managing behavior.

WHO WILL BENEFIT FROM THIS INTERVENTION?

Unstuck and On Target! is designed for 8- to 11-year-old students who have difficulties with flexibility, organization, and planning. Specifically, school-age children who may have autism spectrum disorder (ASD), attention-deficit/hyperactivity disorder (ADHD), anxiety, or other related problems, who also have average IQ and at least a second-grade language and reading level.

WHO SHOULD PROVIDE THIS INTERVENTION?

Unstuck and On Target! is designed for use in a small, school-based weekly group of students led by a professional (teacher, psychologist, social worker, speech-language therapist, occupational therapist, counselor, or highly trained teaching assistant). Those implementing this curriculum should have basic skills in working with students with special needs, including an understanding of positive reinforcement techniques, and should read the entire manual before beginning the curriculum. *Unstuck and On Target!* has also been successfully used by clinicians and parents in small group or individual sessions.

GUIDE TO THE LESSON PLANS

This manual includes 21 lessons, which are divided among six topics.

Topics

Each topic begins with an overview page that summarizes the topic, expected outcomes, and background on the rationale for the topic. The information on this page covers the material for all of the lessons included in that topic. Each topic includes a progress report. This is designed to help monitor student progress throughout the curriculum and communicate progress with parents and caregivers.

Lessons

Each lesson plan has the same structure and includes:

- A statement of the purpose of the lesson
- A list of required materials
- Suggestions for modifications
- Descriptions of each activity
- Handouts

Every lesson has a standard opening and closing routine. The lesson is introduced to the students in a Goal, Why, Plan, Do, Check (GWPDC) format in order to reinforce a key script taught in *Unstuck and On Target!* for completing any multi-step task. Each lesson also begins with a summary of the previous lesson (i.e., Lightning Round), highlighting the vocabulary students have learned. Each lesson ends with the review and completion of the GWPDC.

It is critical that you completely understand the lessons before beginning them with the students. Read through the entire topic before beginning instruction in order to gain a full understanding of the skills being taught and how the lessons fit together, as well as prepare and gather materials. You know your students best, and an overall understanding of the lessons will allow you to pace and adapt lessons as you deem appropriate. Note that some lessons may require you to gather additional materials not typically found in a classroom or school. Those lessons are marked with 🛒 throughout the manual. For other lessons, you may need to spend a bit more time preparing (e.g., cutting materials out), and those lessons are marked with ✂.

Home and Classroom Practice

Each lesson includes a Home Practice handout (available in English and in Spanish) and a Classroom Practice handout. The goal of these handouts is to:

- Provide additional practice opportunities
- Share key scripts, vocabulary, and concepts with families and classroom teachers
- Promote generalization across settings by encouraging families and classroom teachers to use similar language and practice concepts at home and in the classroom.

The students will benefit from going over their Home Practice handout before they take it home. To promote generalization you are encouraged to share the Classroom Practice handout with school personnel who interact with your students.

OVERVIEW OF *Unstuck and On Target!*

The *Unstuck and On Target!* curriculum has the following major goals:

- Teaches *what* flexibility is through concrete, hands-on experiments with physical and cognitive flexibility, and a specific vocabulary (e.g., *flexibility, Plan A → Plan B, stuck*), which is then used consistently throughout the intervention.
- Explains *why* it is important to be flexible. The curriculum provides explicit instruction to students on the benefits of being flexible (e.g., it gives them more choices, it helps them become a better friend).
- Teaches students *how* to be flexible by emphasizing routines and self-regulatory scripts that are continuously practiced and reinforced until they are automatic.
- Teaches *what* goals are and *how* to achieve them. The curriculum contains lessons to help students focus on what their goals are and distinguish major or target goals (e.g., getting good grades, making a friend) from distractors.
- Teaches a routine and script for setting a goal and completing any type of multiple step activity, project, or assignment. GWPDC is a universal strategy that improves executive functioning, efficacy, and independent work habits for a variety of tasks. It promotes goal-directed behavior, sustained effort, problem solving, self-monitoring, and flexibility. It is such a critical strategy that we use it as the framework for every lesson and embed it in activities as often as possible. We invite you to do the same, and we often find that educators experience such success with GWPDC that they integrate it throughout their teaching.
    - *How does GWPDC work?* It makes goal setting explicit and easy to understand. Making the plan explicit helps students learn to plan more effectively and provides an opportunity to build flexibility through the use of Plan A, Plan B, Plan C, and so on. Being explicit about checking the plan fosters self-monitoring and flexibility by detecting when a plan is not producing the desired results and adjusting the plan when needed.
- Teaches students how to cope when being flexible and using goal-directed behavior is hard. Positive reinforcement and humor are embedded throughout the curriculum, as they both have magical powers for shaping the behavior of students. The curriculum also teaches coping strategies for those times when being flexible is especially hard.

WHAT YOU NEED TO KNOW ABOUT EXECUTIVE FUNCTION

What Is Executive Function?

Executive function is a set of brain-based abilities that help people control their behavior (e.g., stay seated at desk) and reach their goals (e.g., finish something with multiple steps, like getting ready for school). There are many different brain-based abilities that make up executive function, including:

- **Initiation** (getting started on something quickly and easily)
- **Inhibition** (impulse control, "putting on the brakes," and "thinking before acting")
- **Flexibility** (shifting from one activity or idea to another, accepting a different way of seeing or doing things)

- **Working memory** (keeping information in mind while performing a task, e.g., remembering directions someone told you while you drive to your destination)
- **Organization** (keeping track of materials, understanding what the main point is, seeing the big picture, and knowing what is top priority at any given time)
- **Planning** (developing, carrying out, and modifying a plan of action, e.g., science fair project)
- **Self-monitoring** (tracking your performance, e.g., "How am I doing?," "Am I doing what I am supposed to be doing?")

This curriculum focuses specifically on four aspects of executive functioning: flexibility, organization, planning, and monitoring skills.

What Is Flexibility?

Students who have biologically based rigidity and inflexibility can have difficulty with the following:

- Making transitions
- Tolerating changes and unexpected events
- Responding to feedback
- Coming up with new ways to approach a problem
- Accepting flexible interpretations of rules or events
- Managing an intense emotional feeling
- Responding to the needs or interests of friends
- Negotiating with others
- Accepting differing viewpoints

In general, flexibility skills are essential for school and social success, and are a primary focus of this curriculum. Sometimes, however, inflexibility is adaptive. For example, most of us have a morning routine that we more or less follow when getting ready to leave the house. This prevents us from leaving the house before realizing we forgot to brush our teeth. Sometimes inflexibility is essential for students with executive functioning problems, who can be easily overwhelmed in social, group, and novel situations. Once overwhelmed, children with executive function difficulties get more anxious, impulsive, or otherwise behave inappropriately. The risks they run at such times are profound, given the social isolation, teasing, and bullying they can experience at the hands of peers and even adults. Ari Ne'eman, co-founder of the Autism Self-Advocacy Network, offers this analogy to explain the protective function of inflexibility:

> "In a mine field, anyone would be very cautious and resistant to making any sudden, unplanned moves. This is similar to what it is like in social situations for those of us with autism." (personal communication)

Thus, inflexibility serves a role in limiting the amount of unexpected events to which the student must respond. For this reason, it is imperative that adults provide predictable structure and routine as described in the Prerequisites for Successful Implementation of *Unstuck and On Target!* section later in this Introduction.

What Is Planning and Organization?

Students who have biologically based problems with planning and organization can have difficulty with the following:

- Setting realistic goals
- Predicting how long something will take
- Following a series of steps to reach a goal
- Integrating information into a unified understanding
- Showing what they know in a timely manner without undue effort
- Understanding that completing homework today will be important for getting a good grade in the future
- Turning in work that has been completed
- Getting started on a multiple step project
- Showing how they calculated an answer when completing a problem
- Supporting ideas in writing
- Following directions in class (especially when they aren't written down)
- Knowing what steps and materials are needed to complete a project
- Drawing inferences

This curriculum shows you how to teach key organizational and planning skills and routines, like goal setting. In addition, just like with flexibility, students also need specific accommodations for these problems. Just as the inflexible student needs to be warned when a change will occur, the disorganized student needs an extra visual reminder in the classroom to turn homework in. Increased communication with parents to help them organize their children at home is also often needed (e.g., an email letting a parent know when a student has not brought homework to school). Breaking a big task down into a series of smaller steps and checking in with the student after each step is completed is another important accommodation for most students with organization/planning problems.

When inflexibility and disorganization combine with other executive function challenges, like problems with self-awareness and self-monitoring, it makes it very hard for children to get even basic tasks done. The following short stories about Michael and Lorraine show what this looks like in real life.

Michael and Lorraine are smart 10-year-old twins. Michael has ADHD. Lorraine does not. Here is an example of how Michael and Lorraine's executive function abilities affect them in school during a reader writer workshop class. They are both articulate children with good spelling and grammar skills. They both generally express good ideas in class discussion and clearly have the verbal knowledge to tackle today's assignment. They are starting a new unit on biography and the assignment is to pick a hero that they want to read and write about. **Table 1** describes what happens when they try to put their knowledge into action.

Table 1. What does flexible, organized, and goal-directed planning look like at school?

Michael	Lorraine
Michael arrives a few minutes late to his class because he is generally ***disorganized*** with his materials, had forgotten his notebook, and had to go back and get it. He doesn't hear the teacher's full introduction but sees on the blackboard that the students are to select a hero to read and write about. He doesn't understand or note the importance of the required task sequence, write anything down about the assignment, or ***plan*** the steps he needs to take to complete it. He *does* decide immediately that he will read all about dolphins. He loves sea mammals and thinks that dolphins are his heroes because they are surviving against all odds.	Lorraine is on time to class, is well ***organized,*** and has a notebook with a section for reader writer workshop in which she writes down the directions as the teacher is both saying them and writing them on the board. Lorraine also writes the draft due dates in her agenda book and makes a ***plan*** about when she needs to complete specific parts of the assignment.
Michael's teacher saw that he arrived late so she checks-in individually with him about whether he understands the assignment and has picked a topic. Michael says yes, although he hasn't written down any details. He says he will write about dolphins and is ***inflexible*** when his teacher says that the hero has to be a human being. He argues with the teacher ***impulsively***. His teacher spends 5 minutes helping Michael calm down, and with her help, Michael agrees to pick Jacques Cousteau, a famous sea explorer who had a special fondness for sea mammals.	*She* ***initiates (gets started on)*** the project easily and thinks about who she could pick for her hero. She considers several options and ***flexibly*** considers each in terms of how easy it will be to get information on the person and also how interesting the person is to her. She picks Marie Curie.
Without a ***plan*** for completing the assignment and still ***stuck*** on dolphins, Michael heads straight for the tiny classroom library, which has a book on dolphins he has been wanting to look at. He knows he needs to investigate Cousteau, but figures that there might be something in this book about him. As he reads the book, however, he is quickly ***distracted from the goal*** of writing a biography and enjoys the pictures of dolphins. He is surprised when the teacher says class is over and is upset because he hasn't finished the book. The teacher sees his distress and again comes to his desk and works out a plan with him so he can take the book home overnight. She also tells him that for homework he needs to research Cousteau on the internet to find 3 sources about him.	*Lorraine* ***checks/monitors*** time and sees that she has 20 minutes left in the class period. She asks the teacher if she can go to the library to search for sources. Lorraine gets permission and uses her library time effectively because she remains ***focused on her goal*** of finding 3 books on Marie Curie. She returns with 3 books as class is ending.
Michael arrives to class the next day without the homework. He is ***distracted*** and starts chatting with a tablemate about dolphins until the teacher checks in 1:1 with him again, and asks if he has found 3 sources yet. He says no, he forgot—so she asks a parent volunteer to help him find 3 books on Cousteau in the library. He finds the books and starts to take notes on one of them. However, he has trouble ***organizing*** and separating the details from the main point. He also hates to write and writes down very little. The next day Michael leaves the books at home. He gets upset and is ***stuck*** on the idea that he can only read the books at home when the teacher sits down with him to suggest getting 1 other book to read that day in class. The teacher e-mails Michael's parents and asks them to help him work on the project over the weekend.	Lorraine arrives at class the next day with the 3 books she has checked out and continues to follow her plan. She reads through 1 of the books and takes notes. Class comes to an end and she ***checks/monitors*** how far she has gotten in the assignment and realizes that tomorrow she will have to complete notes on the other two books, which she does.

Michael	Lorraine
On Monday, Michael comes in with notes he dictated to his mother and his teacher gives him a second copy of the writing prompts for the biography. Michael writes a 4-sentence paragraph with short sentences.	On Monday, Lorraine brings her notes to class, using both her agenda and her good ***working memory*** skills to keep track of the fact that today she will work on her rough draft. She writes a well-***organized*** rough draft using the prompts the teacher has provided and gives it to the teacher to review.
The next day, Michael refuses to make any edits based on the teacher's feedback. His teacher decides to try a new strategy and lets him dictate to a classroom volunteer. He produces much more information this way, but is still ***poorly organized*** and does not follow the rubric.	Lorraine ***flexibly*** incorporates the teacher's edits and turns in a final version of her biography that includes all components described in the assignment rubric.
Outcome: Michael did little reading, learned no new material, and did not respond to the writing prompt. His writing was below grade level and his verbal abilities. His teacher is concerned by his "lack of effort" and motivation to succeed in her class.	**Outcome:** Lorraine got an opportunity to explore a new hero in her area of interest, science. She gained research skills, and practiced her free writing and revising skills. She also enhanced her reputation with her teacher who sees her as an intelligent, hard-working girl.
Amount of 1:1 teacher time required: 60 mins.	**Amount of 1:1 teacher time required:** 10 mins.

PREREQUISITES FOR SUCCESSFUL IMPLEMENTATION OF *Unstuck and On Target!*

This curriculum will teach kids like Michael the skills that made Lorraine so successful on her assignment, but specific supports have to be in place before Michael will be able to learn new skills. Next, we describe basic supports that should be in place within the school, classroom, and teacher–student interactions.

A Flexible and Supportive School Team

Students learn best when there is a good fit between their brain-based abilities and the environmental and task demands of school. When this doesn't occur naturally, there are three possible solutions:

1. The student learns new skills and adapts to the environment. The *Unstuck and On Target!* curriculum is designed to teach students new flexibility, goal setting, and organization skills so that they can be more effective independent learners at school.
2. The school team adapts or adjusts the environment to accommodate the student. Because many students with executive dysfunction are in inclusive environments that are designed for people who are naturally organized and flexible, the match between their brain and the demands of the setting is frequently poor. Just as a student in a wheelchair is entitled to accommodation, so is the student with executive function difficulties. These children need to develop the self-awareness and self-advocacy skills to determine when to ask for accommodation. Mastering these self-awareness and self-advocacy skills is a long-term process that begins with adults providing basic accommodations such as those described below.
3. Selected, unacceptable environments are avoided. There are some situations or tasks that pose unacceptable levels of risk for the student with executive dysfunction. They may require such levels of effort that the student is then incapable of further work. They may overwhelm the student and create high risk for inappropriate behaviors, or they may create high levels of anxiety. The student needs to learn how to recognize these situations and avoid them. For example, it is sometimes best for a student to eat lunch in a classroom rather

than in a large, crowded cafeteria. Early in a student's educational experience, an adult will need to identify these situations or tasks and create suitable alternatives. With time and development, the student will be better able to recognize these moments on his or her own.

A supportive school environment includes these features:

1. The school team doesn't blame or punish a student for a behavior that is not within his or her volitional control. We know that it is not effective to blame a child with dyslexia for not learning to read because it will not successfully change the behavior or foster meaningful progress and it creates a toxic atmosphere that contaminates other teaching activities. In other words, we know that the child ***can't*** learn to read through typical strategies, not that he ***won't*** or chooses not to read. The same is true for executive dysfunction, and it's important for educators to approach executive function difficulties with the same "can't" not "won't" understanding. **Table 2** lists some commonly confused sources of behavior in students with executive dysfunction.

2. The school team provides important accommodations. Commonly needed accommodations include:
   - Preferential seating
   - Maintaining predictable routines, posting schedules
   - Extensive use of priming and visual cues (see next section)
   - Helping with organization of desk and work materials
   - Offering choices whenever possible
   - Reducing the number of staff involved with a student
   - Respecting self-soothing, repetitive routines (e.g., sticking to a schedule, following favored eating rituals) that are not otherwise harmful.
   - Extra contact/collaboration with parents

3. The student has at least one coach or "safe" adult at school. A safe person understands the student and is available to the student on an as-needed basis to review difficult interactions with others, explain confusing situations, and advocate for the student's needs. The safe person also seeks the student out regularly to monitor, teach, and actively coach executive skills.

4. There is a structured behavior management system based on positive behavior supports. A schoolwide positive behavioral interventions and supports system is ideal.

5. The school team works together to reinforce the *Unstuck* vocabulary and scripts and behaviors. The intervention will be successful only if it is consistently implemented throughout the student's environment.

Table 2. Willful misbehavior or different brain?

What looks like "won't"	May actually be "can't"
Opposition, stubbornness	Cognitive inflexibility, effort to avoid being overwhelmed
Lack of will ("He can do it if he wants to")	Difficulty in shifting, variable attention, disorganization
Rudeness	Difficulty controlling impulses
Self-centeredness	Impaired social cognition/ability to take another's perspective
Lack of effort ("She doesn't try")	Poor initiation, impaired planning, or attention
Inability or refusal to put good ideas on paper	Poor fine motor skills, disorganization
Sloppy, erratic work	Poor impulse control, self-monitoring, overload
Refusal to control outbursts	Overload, poor impulse control
Lack of sensitivity to others ("He doesn't care what others think")	Impaired nonverbal social cues, impulsivity
Lack of interest in school	Impaired attention and working memory

A Flexible, Organized, and Supportive Educator

Every educator has an opportunity and a responsibility to establish the culture for his or her classroom. Flexibility and planning, like laughter, are contagious. Children are most likely to thrive and acquire flexibility and planning skills in a classroom culture in which educators and students alike consistently demonstrate and value flexibility, goal setting, and planning. While good teachers may use many of these strategies already, specific ways that educators can explicitly increase their use of these skills in the classroom include the following:

- Make smooth and calm transitions between tasks, activities, and expectations; respond flexibly when changes and unexpected events occur.
- Avoid power struggles. For example, when a teacher makes a request and a student refuses to obey, the teacher refrains from making a second, more demanding request or imposing a consequence that the student refuses.
- Use a high ratio of praise to corrections (target 5:1). Facilitate better performance through positive actions such as instructional scaffolding (providing the supports needed for success), elaboration (expanding on a topic to increase understanding), and modeling (demonstrating a new skill for students to learn by watching) *before* trying to stop inadequate performance with consequences and corrections **(Table 3).**
- Provide active priming, or warnings that something is going to happen. To be effective, priming should occur at least several minutes before a student has to make any change, such as stopping work, changing classes, or interrupting an activity. When priming, it is

Table 3. Positive versus negative: Positive teacher responses can help change the direction of an interaction; negative teacher responses can lead to negative student responses and, ultimately, an entrenched negative cycle.

	Keeping it positive or neutral	Keeping it negative
Teacher	(Calmly) The class is ending in 10 minutes. I'm going to get your schedule so we can prepare for your next class.	(Urgently) Hurry up and finish your worksheet. You need to get your materials for the next class.
Johnny	I'm still working.	I'm still working.
Teacher	You can keep working. Here is your checklist. What do you need to do next?	You should have thought of that when you were talking in class earlier.
Johnny	(Looks at list and puts math book and homework in backpack)	I was bored! I hate math!
Teacher	Great. While you're putting your homework in your backpack, I'll read the next item—check to make sure there are no papers in your desk.	You haven't even put your math work away! You have to hurry up!
Johnny	(Checks desk and puts pencil in backpack)	I hate school. I don't even want to be here.
Teacher	What's next on your checklist?	Fine. Then maybe it's time for you to visit the principal's office.
Johnny	Get out your English book.	(Feeling overloaded) No!
Teacher	Yes! Do you know where it is?	You need to lower your voice inside!
Johnny	Great! Right where it should be! Good thinking, put-ting it back in place yesterday.	That's it. I can't take this anymore! (Storms out of the class)
Teacher	Bye! (Johnny goes to next class)	(Escorts Johnny to the principal's office)

important to provide concrete and explicit direction about what a student needs to do to prepare for the upcoming change. For example, a student may have an easier time stopping a writing task if he or she is directed to finish the specific sentence he or she is working on and is told when he or she may have time to finish the activity.

- Communicate clear, explicit, and specific expectations for the work to be done, expected behavior, and how students should set and achieve goals.
- Provide clear, written, step-by-step instructions for any multiple-step task. Keep white boards near to quickly "make it visual."
- Maintain an organized classroom so that clutter and visual distractions are minimized and there are clear routines for turning in work, getting ready to go home, and making the transition between classes.
- Provide specific visual reminders to students who have trouble following classroom routines.
- Exhibit a calm demeanor, an empathic understanding, a positive outlook, and high expectations. These personality traits are critical for any educator, but especially so for those working with students with executive function difficulties.
- Problem-solve both internally and externally (with students) to detect when and why student performance breaks down. For example, say that a student refuses to write a paragraph on his or her summer vacation. Instead of assuming noncompliance, the educator acknowledges the student's difficulty and works to discover why the student has refused the task. Maybe the student doesn't know where to start, has trouble with fine motor tasks, or doesn't have a pencil. Finding solutions and compromises (a writing rubric, providing a pencil, or allowing the student to work on a computer) are easier once a specific reason has been identified.
- Have self-knowledge. To be an effective educator, you must know yourself in the classroom. What upsets you? Are there certain students or behaviors that are triggers for you? Are you ever rigid or disorganized in the classroom? When? What do you do when you are rigid? Learning your own early signs and applying strategies that work for you will increase your flexibility, organization, and efficacy.
- "Think out loud," or provide explicit instruction. Students with executive function difficulties may not realize that being flexible and setting a goal or following a plan will increase their chances of making a friend or getting better grades, particularly since they have difficulty learning from their own experience or from watching other people. These students do better when key concepts are taught explicitly and are continuously reinforced through the technique of making the implicit executive function demands of situations explicit. By highlighting your own experience of situations that require executive function skill and explicitly identifying flexible, organized responses, you can provide your students with a working framework for how they can resolve other difficult situations. For example, you might say, "I was hoping to use the projector to show you this worksheet, but the bulb is burned out. I am going to be flexible and give you each your own worksheet instead."
- Treat students with respect and as active partners in their education. Collaborative relationships do not require teachers to give in to students or give up their expectations. In fact, they often facilitate increased effort and output from students. Collaborative relationships do require a willingness to give choices within the framework of clear expectations (e.g., allowing a student to choose the topic of an essay). They also require both parties to listen to what the other has to say. One student noted that he really wanted "teachers to

listen to what kids say and not assume things about us, and also take our opinions into account" when appropriate.

- Empower students. As you identify those times of day when a student would benefit from an accommodation (e.g., taking a 5-minute reading break after lunch) or those environments that are a poor fit for the student (e.g., a loud cafeteria), support the student in discovering for him- or herself what he or she needs. This is an essential first step to teaching effective self-advocacy skills. Here are some examples of what you might say:
    - "I noticed that the cafeteria is very loud and you cover your ears when you are in there. That makes it hard for you to talk or eat your food. Can you help me think of a spot that would be less noisy where you could have lunch?"
    - "You have told me that you are really tired when you come in the morning. After you went on the swings yesterday you had a lot more energy and you were able to start your work. What strategy should we use when you come in feeling tired in the morning?"
- Provide an optimal level of support through just-right cuing techniques. Use guided practice with faded cuing to gradually build new skills, one step at a time. Guided practice begins with concrete tasks and a high level of teacher support (i.e., verbal prompting and redirection). The role of the adult is to scaffold behavior only as much as the student needs in order to be successful, not to serve as a crutch or to create a dependency. Thus, teachers should gradually fade support and guidance as soon as students can demonstrate the skill independently. In the case of the *Unstuck and On Target!* intervention, teachers must be prepared initially to prompt the use of scripts and routines but should reduce prompting over time, providing just the level of support needed for success. In this regard, it is helpful to use the Socratic method of asking questions in place of providing answers (e.g., "What do you need to get started?") to find out how much information the student can generate without staff input. This process will enable the student to become independent and automatic in using the new vocabulary and scripts. Automaticity takes time, however, and repeated practice should be expected. Think of it as similar to the model of athletic coaching or music instruction, in which students perform the same drills and routines repeatedly before gaining mastery.

Reinforcement System

The purpose of this reinforcement system is to shape and reinforce student behavior and increase pro-social interactions. The hope is that the reinforcement system will improve the classroom culture by motivating students to stay on task, demonstrate target skills, and make positive contributions to the group. Within the structured reinforcement system there is complete flexibility for you to tailor the motivators to your students—their individual needs and what is most motivating to them (see the Troubleshooting section for tips).

SYSTEM CONSTRUCT

- **Tally Marks**—Every time a student demonstrates a target behavior (uses one of the *Unstuck and On Target!* skills, contributes to the group in a positive way, or demonstrates any skill you would like to see continue), he or she is awarded a tally in a *group goal* box visual. During an *Unstuck and On Target!* session you should aim to deliver at least 10 tally marks.
- **Praise**—A critical component to increasing desired behaviors is to pair the tally with praise. Praise as a reinforcer for positive behavior helps to foster a **positive** and productive **relationship** between students and the teacher. Praise allows you to **tailor your feedback** to the individual social learning needs of the student. The rule of thumb is 5:1 (5 positive praise to every one corrective feedback). Praise should be **specific, true (genuine)**, and **immediate.**

  Example of 5:1 ratio: Please keep your hands in your space (corrective); Great job starting your work (praise); I love that you are keeping your body at least an arm's length from your neighbor (praise); The back table is working so quietly, I can tell everyone is focused (praise)

- **Thermometer**—At the end of every social learning session, count the total number of tallies earned by the group. This amount is recorded on a group thermometer visual.
  - **What will we earn?** As a group, decide what students will earn for filling up the thermometer. As you decide on the group reward, you will want to make sure it is something motivating to the students and something you can sustain (not too time, labor, or financially intensive). When you select the group reward, post it at the

top of the thermometer so that students are constantly reminded of what they are working for.

Examples of group rewards: movies/YouTube clips, snack, game time, free time, homework pass, outside time, a menu of rewards for the students to choose from when they reach their goal

- **Next Steps:** This system is designed to be simple, with very little teacher preparation required. You might create a thermometer on paper and continue using it within the group until the goal is achieved. Or, you may prefer to quickly draw it on a whiteboard / chart paper before each group. You'll usually need to create a fresh tally box for each group—either directly on the whiteboard / chart paper or with a piece of paper taped to the front of the room. If you decide to use paper, remember that you'll need a fresh page each session. After group time, record the number of tallies on the goal thermometer.
- **How long will it take?** It is also important to consider the needs of your group—how long can the students wait for the reward and still remain motivated to earn tickets? This varies from group to group but should generally not be longer than 3 weeks. One reward per topic is probably a good goal.

REINFORCEMENT VISUALS

Group Goal Example

The group goal box and group thermometer visuals are displayed in the front of the room. The tally box starts empty at the beginning of each group.

Room 221's Race to the Top!

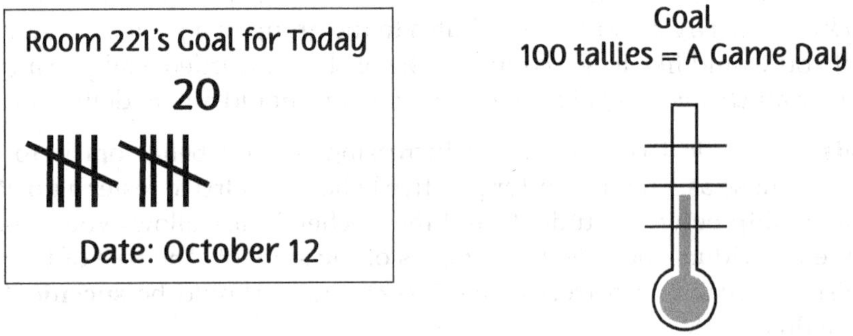

TROUBLESHOOTING

Note: See the Troubleshooting section in the Appendix for more troubleshooting questions/concerns and answers.

Concern: **My students should be motivated to behave; I don't feel like I should have to give them the external reinforcers to behave!**

The internal motivation that works for you and other students won't work in the same way for those with ASD or ADHD, because those rewards aren't always logical or explicit. You need to develop an explicit reward system. Change is hard for any of us, and most of us do better at working toward a big goal if there is a reward at the end, whether it is a chocolate after an unpleasant task or a new outfit when we lose weight. However, rewards are particularly important for students with ASD or ADHD. Both disorders have a profound effect on children's internal motivational systems: many children with ASD or ADHD may be motivated by the things in which they are interested but unable to be motivated to do the things you or other adults are interested in having them do just because you want them to do them.

When you want students to learn something new, especially something that does not come naturally, be sure you are offering a tangible, meaningful reward. When a skill is new, reward your students for each step they are able to perform. As their skills grow and develop, you should reward the ability to perform them independently.

Concern: What do I do if the tally marks are not motivating?

1. Integrate the reinforcement system into the daily routine that rewards expected behavior. Make this reward system as simple, clear, and flexible as possible. The easier it is to use and understand, the more likely you will be to use it. The more you use it, the more powerful the system becomes.
2. Give bonus points! Extra, unexpected points or rewards should be given for extra effort. Intermittent reinforcement is the most powerful kind of reinforcement. This is why slot machines work, or why a surprise $20 gift card for a job well done is more powerful than a $20 raise. Give bonus points for helping a classmate or friend; compromise; negotiate; or any other positive behavior you want to encourage.
3. Change the rewards frequently. Once your students "get used to" your rewards, you will need to change them to keep up their motivating effect. Try to be creative.
4. Your students may need to reach their thermometer goal more frequently. The tally marks will only be reinforcing if it is tied to a reward they are interested in.

Concern: How do I select a prize that is reinforcing to the whole group?

Some groups will have a difficult time agreeing on a prize. When that happens, you may have to choose the prize for them. Choose things you think your students would most enjoy (such as agreeing to wear a silly hat) if they meet their goal. Most elementary students love seeing their teachers do silly things. Other options are picking a list of funny, engaging, and short YouTube clips to watch or having the top-performing student (in groups where competition will not add difficulty) pick a number out of a basket and having that number indicate the prize. Again, try to be creative with the prizes, and change the options frequently.

Concern: Student behavior is not great these days and I am having trouble finding at least 10 things to give tally marks or praise for.

Sometimes an extra prompt, with clear expectation of success, can be helpful. For example, you might pick up your pen and wait silently with your pen poised over the tally box, and start rewarding as soon as you see good behavior. You may say, "I'm ready to see a good group!," "I'm ready to reward!" with a positive tone of voice and facial expression. Be ready to work a little harder to find things to reward, even if it means you are rewarding right before you think a student may do something that would warrant a correction. For example, if you see a student fidgeting and about to get up out of his seat, before he gets up say, "Thank you for sitting and being ready to learn" and give a tally. Usually this will preempt an unwanted behavior.

Also, avoid taking away points. Rewards and praise are much more effective than punishment, particularly for those with ASD (punishment can set off a new cycle of inflexibility, which can actually make things worse).

Concern: I feel like I am bribing my students with this reward system.

Rewards aren't the same thing as bribes: A bribe comes before the action (I pay you to vote a certain way on legislation tomorrow). A reward comes after the action (like your paycheck).

Concern: My students need a more immediate reinforcement, waiting until the thermometer is full is too long.

1. Use lots of visuals. Points should be awarded in a visual, systematic way, such as on a chart or with a tangible reward, and counted frequently throughout the day.
2. Be sure to give daily rewards. Points should be redeemed frequently for something the students find highly motivating (e.g., computer time, video time), and redeemed points can still count on the thermometer.

Icon Glossary

Goal, Why, Plan, Do, Check (GWPDC)

When you see this, there's a good opportunity to help students complete multiple-step activities by breaking them down into smaller, manageable tasks!

Flexible

When you see this, there's a good opportunity to help students recognize the benefits of being flexible in challenging or unexpected situations!

Stuck

When you see this, there's a good opportunity to help students recognize when they're "stuck" on something and think of ways to get "unstuck"!

A→B

Plan A→Plan B

When you see this, there's a good opportunity to help students recognize that if their first plan doesn't work, there are other options (Plans B, C, D, etc.) available to them!

C ?

Choice/No Choice

When you see this, there's a good opportunity to help students identify what is within their power to change and what is not!

D OR d

Big Deal/Little Deal

When you see this, there's a good opportunity to help students learn to distinguish what is important from what is not important!

Compromise

When you see this, there's a good opportunity to help students learn strategies for negotiating with others so both people get part of what they want!

Target Goal

When you see this, there's a good opportunity to help students identify their goals and the steps needed to achieve them!

Script Practice Throughout the Manual

Goal, Why, Plan, Do, Check

- "What is your goal?"
- "Did your plan help you accomplish your goal, or do we need a Plan B?"

Topic 1, Lesson 1: Introduction
Topic 1, Lesson 1: Classroom/ Home Practice
Topic 1, Lesson 2: Activity 1, Activity 2
Topic 1, Lesson 3: Classroom/ Home Practice
Topic 5, Lesson 15: Activity 1
Topic 5, Lesson 15: Classroom and Home Practice
Topic 5, Lesson 16: Activity 1
Topic 5, Lesson 16: Classroom / Home Practice
Topic 5, Lesson 17/18: Activity 1, Activity 2
Topic 5, Lesson 19: Activity 1
Topic 5, Lesson 19/20: Classroom/ Home Practice
Topic 6, Lesson 21: Activity 1, Additional Activity

Flexible

- "We can be flexible and make a Plan B."
- "I love how you were flexible."

Topic 2, Lesson 5: Activity 1, Activity 2
Topic 2, Lesson 5: Classroom/ Home Practice
Topic 2, Lesson 6: Activity 1, Activity 2
Topic 2, Lesson 7: Activity 2

Topic 4, Lesson 13: Activity 1, Activity 2, Activity 3
Topic 4, Lesson 14: Activity 1, Activity 2
Topic 4, Lesson 14: Classroom/ Home Practice
Topic 5, Lesson 17/18: Activity 1, Activity 2
Topic 5, Lesson 17/18: Classroom/ Home Practice
Topic 5, Lesson 17/18: Classroom/ Home Practice
Topic 6, Lesson 21: Activity 1, Additional Activity

Stuck

- "I'm getting stuck on this. How can I get unstuck?"
- "Since you got unstuck, now you can have more choices."

Topic 2, Lesson 7: Activity 1, Activity 2
Topic 2, Lesson 7: Classroom/ Home Practice
Topic 3, Lesson 9, Activity 2
Topic 4, Lesson 13: Activity 1, Activity 2, Activity 3
Topic 5, Lesson 17/18: Activity 1, Activity 2
Topic 6, Lesson 21: Activity 1, Additional Activity

A→B

Plan A→Plan B

- "What is our Plan B?"
- "I'm so glad we had a Plan B, so we could still accomplish our goals."

Topic 3, Lesson 8, Activity 1, Activity 2, Activity 3
Topic 3, Lesson 8: Classroom/ Home Practice
Topic 4, Lesson 13: Activity 1, Activity 2, Activity 3
Topic 5, Lesson 17/18: Activity 1, Activity 2
Topic 5, Lesson 17/18: Classroom/ Home Practice
Topic 6, Lesson 21: Activity 1, Additional Activity

C ?

Choice/No Choice

- "You have a choice. Let's look at all of your choices."

Topic 3, Lesson 11: Activity 1, Activity 2
Topic 3, Lesson 11: Classroom/ Home Practice
Topic 6, Lesson 21: Activity 1, Additional Activity

D OR d

Big Deal/Little Deal

- "How can we turn this big deal into a little deal? Let's make a plan."
- "I can tell this feels like a big deal. I have a suggestion for how we can turn it into a little deal."

Topic 3, Lesson 10: Activity 1, Activity 2, Activity 3
Topic 3, Lesson 10: Classroom/ Home Practice
Topic 6, Lesson 21: Activity 1, Additional Activity

Compromise

- "Let's compromise so we can both get some of what we want."
- "Something is better than nothing."

Topic 3, Lesson 9: Activity 1, Activity 2
Topic 3, Lesson 9: Classroom/ Home Practice
Topic 5, Lesson 17/18: Activity 1, Activity 2
Topic 5, Lesson 17/18: Classroom/ Home Practice
Topic 6, Lesson 21: Activity 1, Additional Activity

Target Goal

- "What is my Target Goal?"
- "Is that your Target Goal or a distracting goal?"

Topic 5, Lesson 16: Additional Activity
Topic 5, Lesson 16: Classroom / Home Practice
Topic 5, Lesson 17/18: Activity 1, Activity 2
Topic 5, Lesson 17/18: Classroom/ Home Practice
Topic 6, Lesson 21: Activity 1, Additional Activity

Expect the Unexpected

- "You were super flexible when we had to make that change—how did you do it?"
- "You really knew how to expect the unexpected!"

Topic 3, Lesson 12: Activity 1, Activity 2
Topic 3, Lesson 12: Classroom/ Home Practice

TOPIC 1

Foundational Skills

SPECIAL INSTRUCTIONS: Although it is important to provide the vocabulary and frameworks set forth in this topic, the group leader is expected to modify the activities as necessary to better meet the students' needs.

Summary: Topic 1 introduces foundational skills that promote successful participation in group sessions and implementation of the *Unstuck and On Target!* curriculum. It introduces a Code of Conduct (ground rules) for the group sessions and a universal script (or routine) for completing work and organizing the group sessions called Goal, Why, Plan, Do, Check (GWPDC). Topic 1 also teaches students how to use a visual rating tool to identify their feelings (Feelings Target), how to link feelings to behaviors and outcomes (Feelings Chain), and common coping techniques for managing overwhelming feelings (e.g., deep breathing).

Prerequisite skills: None

Related skills: Awareness of body, use of visual rating tool

OUTCOME—CRITERIA FOR MASTERY

1. The student understands and attempts to follow the code of conduct for group sessions.
2. The student can state the meaning of the goal and plan and check phases of the Goal, Why, Plan, Do, Check (GWPDC) routine.
3. Using a visual chart, the student can rate his or her current feeling state.
4. The student can identify and access several coping strategies and use them when needed.

TOPIC BACKGROUND AND RATIONALE

This topic introduces several foundational skills as well as a set of ground rules for behavior in the group sessions. Students are taught a standard operating procedure for reaching goals known as the Goal, Why, Plan, Do, Check (GWPDC). GWPDC is a fundamental script that underlies every session of *Unstuck and On Target!* It is a generic and widely applicable self-regulatory/problem-solving script that provides a template for approaching a problem, situation, or project. The first part of this script is an introduction to the concept of a goal. Making the definition of goal explicit is a very important step for students with executive dysfunction because they can easily over-focus on details and lose sight of the main reason for, or goal of, their activity. GWPDC breaks down any activity into small, achievable chunks, helping the student to focus on the right goal from the beginning. It promotes flexibility by encouraging the development of a plan, revision of the plan, and development of an alternative plan (Plan B). Students are encouraged to try things out (their plan) and then go back and check on the success of the plan. This provides a prompt for the self-monitoring that is often difficult for them. An additional virtue of this approach is that the focus is on the plan, not on the student's difficulties; therefore, a breakdown in the situation can be blamed on an unhelpful plan rather than on the student.

Topic 1 also introduces foundational skills for identifying feelings, linking feelings to actions and events, and using coping strategies effectively to manage overwhelming feelings. *Unstuck* teaches routines for regulating behavior in the face of flexibility demands and expectations for independent, goal-directed work (e.g., completing homework). These are hard skills for students with executive dysfunction and can be hindered by overwhelming feelings. Furthermore, students often struggle with identifying their feelings. As a result, they can fail to recognize their own stress until it is very high and they feel overwhelmed. It is important that instruction in executive function skills be accompanied by active support for increasing coping skills that will help students know what they feel and will give them strategies for managing overwhelming feelings.

Lesson 1 Get to Know You

PURPOSE

The purpose of this lesson is to welcome the students into the group, help them get to know one another, and generate a Code of Conduct. The Code of Conduct should serve as the guidelines for how students can be successful group members. The Code of Conduct creates a common language around behaviors and expectations. There are two activities in this lesson.

Materials Required for All Activities

Not Included

- Whiteboard or chart paper
- Regular markers (if using chart paper) or dry erase markers (if using a whiteboard and when using the poster; see Included list at right)
- Pencils
- Group Reinforcement Visual (i.e., group goal/tally box and thermometer)
- One full-size three-ring binder for each student to use as his or her *Unstuck and On Target! (UOT) Notebook*

Included

- GWPDC for Lesson 1
- Handout: All About Me!
- Code of Conduct poster
- Classroom Practice 1
- Home Practice 1

INTRODUCTION

Preview: GWPDC

Review
~3 minutes

Materials

Not Included

- Whiteboard or chart paper
- Regular markers (if using chart paper) or dry erase markers (if using a whiteboard and when using the poster; see Included list at right)

Included

- GWPDC for Lesson 1

Instructions

At the beginning of every session, post the Goal, Why, Plan, Do, Check (GWPDC) on the board before the lesson begins. Since this is your students' first time seeing a GWPDC, you will want to briefly explain that... *each time the group comes together you will have something you want to accomplish or a goal. The "W" stands for why. It is always useful to know why we want to achieve this goal. In order to accomplish the goal you will need to follow a plan and think about why the goal is important. Once you follow the plan, you always want to come back and check to see if your plan worked. This is what we will do when we get to the check section.*

For this first exposure to GWPDC we have chosen a *goal* or target number of tallies (20 tallies) the students will earn during group. This was designed to motivate students. Please select a number of tallies you think your students will be able to achieve. It is imperative the students experience success on this first day and see the benefits of their efforts to create buy-in for the program and establish motivation for continuing to earn tallies in future.

Review the GWPDC with the group.

Tips

★ As you move through the lesson, check off each step of the plan.

★ Integrate GWPDC language into your lesson. ("Wow, we are really working hard and getting closer to accomplishing our goal." "That was a great answer and definitely helping us accomplish our goal." "Remember, this goal is important because ________." "I am so glad we are staying on track and moving through our plan." "What is the next step in our plan?" "That fire drill was unexpected and we were unable to make it through all the steps of our plan.")

★ To keep students engaged have them check off steps of the plan as they are accomplished.

★ If students veer off topic, have them read the goal and ask if that conversation or activity will help the group accomplish the goal.

★ Use colors for each of the key words (e.g., Goal=red; Why=orange; Plan=blue; Do=green; Check=black); keep these consistent throughout the intervention. This consistency will help students more easily identify the part of the process they need to focus on.

★ Select a "target" number of tallies you think your students will be able to achieve.

G W P D C

Goal: Get to know the group and earn 20 tallies.

Why: We are working together to learn and earn our group reward. What you do in our group affects you, others, and the success of the group, and our code of conduct will help us each have a positive effect on the group. We need to know how to earn our reward, and if we know each other a little better, it will help us work together and earn our reward!

Plan:

1. Create the Code of Conduct
2. Finish All About Me! handout
3. Play Who Knows Whom? game
4. Review Home Practice
5. Check

Do: Follow the plan and earn tallies.

Check: How did it go? Did we accomplish our goal? Which Code of Conduct item was the easiest to follow? Which one was the hardest?

ACTIVITY 1

Code of Conduct

Group Brainstorm
~10 minutes

Materials

Not Included

- Whiteboard or chart paper
- Regular markers (if using chart paper) or dry erase markers (if using a whiteboard and when using the poster; see Included list at right)
- Group Reinforcement Visual

Included

- Code of Conduct poster

Code of Conduct Example

The Code of Conduct poster should be placed in the front of the room, displayed during each group. Leave room to add to it throughout intervention. Feel free to use language and items that will be meaningful and relevant to your group of students.

Group Rules

1. Listen when others are talking.
2. Respect other people's ideas.
3. Follow directions.

Group Goal Example

Use markers and chart paper (or dry erase markers and a whiteboard) to display the Group Reinforcement Visual. The reinforcement visual should include the group goal/tally box and a goal thermometer as described in the "Reinforcement System" section. The tally box starts empty at the beginning of each group. Please feel free to modify these to meet the needs of the students in your group (language, interests, etc.).

Room 221's Race to the Top!

Room 221's Goal for Today
20
Date: October 12

Goal
100 tallies = A Game Day

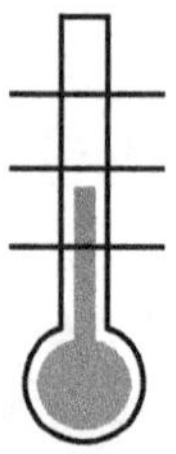

In this lesson students will generate components of the code of conduct by thinking about what behaviors the group *should* demonstrate to make the group successful. Students will also have the opportunity to decide how they would like to celebrate filling their *group goal thermometer*. Before the start of the lesson determine the parameters and structure for helping students determine their prize (see Reinforcement System overview).

Reinforce!

Give a tally for each student's contribution

"Great suggestion!"

Reinforce!

Tallies for demonstrating Code of Conduct behavior

"I like the way you were respectful of his idea!"

1. Code of Conduct—Explain to students that what they do affects themselves, each other, and the ability of the group to be successful. Ask students to think about what they do to make a successful group (i.e. raise your hand, listen to others, be respectful of other people's ideas—everyone has their own opinion). Use dry erase markers to record their answers on the Code of Conduct poster. Reinforce the idea that when we all follow the code of conduct we are able to accomplish our group goals, have more fun together, and people will want to be around us.

   Tips

   ★ If generating the items from scratch will be too challenging for your students, you can create the "code" in advance of the lesson. Students can then act out what it means to follow each part of the code.

   ★ Students may benefit from you asking leading questions or linking it to their past experiences and providing examples to generate responses and code of conduct items.

   ★ Students often tell you what not to do ("Don't call out"); help them shape their responses to indicate what to do ("Raise your hand").

   ★ Provide a copy of the Code of Conduct for students to take home. Most teachers find it easiest to take a digital photo and either print it out or send it electronically using whatever system adopted by the school.

2. Review the game—Tell students they will be playing a game called Who Knows Whom? Tell students that they will be responsible for answering some questions about themselves and then sharing that information with the class (your favorite food, what you like to do after school, etc.). Let students know they will have to listen carefully because once their classmates and teachers are finished presenting there will be a quiz show to find out who remembers the information they just learned.

   Now that students have heard how the game is going to be played, ask them if there is anything they want to add to the Code of Conduct that will help make the game successful.

3. Reinforcement—Draw a box on the board and label it "Group Goal." (In subsequent sessions the group might want to come up with their own name for the tally box.) This is the group reinforcement box. Each time a student displays a behavior from the code of conduct or does something you want to reinforce, put a tally in the box. At the beginning of each group let students know how many tallies they are trying to earn for that group. Tell the students that each day we will add the total number to our thermometer, and when we reach 100, or a number you decide is appropriate, we will have a group celebration or shared group prize.

4. As a group decide on what you would like the prize to be. The first time it might help to offer 2 to 3 choices and have the group vote. We want this to be motivating for all students (see Reinforcement System overview for tips). Write the reward on the board above the thermometer. This will serve as a constant reminder and motivator.

   Tips

   ★ Open-ended options can be difficult. Pick a theme (e.g., snack, video) then have students make suggestions within that theme.

   ★ If your students have trouble voting, force a compromise by picking the item and giving each student a choice within (e.g., video—each student can pick 1 appropriate YouTube clip to watch; snack—each person can pick 1 ingredient for the trail mix; homework pass—each student selects the class where they will use the pass), or create a menu of prize options each student can select from.

   ★ Give at least 10–20 tallies a class period.

ACTIVITY 2

Who Knows Whom?

Worksheet & Game
~15 minutes

Materials

Not Included

- Pencils (1 per student)

Included

- Handout: All About Me!

Instructions

Students and teachers will fill out a questionnaire about themselves. They will use this information to play the game Who Knows Whom?

1. Pass out the handouts All About Me! Ask students to answer the questions. Teachers should take the time to fill out a questionnaire too.
2. After students have completed the questionnaire, have students go around the room and read through their answers. Remind group members to listen carefully because this information will be used in the game.
3. Once students have shared their answers, collect the worksheets. Tell students they will be working together to answer questions about their classmates. Go around the room to each student and generate a question from the worksheet ("This student's favorite food is Mexican."). The student has the chance to answer, or use a lifeline and select another classmate for help. Encourage students to try their best and work together to earn tallies and reach the group goal.
4. Continue to play until all of the students have had at least 2 turns or they've reached their goal.

Tip

★ As instructors are still getting to know their students' level of comfort with writing, they have the option to have students work in partners to avoid using writing worksheets. Students should be paired up and asked to interview a partner. If students have difficulty coming up with questions, teachers can provide suggestions on the whiteboard or verbally to direct the interviews. Once enough time has been allocated to get to know their partner, students will be asked to take turns presenting their partner to their fellow classmates. Once all students are introduced, students can work together to answer questions about their classmates.

Reinforce!

Give out tallies for completing worksheet, speaking clearly, good listening, and trying to answer the question.

"I can tell you were listening because you were looking at the speaker."

TOPIC 1

All About Me!

Name: ______________________ Date: ______________________

My favorite food is:

____

My favorite television show is:

____

My favorite animal is:

____

After school I like to:

____

____

____

____

____

CLOSING

Review: Classroom & Home Practice

Wrap-Up
~5 minutes

Materials

Not Included

- Pencils (1 per student)
- Group Reinforcement Visual
- Each student's *UOT Notebook*

Included

- Classroom Practice 1
- Home Practice 1

Instructions

Students will review the Home Practice sheet and complete the *check* portion of the Goal, Why, Plan, Do, Check (GWPDC).

1. Hand out the Home Practice sheets. Read the goal aloud. Ask students to think about who will work on their Home Practice (HP) with them. Let students know they will each earn a tally for bringing the completed HP with them next time you meet.

   This HP focuses on the Code of Conduct. Students should write the Code of Conduct on the HP prior to taking it home. If writing is a laborious or challenging task for your students, have them write a key word for each item or fill in the worksheet for your students.

   Tip

   ★ Establish a consistent routine with the HP to support students (e.g., review Home Practice sheets, monitor all students as they put it in their homework folder, monitor all students as they write it in their homework planner).

2. Guide students to file all worksheets from the session in their *UOT Notebook*.
3. Read the goal for Lesson 1 (from the GWPDC) aloud to the class. Ask students if they were able to accomplish the goal. Ask students to identify what helped them accomplish the goal.

   Tip

   ★ During the first few lessons make sure students are able to accomplish the goal so that they feel a sense of success and develop an understanding of how to earn tallies.

4. Review the plan. Ask students if they were able to accomplish the plan. Were there steps that we were not able to accomplish? Did we need to revise the plan in any way?

   Tip

   ★ Sometimes plans have to change. An unexpected fire drill or a great discussion takes too long and you have to alter the plan. Celebrate these changes and let students know that even though the *unexpected* happened they were flexible and made a new plan. This concept will be taught in greater detail in future lessons.

5. Remind students they are working towards a large group prize. Each day you will add their tally marks to a bank. When they reach ______ tallies they will get a group celebration or prize.

   Tips

   ★ Determine what this prize or prize options will be ahead of time. See Troubleshooting section for suggestions.

   ★ When selecting how many tallies your students need to earn, consider how many they will earn on a given day (no fewer than 10), and how long they can wait for the reinforcement and still maintain motivation (no longer than 3 weeks).

- ★ Post the tally bank in the front of the classroom so students are constantly reminded of how close they are to their goal (i.e., a goal thermometer).
- ★ Have fun, get silly, demonstrate enthusiasm as you reflect on their accomplishments and their progress towards the group goal.
- ★ If students have a challenging group, reflect on what might happen differently in future groups to be more successful.

6. Distribute the Classroom Practice handout to all instructors who interact with your students and would benefit from supporting students as they work on their new skills.

TOPIC 1

Classroom Practice 1

Dear Teachers:

Your student, ________________________________, had his/her first group meeting of *Unstuck and On Target!* today. *Unstuck and On Target!* will teach your student to be more flexible, set goals, and make plans. We will be meeting almost every week this school year. We will be having fun in groups, but also working on new skills. Your student will need some extra help from you to be able to use these skills. Every week we meet, you will get a Classroom Practice sheet like this one (except shorter) so you can help your student use the *Unstuck and On Target!* vocabulary and skills in class. It will help if you treat Classroom Practices as fun and positive activities.

I'm really looking forward to working with you and your student this year. Please let me know if you have any questions.

Sincerely,

____

Group leader

Phone: ____

E-mail: ______________________________

Summary: The students just created a group Code of Conduct, and they played a get to know each other game. The students are working together to earn a group prize.

What you can do to support your student's learning and generalization:

1. Ask your student to tell you about his/her group.
2. Help your student experience success as a group member. You can help your students master their ability to participate in groups by connecting their actions to their own success and the success of the group. The more you use this language with your students, the better they'll be able to contribute to the many different group situations in your class. Refer to the attached icons and key vocabulary as a reminder.
   a. For example:
      i. *"Thank you for respecting other people's ideas. When you respect others' ideas, you make your friendships stronger."*
      ii. *"Thank you for working toward our goal together today!"*
      iii. *"When you each stay quiet like this, we make so much progress—thank you!"*
      iv. *"You did a great job following directions!"*

You may already be doing something like a Code of Conduct, but if it's something you're thinking about adding, please see the next page.

(continued)

TOPIC 1

Classroom Practice 1

4 Steps to a Classroom Code of Conduct

Step 1: Create your classroom's code. Keep the language simple. You can include your students in the creation of the Code of Conduct. Here is an example:

Group Rules

1. Listen when others are talking.
2. Respect other people's ideas.
3. Follow directions.

Step 2: Display the Code of Conduct where it is easy for everyone to see.

Step 3: Use your daily language to reinforce your students' efforts and encourage them to keep following the Code of Conduct.

Step 4: Reward desired behavior by creating a class goal. It could be a special event or activity—something that will motivate your students to follow the Code of Conduct. Display the reward chart and daily tracking next to the Code of Conduct. Here are examples:

Room 221's Race to the Top!

Goal
100 tallies = A Game Day

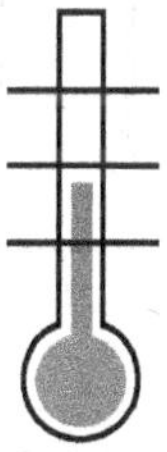

(continued)

TOPIC 1

Classroom Practice 1

Key *Unstuck and On Target!* Scripts & Icons

Goal, Why, Plan, Do, Check

When you see this, there's a good opportunity to help students complete multiple-step activities by breaking them down into smaller, manageable tasks!

Flexible

When you see this, there's a good opportunity to help students recognize the benefits of being flexible in challenging or unexpected situations!

Stuck

When you see this, there's a good opportunity to help students recognize when they're "stuck" on something and think of ways to get "unstuck!"

Plan A→Plan B

When you see this, there's a good opportunity to help students recognize that if their first plan doesn't work, there are other options (Plans B, C, D, etc.) available to them!

Choice/No Choice

When you see this, there's a good opportunity to help students identify what is within their power to change and what is not!

Big Deal/Little Deal

When you see this, there's a good opportunity to help students learn to distinguish what is important from what is not important!

Compromise

When you see this, there's a good opportunity to help students learn strategies for negotiating with others so both people get part of what they want!

Target Goal

When you see this, there's a good opportunity to help students identify their goals and the steps needed to achieve them!

TOPIC 1

Home Practice 1

Dear Parents:

Your child participated in the first group meeting of *Unstuck and On Target!* today. *Unstuck and On Target!* will teach your child to be more flexible, set goals and make plans. We will be meeting almost every week this school year. We will be having fun in groups, but also working on new skills. Your child will need some extra help from you to be able to use these skills at home. Every week we meet, you will get a Home Practice sheet like this one so you can help your child use the *Unstuck and On Target!* vocabulary and skills at home. It will help if you treat Home Practices as fun and positive activities.

I'm really looking forward to working with you and your child this year. Please let me know if you have any questions.

Sincerely,

____

Your child's group leader

Phone: ____________________________________

Email: ____________________________________

Summary of today's group: Your child learned that his or her behaviors affect himself or herself, others, and the success of the group. In order to have a positive effect, your child helped create a Code of Conduct today. Then, the group played a game to get to know each other. The whole group is working together to earn a prize.

What you can do at home:

1. Ask your child to tell you about his/her group.
   - Can your child remember any of the group members' names?
   - Anything they like or share in common?
   - Anyone they'd like to see outside of group?
2. Help your child practice good behavior and connect good behavior to positive effects on himself or herself and others.
   - For example, say to your child:
     - *"Thank you for listening. Your listening helped us finish more quickly."*
     - *"You worked really hard on that!"*
     - *"Great job following directions!"*
3. Post the attached sheet of key vocabulary words as a reminder.

(continued)

TOPIC 1

Home Practice 1

Key *Unstuck and On Target!* Scripts & Icons

Goal, Why, Plan, Do, Check

When you see this, there's a good opportunity to help students complete multiple-step activities by breaking them down into smaller, manageable tasks!

Flexible

When you see this, there's a good opportunity to help students recognize the benefits of being flexible in challenging or unexpected situations!

Stuck

When you see this, there's a good opportunity to help students recognize when they're "stuck" on something and think of ways to get "unstuck!"

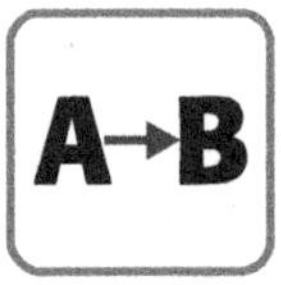

Plan A→Plan B

When you see this, there's a good opportunity to help students recognize that if their first plan doesn't work, there are other options (Plans B, C, D, etc.) available to them!

Choice/No Choice

When you see this, there's a good opportunity to help students identify what is within their power to change and what is not!

Big Deal/Little Deal

When you see this, there's a good opportunity to help students learn to distinguish what is important from what is not important!

Compromise

When you see this, there's a good opportunity to help students learn strategies for negotiating with others so both people get part of what they want!

Target Goal

When you see this, there's a good opportunity to help students identify their goals and the steps needed to achieve them!

Lesson 2 Introduction to Goal, Why, Plan, Do, Check

TOPIC 1

PURPOSE

Students are introduced to the Goal, Why, Plan, Do, Check (GWPDC) structure and language. They will practice following and create a GWPDC of their own. There are two activities in this lesson.

Materials Required for All Activities

Not Included

- Whiteboard or chart paper
- 3 pieces of paper (each labeled with a number 1, 2, or 3)
- Tape
- Colored dry/wet erase markers or markers
- Water fountain
- Pencils
- Group Reinforcement Visual
- Each student's *UOT Notebook*

Included

- GWPDC for Lesson 2
- Lightning Round Questions
- Handout: Wacky GWPDC
- Classroom Practice 2
- Home Practice 2

INTRODUCTION

Preview: GWPDC & Lightning Round

Review & Game
~5 minutes

Materials

Not Included

- Whiteboard or chart paper and suitable markers
- 3 pieces of paper (each labeled with a number 1, 2, or 3)
- Tape

Included

- GWPDC for Lesson 2
- Lightning Round Questions

Instructions

1. Post the GWPDC on the board before the lesson begins.
2. Review the GWPDC with the group.
3. Complete the Lightning Round activity.

At the beginning of each lesson students will play a *Lightning Round.* There are several reasons for starting the lesson with this activity. By answering questions about the previous lesson's material you will be able to gauge what information students retained and what concepts are still unclear. Students activate their prior knowledge when previously taught concepts are brought up and the fun, playful nature of the game provides a hook for getting kids engaged. Finally, since every lesson begins with a *Lightning Round,* it offers a predictable routine and structure to the group.

Reinforce...
Memory
"Great job remembering that from our last group, I can tell you were really paying attention."

Set-up: Write the 3 questions below on the board and cover each one up with a sheet of paper that has "1", "2," or "3" written on it. The numbers equate to the number of tallies the students will earn if they answer the question correctly. Students select a question, "I want the question for 3 tallies." Read the question aloud. Students can answer the question or ask for a lifeline and call on a classmate for help. If the question is answered correctly, award the group that number of tallies in the *Group Goal* box.

Tips

★ Before beginning the Lightning Round, direct the students to "Raise your hand if you showed the Home Practice to a grown-up at home." Reward the group with a tally for each student who raised their hand.

★ If you would like each student to answer a question each day, you can create additional questions.

★ This should be a very quick activity and take no more than 5 minutes.

★ Reinforce students working together to answer a question for their good effort.

★ If students have difficulty not being called on first, leave it up to chance—write everyone's name on a popsicle stick and put them in a jar. Randomly select a stick and call on that student.

G W P D C	**Goal:** Learn and Practice Goal, Why, Plan, Do, Check (GWPDC) and earn 20 tallies. **Why:** Learning how to achieve goals helps us get what we want, and earning tallies helps us earn our group reward. **Plan:** 1. Lightning Round 2. Practice GWPDC 3. Write your own GWPDC 4. Review Home Practice **Do:** Follow the plan and earn tallies. **Check:** How did it go? Did we accomplish our goal? Which Code of Conduct item was the easiest to follow? Which one was the hardest?

Lightning Round Questions

1. Name 1 item from our Code of Conduct.
2. Why do students earn tallies in our group?
3. What happens when group members follow the Code of Conduct?

Don't forget to check off this step on the GWPDC!

ACTIVITY 1

Introduction to GWPDC

Activity
~10 minutes

Materials

Not Included

- Whiteboard or chart paper and suitable markers
- Water fountain

Instructions

1. Write the words *goal, why, plan, do, check* on the board; use the same colors you used for the lesson Goal, Why, Plan, Do, Check (GWPDC).
2. Begin by telling students that there are different kinds of goals. In sports, you can score a goal, but we're talking about a different kind of goal.
3. Tell students that they may not know it but during the day they set many goals for themselves and create lots of plans to help them accomplish their goals. Then whether they realize it or not they check those plans and decide if it helped them accomplish their goal or not. Share an example of this process in action (feel free to tailor the example to meet the needs/interest level of your students).

    Example: You are heading out to the playground and you are excited to have a good time—having fun is your goal. You think to yourself soccer is fun, my plan is to play soccer. When you get outside you realize there is already a game going on, and you realize your original plan is not going to work so you decide to go on the swings instead. On your way in from recess you check or think to yourself, that was fun, and you have accomplished your goal.

4. Read aloud these 5 definitions and ask your students to label aloud whether it defines Goal, Why, Plan, Do, or Check.
    - What do you want to do or accomplish? (GOAL)
    - What makes the goal important? (WHY)
    - How will you do it? (PLAN)
    - Try your plan. (DO)
    - Stop and think. Did my plan work? Do I need a different plan? (CHECK)
5. Tell students you are very thirsty and you really need a drink of water. Have them help you write a GWPDC to accomplish your goal of getting a drink of water. *You may need to modify this activity if you don't have access to a water fountain.*

    GOAL: To get a drink of water from the water fountain.
    WHY: I am *very thirsty* and I like water.
    PLAN:

    1. Stand up
    2. Walk to the door
    3. Open the door
    4. Walk down the hallway, past 4 classrooms
    5. Turn to the left and stand in front of the fountain

Reinforce!

Attempts to identify whether the description is a GOAL, WHY, PLAN, DO, or CHECK

6. Press the button
7. Lean down and drink water

DO: Follow the plan.
CHECK: How did it go? Do I need a different plan?

Depending on time, have students watch you follow the plan or have each student try it out. After you have completed the plan, complete the check and reflect on how the plan went.

*OPTION: Combine Activities 1 and 2; instead of having students create their own wacky ways of getting to the water fountain, as part of Activity 1 the class will create a "funny" Plan B to get to the water fountain

Remember to check off this step on the GWPDC!

ACTIVITY 2
Wacky GWPDC

Activity
~10 minutes

Materials

Not Included
- Whiteboard or chart paper and suitable markers
- Water fountain

Included
- Handout: Wacky Goal, Why, Plan, Do, Check

Instructions

1. Distribute the Wacky Goal, Why, Plan, Do, Check (GWPDC) handout to each student.
2. Tell them they are responsible for writing their own plan to get to the water fountain. Let them know they can be as silly as they want but need to be safe. Remind them that although they might be silly, the object of the game is to accomplish the goal. *Make sure to set parameters so that students will not be able to try any unsafe options (e.g., running, jumping on furniture). Feel free to modify the task to meet the needs of your students (e.g., select a task that keeps them in the classroom).*
3. Students fill in the worksheet with their plan for how they are going to get to the water fountain and accomplish their goal of getting a drink of water (hop, jump, crawl, walk backwards).

   Example:

   GOAL: To get a drink of water from the water fountain.
   WHY: I am thirsty.
   PLAN:
   1. Stand up
   2. *Hop* to the door
   3. Open the door
   4. *Crawl* down the hallway, past 4 classrooms
   5. *Turn around 3 times* and stand in front of the fountain
   6. Press the button
   7. Lean down and drink water

   DO: Follow the plan.
   CHECK: How did it go? Do I need a different plan?
4. Give each student a chance to try out his/her plan.
5. After each student has tried his/her plan, check to see how it went. Did they accomplish their goals? Would they like a new plan?

Reinforce!
Staying safe, and reflecting honestly during the "check"—how the plan went

Remember to check off this step on the GWPDC!

Tips

★ Some plans will take too long, or be too tiring, so celebrate the need for a different plan. We will focus on making a Plan B later in the curriculum.

★ If the instructor would prefer to implement the GWPDC as a group activity, they can suggest the students pretend he/she is a robot and they must provide explicit instructions on how the "robot" can get to the water fountain. Since the instructor must follow the students' exact instructions, the students can brainstorm different methods to accomplish their goal and enjoy being a little silly in the classroom as the "robot" must follow their instructions. After the activity, students can reflect on their plan and if it was the best way to accomplish their goal as in the individual activity.

TOPIC 1

Wacky GWPDC

	GWPDC
GOAL	
WHY	
PLAN(S)	
DO	
CHECK	Did I accomplish my goal? How did it go? 1 2 3 4 5 No, not so good Part, OK Yes, great

CLOSING

Review: Classroom & Home Practice

Wrap-up
~5 minutes

Materials

Not Included

- Pencils (1 per student)
- Group Reinforcement Visual
- Each student's *UOT Notebook*

Included

- Classroom Practice 2
- Home Practice 2

Instructions

Students will review the Home Practice and complete the *check* portion of the Goal, Why, Plan, Do, Check (GWPDC).

1. Hand out the Home Practice sheets. Read the goal aloud. Ask students to think about who they will work on their Home Practice (HP) with. Let students know they will each earn a tally for bringing the completed HP with them next time you meet. This HP focuses on GWPDC.

   Tip

   ★ Follow the same procedure every day for reviewing and completing HP (e.g., review Home Practice, monitor all students as they put it in their homework folder, monitor all students as they write it in their homework planner).

2. Guide students to file all worksheets in their *UOT Notebook.*
3. Read the goal from Lesson 2 aloud to the class. Ask students if they were able to accomplish the goal. Ask students to identify what helped them accomplish the goal.

   Tip

   ★ During the first few lessons make sure students are able to accomplish the goal so that they feel a sense of success and develop an understanding of how to earn tallies.

4. Review the plan. Ask students if they were able to accomplish the plan. Were there steps that we were not able to accomplish? Did we need to revise the plan in any way?

   Tip

   ★ Sometimes plans have to change: an unexpected fire drill or a great discussion takes too long and you have to alter the plan. Celebrate these changes and let students know that even though the *unexpected* happened, they were flexible and made a new plan. This concept will be taught in greater detail in future lessons.

5. Remind students they are working towards a large group prize. Each day you will add their tally marks to a bank. When they reach ____ tallies they will get a group celebration or prize.

   Tips

   ★ Determine what the prize or prize options will be ahead of time. See Troubleshooting section for suggestions.

   ★ When selecting how many tallies your students need to earn, consider how many they will earn on a given day (no fewer than 10), and how long they can wait for the reinforcement and still maintain motivation (no longer than 3 weeks).

   ★ Post the tally bank in the front of the classroom so students are constantly reminded of how close they are to their goal (i.e., a thermometer).

6. Distribute the Classroom Practice handout to all instructors who interact with your students and would benefit from supporting students as they work on their new skills.

TOPIC 1

Classroom Practice 2

Summary: Today the students learned about setting goals and making plans. They are using a simple script called Goal, Why, Plan, Do, Check (GWPDC). Many teachers have used this script in their classrooms to help support the executive functioning skills of all of their students.

What you can do to support your student's learning and generalization:

1. Integrate goal, why, plan, do, check language into your lessons.
   - *"Wow, we are really working hard and getting closer to accomplishing our* ***goal****."*
   - *"****Why do we want to*** *learn about this today?"*
   - *"I am so glad we are staying on track. What is the next step in our* ***plan****?"*
   - *"Let's* ***check*** *on our progress."*
2. You may already be doing something like a daily schedule, but if you'd like to try a GWPDC in an academic lesson, an example is below:

   GOAL: To practice our math facts.

   WHY: Once we memorize our math facts, math is much easier.

   PLAN:

   1. Complete 2 minute time trial.
   2. Compare your answers to the answer key.
   3. Track how many you got right on your graph.

   DO: Follow the plan.

   CHECK: Check time trial. How did it go? Did I get more right than I did last time? Do I need a different plan (more practice with math games online, flashcards, time trials for homework)?

TOPIC 1

Home Practice 2

Your child participated in the second session of *Unstuck and On Target!* today.

Summary: Your child was introduced to setting goals and making plans. Your child learned how to use a simple routine called Goal, Why, Plan, Do, Check (GWPDC). Your child will come back to this topic again in their 15th session.

Here's an example of how GWPDC might be used at home:

GOAL: To eat together as a family once this weekend.

WHY: We are hungry and actually enjoy talking to each other once in a while.

PLAN:

1. Find a time that works.
2. Figure out what we want to eat and what's in the fridge.
3. One of us sets the table.
4. One of us cooks.
5. One of us cleans up.

DO: Follow the plan. (Let's eat!)

CHECK: How did it go? Do we need a different plan?

What you can do at home:

1. Help your child see what it is like setting goals and making plans by being a model. Say your plans and goals out loud.

- For example:
  - *"My **goal** is for us to get to __________ on time." (church/school/Scouts/practice/Grandma's)*
  - *"Well, this isn't how **I planned it.**"*
  - *"My **goal** is to make it to Back to School Night this year. I **plan** to leave work early."*
  - *"My **plan** to go to the grocery store tonight is still possible."*

Lesson 3 Emotional Identification

PURPOSE

If students can identify the emotion they are feeling and with what intensity they are feeling it, they can make better choices about what to do next. This lesson builds on the concept that what students do affects themselves and others, enriching their understanding of the social world and its reciprocal influence on them. In addition, this understanding helps build motivation to use positive, active emotional regulation strategies. To this end, Lesson 3 includes three activities to support each student's skill acquisition. At the conclusion of this lesson, students will have expanded their understanding of the full range of a variety of emotions and begun to develop a broader vocabulary of terms related to emotional states.

Materials Required for All Activities

Not Included

- Whiteboard or chart paper
- 3 pieces of paper (each labeled with a number 1, 2, or 3)
- Tape
- Dry/wet erase markers or markers
- Pencils
- Group Reinforcement Visual
- Each student's *UOT Notebook*

Included

- GWPDC for Lesson 3
- Lightning Round Questions
- Visual: Feelings Target
- Materials: Feelings Target Cards
- Visual: Feelings Chain Scenarios
- Handout: Feelings Chain Blank
- Classroom Practice 3
- Home Practice 3

ESSENTIAL NOTES:

1. This lesson, coupled with Lesson 4, provides the initial building blocks for understanding the complexity of social interaction and expands on the fundamental understanding that what you do affects you and others. You can help your students understand this complexity better by expanding on the foundation of Lessons 3 and 4 through ongoing use of the Feelings Target; a rich vocabulary reflecting a variety of emotions; making the implicit explicit, especially related to the dynamics of social exchange and emotions; and the Feelings Chain.
2. Because we are addressing a social exchange, we would be missing something if we didn't talk about the social partners and group members your students will meet outside of your intervention sessions.
   a. Sometimes other children are less tolerant of children on the autism spectrum because children on the autism spectrum so often behave in ways that diverge from social expectations. You can improve acceptance of neurodiversity by focusing on the strengths of all students and cultivating an acceptance of social and thinking style differences within the classroom and the school. This can be done by highlighting the advantages of such diversity and that each person has a different brain and different types of strengths, ways of doing things, and difficulties. We can enhance the flexibility of social expectations within the school culture just as we create physical settings that are more accessible for students who must use a wheelchair.
3. Some students may make direct connections between their behavior and consequences and how others feel for the first time, and you may be the first person to hear about experiences that they have had at school or at home. Children may report being bullied, to which an immediate and proactive response is critical. If a child reports being physically abused, immediately follow your school's protocol for reporting such instances. In both cases, it's critical that the student understand that he or she is not at fault for the abusive behavior of others, and accessing available school resources (e.g., school counselor or psychologist) to support the student is essential.

INTRODUCTION

Preview: GWPDC & Lightning Round

Review & Game
~5 minutes

Materials

Not Included

- Whiteboard or chart paper and suitable markers
- 3 pieces of paper (each labeled with a number 1, 2, or 3)
- Tape

Included

- GWPDC for Lesson 3
- Lightning Round Questions

Instructions

1. Post the GWPDC on the board before the lesson begins.
2. Review the GWPDC with the group.
3. Complete the Lightning Round activity.

**For a complete set of instructions and tips, refer to the GWPDC and Lightning Round instructions (Topic 1, Lesson 2).*

Reinforce...
Participation
"Good job raising your hand, I can tell you are ready and excited to play our game."

G W P D C	**Goal:** Identify the many different feelings we have and think about how we react when we feel them. **Why:** I feel many different ways throughout the day. Depending on how I feel I may react in different ways. What I do affects me and others, and it can affect how others feel about and respond to me. I can control the way I react and positively affect my friends, teachers, parents, and others. I can also control my reaction and affect the choices available to me and how others feel about me. **Plan:** 1. Lightning Round 2. Feelings Target 3. Play How Does It Make Me Feel? 4. Construct a Feelings Chain 5. Review Home Practice **Do:** Follow the plan and earn tallies. **Check:** How did it go? Did we accomplish our plan? Look at the Feelings Target—at this moment how are you feeling?

Lightning Round Questions

1. When we decide what we want to do or what we want to accomplish, we call this our _____? (Goal)
2. When we decide how we are going to accomplish our goal, this is called our _____? (Plan)
3. What are three ways I can earn tallies in class?

Don't forget to check off this step on the GWPDC!

ACTIVITY 1

Feelings Target

Activity
~10 minutes

Materials

Not Included

- Tape

Included

- Visual: Feelings Target poster
- Handout: Feelings Target
- Materials: Feelings Target Cards

Instructions

Set-up: Place the Feelings Target poster in the front of the room. This should stay up for the remainder of the intervention.

1. Introduce students to the Feelings Target poster or Visual: Feelings Target printed and displayed. Ask them if they have ever played darts before. Let them know that the purpose of the game is to hit the bullseye or the center point. The center point of our Feelings Target means "just-right" or "on target." Ask students to think about what they are able to do when they are feeling just-right (do school work, play with friends). What are some words they would use to describe themselves when they are just-right or on target (happy, calm, cool, good)?
2. Hand out an equal number of emotion cards to each student. Keep a few cards for yourself and demonstrate what level the emotions on the cards are by attaching the card with tape to the level it goes with. Go around the room and let each student attach his or her cards to the Feelings Target at the level that fits or use a dry erase marker to write the emotion words on each level of the Feelings Target. Encourage your students to think of additional words that describe how they might feel at each level (example: #1=calm, happy, just-right, on target, feeling good; #2=okay, fine, feeling pretty good, so-so; #3=nervous, annoyed, grumpy; #4=mad, scared, frustrated, anxious; #5=overwhelmed, out of control, furious, very upset, really anxious). If your students prefer a different word you can write that on the back of the card.
3. After you finish the activity, leave the group-generated words on the Target. The Completed Target should stay up for the remainder of the intervention.

Reinforce!

Provide tallies for participation.

"Excellent suggestion, I think ____ describes a level ____ emotion."

*Encourage classroom teachers to use the target throughout the day (priming for an event, debriefing from an event, analyzing literature, etc.).

TOPIC 1

Feelings Target

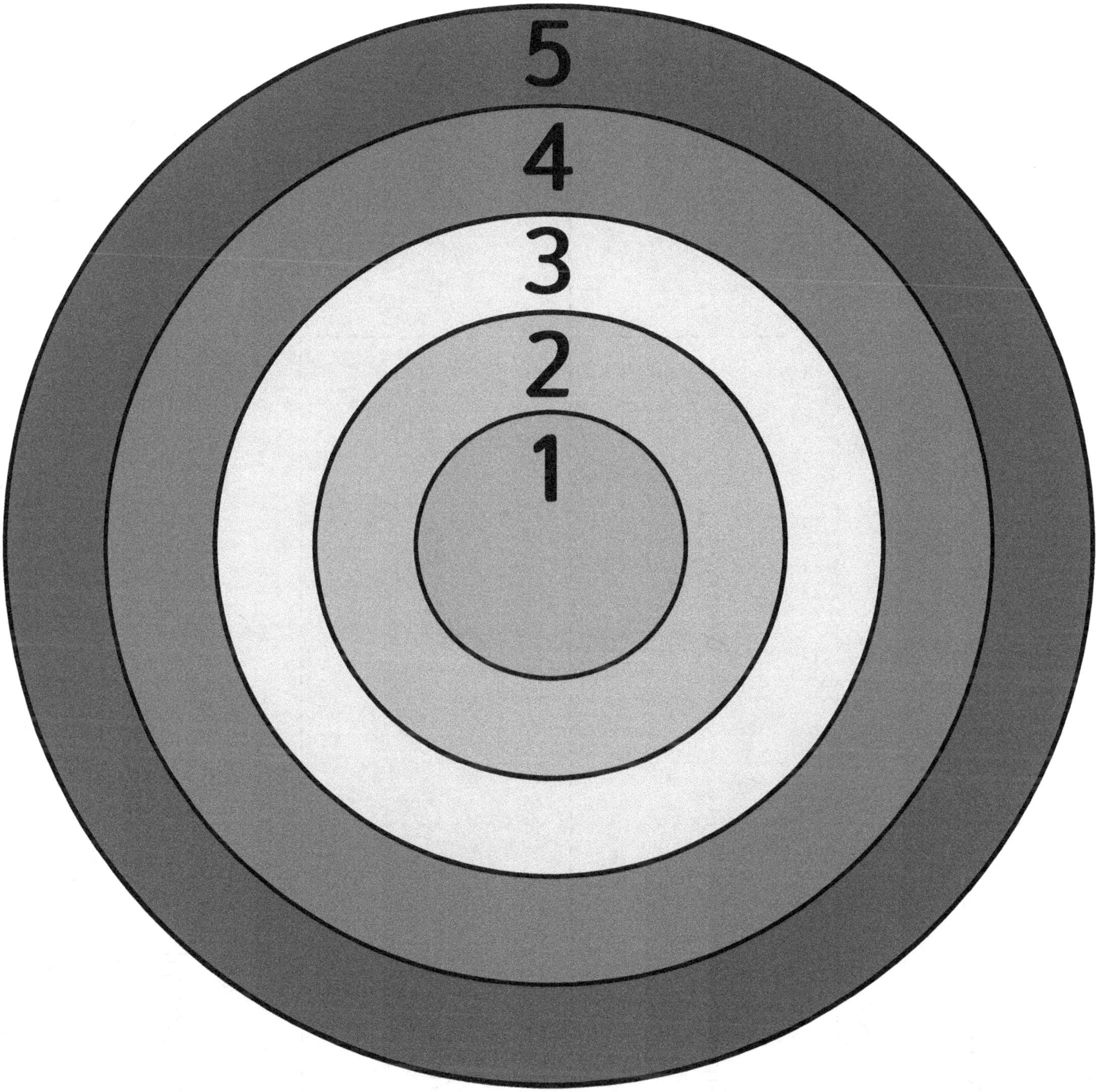

Happy	Calm	Okay
Fine	Annoyed	Nervous
Mad	Scared	Overwhelmed
Out of Control	Excited	Embarrassed/ Disappointed

ACTIVITY 2

How Does It Make Me Feel?

Activity
~5 minutes

Materials

Not Included

- Whiteboard or chart paper and suitable markers

Included

- Completed Feelings Target

Instructions

Reinforce!

Highlight and reinforce students when they share their ideas and celebrate when they have different ideas from one another.

"A trip to an amusement park makes some people feel like a #1 and others like a #5. We all experience different emotions."

Set-up: Make sure the Feelings Target that was created in Activity 1 is posted for all students to see.

1. Read students a list of scenarios and ask them to rate what number they would be on the Feelings Target. Remind students that #1 is just-right, the farther out they go on the chart, the more extreme the emotion. Encourage students to articulate what they act, look and feel like when they are experiencing that emotion (i.e., "I get really frustrated when my computer doesn't work and I scrunch up my face and yell sometimes I get so nervous that my stomach hurts."). Try to encourage a variety of different emotional responses (e.g., worried, excited, happy, calm, elated, anxious, angry, a little upset). There is no right answer for each statement; students may have different opinions. It may be helpful for you to use your own experiences. You can describe an event, the emotion you felt, how that emotion feels in your body, and how it looks. You can also use examples from books that the students have recently read or a popular movie. Use the whiteboard/chart paper to highlight important insights created by the group to make it visual.

Scenarios:

- I found out there will be no recess for the rest of the year.
- I found out there will be an ice cream party at the end of class today.
- I just heard that the cafeteria is serving a lunch that I like today.
- I lost my homework.
- My friend is coming over to spend the night.
- The cell phone is not working.
- I got an A on my math test.
- I lost my pencil.
- My mom packed my favorite lunch.
- I have no homework for the rest of the week.
- My dog died.
- I just found out we are going to an amusement park (Six Flags, Kings Dominion) tomorrow.

ACTIVITY 3

Feelings Chain

Activity

~10 minutes

Materials

Not Included

- Whiteboard or chart paper and suitable markers"
- Dry/wet erase markers or markers

Included

- Completed Feelings Target
- Visual: Feelings Chain Scenarios
- Handout: Feelings Chain Blank

Instructions

Reinforce!

Students for referencing the Feelings Target when completing their Feelings Chain

Set-up: Make sure the completed Feelings Target is visible to all students.

1. Tell students that our feelings can cause us to act a certain way. Ask students to visualize or picture themselves the last time they were really excited: what did they do (jump, smile, run around, laugh)? How about when they were really mad (yell, clench fists, run out of the room)?
2. Tell students that a chain of events happens every time we have an emotion.
3. Distribute one Feelings Chain to each student.
4. Walk students through the Feelings Chain.
5. Take students through the following scenario and reference the Feelings Chain, using the Visual: Feelings Chain Scenario as a support.

Scenario 1:

I was walking home from school yesterday, feeling great because I had no homework. I had plans to watch my favorite show on TV with my friend when I got home. When I arrived home, my mom said the power was out and we couldn't watch TV. I was furious. I was incredibly angry, so angry in fact that I started stomping my feet and yelling. I could not calm down. My mom tried to help, but I just kept yelling. She told me that because I was being so disrespectful, I would not be able to have dessert after dinner.

Event

Power is out, can't watch TV

Feeling

Furious (4)

Action

Yelling   Stomping my feet

How Others Feel

Frustrated

Consequence

Friend went home

I Feel

More disappointed (5)

Scenario 2:

Now show students how to create a chain with a different outcome. Re-read the scenario, but highlight that instead of screaming and yelling you decide to go and ask your mom if she can fix it. She says she can't figure out why the power is out, but she will take you both to the basketball court so you can play because you handled the disappointment so well.

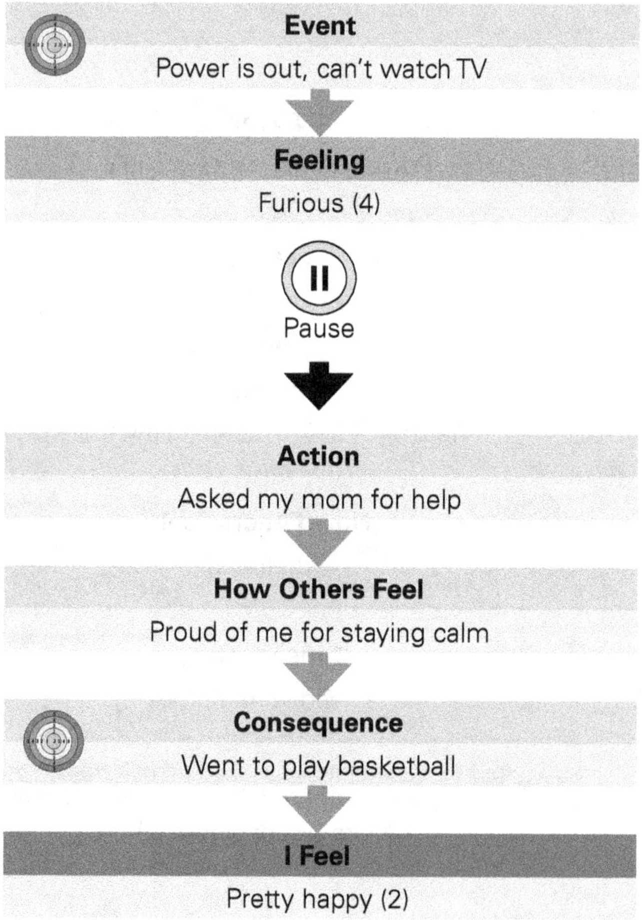

Ask students which Feelings Chain ended with the better outcome. Ask them to look at the 2 chains, which step changed (the action). Highlight that it was still really frustrating that the power was out but that when you chose to ask for help instead of screaming, the consequence was a much better one, and everyone left feeling good. Share with students that often it's important to remember to pause when experiencing strong emotions. Pausing can put a situation on hold and give you time to make a choice about what to do next. Pausing is better than your feelings causing you to act in a way that makes a difficult situation even worse.

Tips

★ Look for opportunities to use the Feelings Target and the Feelings Chain at other times, with other scenarios during the session and through school day. We have provided a blank template for you to use in such opportunities.

★ Reinforce students for referencing the Feelings Target and Feelings Chain outside of group time.

TOPIC 1

Feelings Chain Scenarios

Scenario 1

Event
Power is out, can't watch TV

Feeling
Furious (4)

Action
Yelling   Stomping my feet

How Others Feel
Frustrated

Consequence
Friend went home

I Feel
More disappointed (5)

Scenario 2

Event
Power is out, can't watch TV

Feeling
Furious (4)

Pause

Action
Asked my mom for help

How Others Feel
Proud of me for staying calm

Consequence
Went to play basketball

I Feel
Pretty happy (2)

TOPIC 1

Feelings Chain Blank

Scenario 1: Use the first example to create a Feelings Chain based on a situation when feelings drove actions, and the situation did not improve.

Event

↓

Feeling	
Feelings word:	Number:

↓

Action

↓

How Others Feel

↓

Consequence

↓

I Feel	
Feelings word:	Number:

(continued)

Feelings Chain Blank

Scenario 2: Use the second example to create a Feelings Chain based on a situation when actions drove feelings, and something positive happened.

Event

Feeling

Feelings word: Number:

Pause Pause

Action

How Others Feel

Consequence

I Feel

Feelings word: Number:

CLOSING

Review: Classroom & Home Practice

Wrap-up
~5 minutes

Materials

Not Included

- Pencils (1 per student)
- Group Reinforcement Visual
- Each student's *UOT Notebook*

Included

- Classroom Practice 3
- Home Practice 3
- Feelings Target
- Blank Feelings Chain

Instructions

Students will review the Home Practice and complete the *check* portion of the Goal, Why, Plan, Do, Check.

1. Hand out the Home Practice sheets. Read the goal aloud. Ask students to think about who they will work on their Home Practice (HP) with. Let students know they will each earn a tally for bringing the completed HP with them next time you meet.

   Tip

   ★ Follow the same procedure every day for reviewing and completing HP (e.g., review HP sheet, monitor all students as they put it in their homework folder, monitor all students as they write it in their homework planner).

2. Guide students to file all worksheets in their *UOT Notebook.*
3. Read the goal of Lesson 3 aloud to the class. Ask students if they were able to accomplish the goal. Ask students to identify what helped them accomplish the goal.
4. Review the plan. Ask students if they were able to accomplish the plan: "Were there steps that we were not able to accomplish? Did we need to revise the plan in any way?"

   Tip

   ★ This particular lesson is chock full of rich emotional regulation skills and strategies. Depending on a group of students' experience in this area, this lesson may take 2 days to complete. These emotional regulation concepts are foundational and will resurface throughout the intervention.

5. Remind students they are working towards a large group celebration or prize. Each day you will add their tally marks to a bank. When they reach _____ tallies they will get a group celebration or prize.

   Tip

   ★ Think about whether the prize is still meaningful and whether students are able to sustain motivation for the duration of the time it will require to access the celebration or prize.

   ★ Feel free to use the same system to reinforce the same behaviors throughout the rest of the day. This will help students generalize the skills across settings and provides the classroom with a common language.

6. Distribute the Classroom Practice handout to all instructors who interact with your students and would benefit from supporting students as they work on their new skills.

TOPIC 1

Classroom Practice 3

Session Summary: The students learned today about how our thoughts/events, feelings and actions all relate to each other and about how to figure out how intense their feelings are. If students can identify the emotion they are feeling and with what intensity they are feeling it, they can make better choices about what to do next.

What you can do to support your student's learning and generalization:

1. Identify your own feelings in front of students at least once a day, using instructive self-talk. For example:
   - "I **felt** unbelievably **proud** when I saw Devin share his favorite toy with Sam. I could tell by Sam's smile that he **felt happy** because he smiled and thanked Devin three times!"
   - "I **feel happy** when I get to read this Roald Dahl book. He is my favorite author."
2. Connect a character's thoughts, feelings, and actions, or how what one character does connects to what another feels in the classroom when you read a story or watch a video. For example:
   - "How did _______ **feel** when her father said _______?"
   - "Why did he do that? What was he **thinking** or **feeling**?"
   - "When he _______, how did that make her **feel**?"

Home Practice 3

Your child participated in the third session of *Unstuck and On Target!* today.

Session Summary: Your child learned today about how thoughts/events, feelings, and actions are connected. We also worked on figuring out how strong his or her feelings are. If your child can identify the emotion he or she is feeling and how strong it is, he/she can make better choices about what to do next.

Thoughts/ Events → Feelings → Actions

What you can do at home:

1. Identify your own feelings in front of your child at least once a day. For example:
   - "I felt so **proud** of you today."
   - "I feel **happy** when I get to talk to Aunt Nina. She always makes me laugh."
   - "I feel **sad** sometimes when I miss Grandma."
2. Try to use a variety of feelings, like:
   - Happy
   - Frustrated
   - Blah
   - Sad
   - Worried
   - Disappointed
   - Proud
3. Try to connect your thoughts, feelings and actions. Or, you can do this while watching TV or reading with your child about the characters:
   - "When I **think** you might hurt yourself, I **feel** scared and I yell."
   - "He **thought** his mom was **mad** at him, so he was **scared** and he hid from her."
   - "When I saw you eat all of your dinner, I **felt happy** and I decided we should have dessert."

Lesson 4 What Can You Do to Feel Better?

TOPIC 1

PURPOSE

This lesson helps students learn coping strategies to feel just right when feelings are intensifying, especially when being flexible is really difficult. There are four activities in this lesson (1 optional activity).

Materials Required for All Activities

Not Included

- Whiteboard
- Tape
- 3 pieces of paper (each labeled with a number 1, 2, or 3)
- Cup
- Water
- Gum
- Access to space for running
- Access to swings
- Five blank index cards for each student and for the teacher
- Markers
- Access to clipart, a computer, or magazines with lots of pictures
- Hole punch
- String or D-ring to hold cards together
- Pencils
- Group Reinforcement Visual
- Each student's *UOT Notebook*

Included

- GWPDC for Lesson 4
- Lightning Round Questions
- Handout: Disappointment and Coping
- Handout: How to Feel Just-Right
- Handout: Just-Right Strategies Investigation
- Handout: My Mission to Get Back to Just-Right
- Handout: Deep Breathing
- Handout: Strategy Card Examples
- Classroom Practice 4
- Home Practice 4

INTRODUCTION

Preview: GWPDC & Lightning Round

Review & Game
~5 minutes

Materials

Not Included

- Whiteboard or chart paper and suitable markers
- Tape
- 3 pieces of paper (each labeled with a number 1, 2, or 3)

Included

- GWPDC for Lesson 4
- Lightning Round Questions

Instructions

1. Post the GWPDC on the board before the lesson begins.
2. Review the GWPDC with the group.
3. Complete the Lightning Round activity.

**For a complete set of instructions and tips, refer to the GWPDC and Lightning Round instructions (Topic 1, Lesson 2).*

Reinforce...
Flexibility
"I know you wanted to go first, thank you for being flexible and letting your classmate go first."

G W P D C	
	Goal: Learn how to feel okay when unexpected things happen. **Why:** I have more choices and can be more flexible when I'm not upset. When I'm more flexible and calm I am more likely to get what I want. **Plan:** 1. Lightning Round 2. What can I do when I feel disappointed? 3. Coping Strategies Investigation 4. Strategy Cards 5. Coping Choices (if we have time) 6. Review Home Practice **Do:** Follow the plan and earn tallies. **Check:** How did it go? Did we accomplish our plan? What is one thing you can do if you are feeling upset or disappointed?

Lightning Round Questions

1. Think about the Feelings Target. What number and color do we use when you're feeling just-right?
2. When your emotions are at their strongest or most intense what number and color do we use?
3. Think about the Feelings Chain. What are the steps of the Feelings Chain? (Hint: It starts with an event.)

ACTIVITY 1

Disappointment and Coping

Group Activity
~5 minutes

Materials

Included

- Visual: Feelings Target
- Handout: Disappointment and Coping (one copy for group)

Instructions

1. Discuss the word *disappointment*: When what you want does not match what happens. *(You may need to provide some examples.)*
2. Ask students to identify feelings they have and/or words they think of when they are disappointed (e.g., *sad, frustrated, mad, angry*). Ask them to think about how their body feels when they are disappointed (e.g., *face gets hot, stomach hurts, teeth clench, fists clench*).
3. Relate different scenarios, and have each student rate the intensity of his or her feelings for each of those scenarios on the Feelings Target. Scenarios might include the following: *I really wanted the new Wii game, but the store was sold out or I wanted to play with Susie at recess, but she chose to play with Ann.* You may also use examples from your classroom.
4. Display Handout: Disappointment and Coping. (Keep this activity moving, students will have the opportunity to dig deeper into this topic with the next activity.) Help students brainstorm ideas for what they can do when they cannot get what they want and they feel disappointed or frustrated (i.e., use coping skills). Ideas might include getting more information, asking an adult for help, requesting downtime, requesting to meet with an adult at school who helps them (e.g., counselor), using thought-stopping skills, breathing deeply, thinking about something that makes them really happy, and politely advocating for a change. Write these ideas on Handout: Disappointment and Coping and post the handout on the wall while you complete Activity 1.

TOPIC 1

Disappointment and Coping

Feeling:

Disappointment

Action:

Coping skills

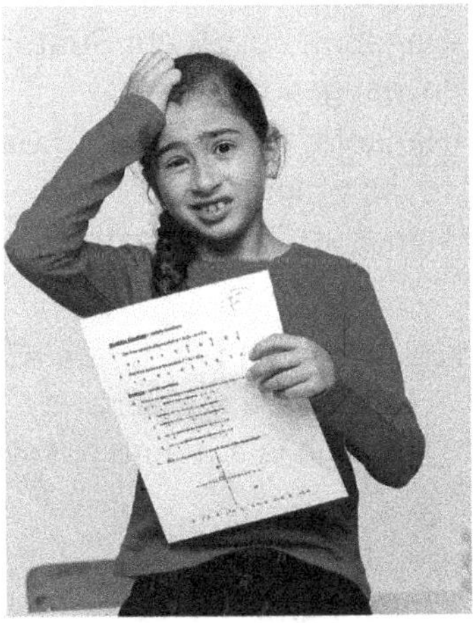

Can you think of anything that would help you feel less disappointed?

- Go outside
  - o Run a lap
  - o Swing
  - o Bounce a ball
- Reading
- Take a break
  - o Deep breathing
  - o Headphones
  - o Soft pillow
  - o Fidget object
  - o Drink of water
  - o Run an errand to the office
- Music
  - o Listening with headphones
  - o Humming
- Drawing
- Journaling
- Thinking strategies
  - o Helpful thoughts
  - o It's okay, I made a mistake
  - o Count to 30
  - o Think of my favorite place or activity

ACTIVITY 2

Coping Skills Investigation

Experiment
~10 minutes

Materials

Not Included

- Cups
- Water
- Gum
- Access to space for running
- Access to swings

Included

- Visual: Feelings Target
- Handout: How to Feel Just-Right
- Handout: Just-Right Strategies Investigation
- Handout: My Mission to Get Back to Just-Right
- Handout: Deep Breathing

Instructions

1. Read Handout: How to Feel Just-Right. Discuss with students what feels like a #5. Have they ever felt like a #5? Share a time when you have felt like a #5. Remind them that everyone feels like a #5 every now and then. Their job is to figure out what strategies help them get back to "just-right."

   Tip

   ★ Emphasize why you want to move from a #5 to a #1/just-right: You feel horrible at a #5, likely to make other people upset when you are at a #5, people are less likely to give you what you want/need when you are at a #5.

2. From the list of brainstormed ideas from Activity 1 or Handout: Just-Right Strategies Investigation, have students choose some of the coping skills and try them. Students will rate how helpful the strategy was for them.
3. Demonstrate deep breathing using Handout: Deep Breathing. Have the students rate this technique on the Handout: Just-Right Strategies Investigation.
4. If you have time, read through Handout: My Mission to Get Back to Just-Right. Have students brainstorm what strategies they would use to get back to "just-right."

TOPIC 1

How to Feel Just-Right

Sometimes I feel like a #5.

I can be #5 because I am feeling angry.
I can be a #5 because I am feeling upset.
When I am a #5, it is harder for me to do my work or pay attention.

When I am a #5, I need to use my strategies to cool myself down to "just-right."

I am going to be a detective.
I am going to be a "just-right detective."

TOPIC 1

Just-Right Strategies Investigation

Try these out and see how you feel:

Just-Right Strategy	How much does this strategy help me get to "just-right"? 1 None	2 A little	3 Some	4 A lot	5 I feel just-right	I like this strategy	I don't like this strategy
Take five deep breaths.							
Close your eyes and think of a "happy place" (e.g., the beach).							
Close your eyes and think of your favorite activity.							
Run outside.							
Think to yourself over and over, "I am okay; I feel calm."							
Have a drink of water.							
Ask to take a break.							
Try the deep breathing script.							
Read.							
Count to 30.							
Draw.							
Sing or hum.							
Swing on the swings.							
Make your own strategy:							
Make your own strategy:							

TOPIC 1

My Mission to Get Back to Just-Right

My mission: to figure out what strategies I like to use to get back to just-right.

I get to select the strategies that I like. These will be my just-right strategies.

I can use these strategies any time I am feeling really upset like a #3, #4, or a #5.

All I have to do is ask my teacher. My teacher will be very proud of me for using my strategies. I will feel very proud of myself for getting back to just-right or a #1.

I will earn bonus points for using my strategies when I need them.

Mission 1

During lunch, I realize I do not have enough money to buy the snack I want. This makes me feel very angry. I am a #5.

Mission 2

In the library, I realize the book I want to read is being used by someone else. I feel very upset. I am a #4.

Mission 3

I yelled when I was using my computer. My teacher had to take my computer away from me. I feel very angry. I am a #5.

Mission 4

My friends and I were making jokes. They made me laugh a lot. I can't stop laughing. I am a #3.

TOPIC 1

Deep Breathing

Focus on your stomach, and imagine a small balloon inside. Breathe in slowly and deeply through your nose, imagining the balloon getting slowly bigger. Hold your breath for a few seconds, then slowly breathe out through your mouth, imagining the balloon gently getting smaller. Repeat five or more times.

See how different your body feels. Are you more relaxed? Do you feel lighter? Great! Practice this exercise several times a day, even while sitting at your desk, and soon your body will develop the habit. Then, when it is hard to be flexible, you can take five or more deep breaths and your body will automatically go into the relaxation mode.

ACTIVITY 3

Strategy Cards

Individual Activity
~10 minutes

Materials

Not Included

- Five blank index cards for each student and for the teacher
- Markers
- Access to clipart, a computer, or magazines with lots of pictures
- Hole punch
- String or D-ring to hold cards together

Included

- Handout: Just-Right Strategies Investigation
- Handout: Strategy Card Examples

Instructions

1. Each student will identify five just-right strategies that he or she thinks will work best in when feelings start getting overwhelming based on his or her responses to Handout: Just-Right Strategies Investigation. Students will make a strategy card for each strategy they choose, showing the strategy in words and images. Make cards for yourself in advance, and show them to the students. Following are some examples (see also Handout: Strategy Card Examples).
   a. Picture of something that represents deep breathing
   b. Picture of the student hugging a loved one
   c. Picture of the words *Ask for help*
   d. Picture of something that represents taking a break
   e. Picture of the student's favorite place or activity
2. For each strategy, students should write a word or phrase and draw, cut out, or download a picture to put on the strategy card. Have them punch a hole in each index card and bind the cards with a loop or ring. Students may use other visual strategies to capture their Just-Right Strategies if they prefer; they do not have to use the strategy cards.

TOPIC 1

Strategy Card Examples

Get a drink of water

Take a break

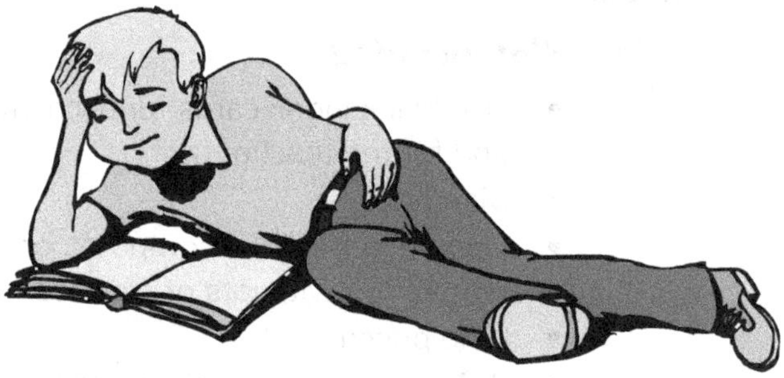

Ask someone for help

Take five deep breaths

Think of my favorite things/activities

Think of my favorite place

ADDITIONAL ACTIVITY

Coping Choices

Skits
~20 minutes

Use this lesson if you feel your students could benefit from additional practice rating their emotions and accessing coping strategies.

Instructions

1. Read aloud or act out the scenarios at the end of this activity using plenty of humor.
2. Ask students to give examples of helpful and unhelpful coping strategies in response to each scenario, or you may choose to read or act out the sample strategies that follow each scenario. Ask the students to indicate whether each coping strategy is a helpful choice or an unhelpful choice. If the strategy is an unhelpful choice, ask students to suggest alternatives.
3. Have students practice the scenarios using the just-right strategies they have selected for their strategy cards. Ask students watching to indicate whether the participants showed good use of the coping strategies.

Scenarios and Sample Strategies

(Please modify scenarios to meet the needs and interests of your students.)

Scenario: You are in math class and cannot figure out how to do a problem. You can feel yourself becoming very frustrated.

- *Coping strategy 1:* You ask to take a break, then return to the math class. Now you can figure it out.
- *Coping strategy 2:* You scream and throw your book on the floor and get sent to the principal.

Scenario: You are in science class, and your body feels like it has a lot of extra energy. You cannot sit still in your seat.

- *Coping strategy 1:* You take a long, deep breath and feel calmer, and you are able to pay attention.
- *Coping strategy 2:* You get more and more wound up and get up and run around the room.

Scenario: You are in the classroom, and your friend is reading the book you wanted to read during free time. You are feeling very upset.

- *Coping strategy 1:* You try to grab the book from your friend and get in trouble.
- *Coping strategy 2:* You look at your list of just-right strategies and decide to read a comic book instead.

Scenario: You are in science class and your friend gets to answer a question you wanted to answer.

- *Coping strategy 1:* You interrupt and do not earn your points.
- *Coping strategy 2:* You wait for the next question and try again.

You can do a Feelings Chain for each of these examples (see Topic 1, Lesson 3). You can use the Feelings Chain to make predictions about "what would happen if…" or to replay a problematic scenario and then rewrite the scene the way the student wishes it had gone. Note when the student should have used a coping strategy.

CLOSING

Review: Classroom & Home Practice

Wrap-up
~5 minutes

Materials

Not Included

- Pencils (1 per student)
- Group Reinforcement Visual
- Each student's *UOT Notebook*

Included

- Classroom Practice 4
- Home Practice 4

Instructions

Students will review the Home Practice and complete the *check* portion of the Goal, Why, Plan, Do, Check.

1. Hand out the Home Practice sheets. Read the goal aloud. Ask students to think about who they will work on their Home Practice (HP) with. Let students know they will each earn a tally for bringing the completed HP with them next time you meet.

   Tip

   ★ Follow the same procedure every day for reviewing and completing HP (e.g., review Home Practice sheets, monitor all students as they put it in their homework folder, monitor all students as they write it in their homework planner).
2. Guide students to file all worksheets in their *UOT Notebooks.*
3. Read the goal for Lesson 4 aloud to the class. Ask students if they were able to accomplish the goal. Ask students to identify what helped them accomplish the goal.
4. Review the plan. Ask students if they were able to accomplish the plan. Were there steps that we were not able to accomplish? Did we need to revise the plan in any way?
5. Remind students they are working towards a large group celebration/prize. Each day you will add their tally marks to a bank. When they reach _____ tallies they will get a group celebration or prize.

   Tip

   ★ During the lesson if you find students sticking to the plan or following the Code of Conduct remind them what they are working for and reinforce accordingly. ("Great job using respectful words and earning tallies. Our tallies get us closer to our flexibility party.")
6. Distribute the Classroom Practice handout to all instructors who interact with your students and would benefit from supporting students as they work on their new skills.

TOPIC 1

Classroom Practice 4

Session Summary: The students chose and practiced coping strategies in group.

What you can do to support your student's learning and generalization:

1. Identify your own coping strategies in front of students at least once a day, using instructive self-talk. For example:
   - *"I am frustrated that this isn't working today! I'm going to **ask for help.**"*
   - *"I am disappointed we aren't going to get to do that today. I'm going to **take five deep breaths**, and think about how fun it will be to do it tomorrow."*
2. If your student has any trouble in your class, remind your student to leave their coping strategy cards out on or in his or her desk. Each student made coping cards with examples of things to do to stay calm (take a deep breath, ask for a break, etc.). Please reward your students when they try to use coping strategies, even when your students aren't totally successful.
   - *"Let's all take a **deep breath** together and focus on our goal."*
   - *"This isn't working. Let's **take a break** and come back to it fresh."*
   - *"This is a good time to check your **coping strategies.** Should we pick one to try?"*

Home Practice 4

Your child participated in the fourth session of *Unstuck and On Target!* today.

Session Summary: Your child learned today about how to calm down when feeling upset, disappointed or frustrated. Your child made coping strategy cards to use as reminders to try to do things to calm down.

What you can do at home:

1. Identify your own coping strategies in front of your child a couple of times this week. For example:
   - *"I am frustrated that this isn't working today! I'm going to* ***ask for help.****"*
   - *"I am disappointed we aren't going to get to do that today. I'm going to* ***take five deep breaths*** *and think about how fun it will be to do it tomorrow."*
2. Take a look at your child's coping strategy cards. These are reminders for things your child can do to calm down. Ask your child which strategy he or she thinks will work the best. You can also remind your child to bring the cards to situations/places that trigger meltdowns.
   - *"Sometimes you get frustrated in the grocery store. How about bringing your* ***coping cards*** *with you and trying some of the strategies?"*
   - Reward your child anytime he or she tries a coping strategy.
3. Your child is going to teach you to try a deep breathing script (see below). It should only take a few minutes, and you might be surprised how helpful it is.

Deep Breathing Script

Focus on your stomach, and imagine a small balloon inside. Breathe in slowly and deeply through your nose, imagining the balloon getting slowly bigger. Hold your breath for a few seconds, then slowly breathe out through your mouth, imagining the balloon gently getting smaller. Repeat five or more times.

TOPIC 1

Topic 1 Progress Report

Student Name: ______________________ Date: ______________________

Teacher Name: ____

Over the last few weeks we have covered the following skills and concepts in Topic 1:

- Code of Conduct
- Goal, Why, Plan, Do, Check
- Feelings Target
- Feelings Chain
- Disappointment
- Feeling Just-Right
- Coping Strategies

Topic 1 Skills	**All of the time**	**Some of the time**	**None of the time**
1. Follows the Code of Conduct			
2. Is able to create a Goal, Why, Plan, Do, Check			
3. Is able to say how s/he feels			
4. Is able to identify how their actions might make others feel			
A success in group:			
Something we will continue to work on:			
Additional Notes:			

X ______________________________________ (Teacher)

(please detach and return the signed slip, acknowledging you have received the progress report)

- -

I have received the *Unstuck and On Target!* Progress Report

X ______________________________ Date: ______________

TOPIC 2

What Is Flexibility?

SPECIAL INSTRUCTIONS: Topic 2 provides students with a deep and specific understanding of the meaning of flexibility, rigidity and being stuck. To teach the students most effectively, a common vocabulary is vital. The same words must be used over and over and be used consistently between home and school. The group leader should modify activities as necessary to best meet students' needs.

Summary: Topic 2 defines *flexible, rigid,* and *stuck*. In addition, the lessons within this topic provide a conceptual foundation for *flexibility* through concrete, playful activities. This topic builds on the foundational understanding of flexibility as a physical property by expanding the concept to include *cognitive* flexibility. Students, teachers, and parents learn and teach a new vocabulary which they all use in the same way.

Prerequisite skills: Understanding and buy-in of the Code of Conduct and GWPDC routine. Ability to use Feelings Target and Feelings Chain (Topic 1).

Related skills: Core language comprehension, ability to participate in group discussion and role play.

OUTCOME—CRITERION FOR MASTERY

1. The student defines flexibility and stuck with their minds.
2. The student defines *flexibility* and *rigidity* in physical, concrete terms.
3. The student identifies whether an object is flexible or rigid.
4. The student demonstrates an understanding of the advantages that flexibility offers to a physical object and thinking/problem solving skills.

TOPIC BACKGROUND AND RATIONALE

Cognitive instruction is the first element of *Unstuck and On Target!* In cognitive instruction, students, teachers, and parents learn and teach new vocabulary related to physical and cognitive flexibility. Cognitive flexibility is a difficult, abstract concept; therefore, it is important to make sure that elementary school students understand its meaning and value—its usefulness—in the concrete, physical world first, then it is important to build on that foundation and expand the concept to *cognitive flexibility*. The primary goal of this lesson, building a common flexibility vocabulary, is vital because it allows teachers, parents, and students to gain access to, with one word or phrase (e.g., "Are you stuck?"), all the teaching and experiences that are provided throughout this intervention. This common vocabulary serves as an essential foundation on which all future work in this curriculum is built.

TOPIC 2

Lesson 5 Flexibility Investigation

PURPOSE

The purpose of this lesson is to introduce the concept of *Flexibility* and bring salience to its definition. The activities included in this lesson are designed as hands-on opportunities to explore Flexibility in its physical form, and how approaching tasks Flexibly is more efficient. There are two activities in this lesson.

Materials Required for All Activities

Not Included

- Whiteboard or chart paper
- Tape
- 3 pieces of paper (each labeled with a number 1, 2, or 3)
- Dry/wet erase markers or markers
- 2 rigid objects (ex., ruler, pencil)
- Bag or bin for objects
- 2 flexible objects (ex., straw, string)
- Scrap paper
- Pencils
- Group Reinforcement Visual
- Each student's *UOT Notebook*

Included

- GWPDC for Lesson 5
- Lightning Round Questions
- Classroom Practice 5
- Home Practice 5

INTRODUCTION

Preview: GWPDC & Lightning Round

Review & Game
~5 minutes

Materials

Not Included

- Whiteboard or chart paper and suitable markers
- Tape
- 3 pieces of paper (each labeled with a number 1, 2, or 3)

Included

- GWPDC for Lesson 5
- Lightning Round Questions

Instructions

1. Post the GWPDC on the board before the lesson begins.
2. Review the GWPDC with the group.
3. Complete the Lightning Round activity.

**For a complete set of instructions and tips, refer to the GWPDC and Lightning Round instructions (Topic 1, Lesson 2).*

Reinforce...
Memory
"Great job remembering that from our last group, I can tell you were really paying attention."

G W P D C

Goal: Figure out the difference between Flexible and Rigid. Decide which one is more efficient. Earn 10 tallies.

Why: Learning more about the difference between Flexible and Rigid helps me learn how to be Flexible at school and in life, which helps me get more of what I want and earn tallies to help us get our group reward.

Plan:
1. Play Lightning Round
2. Flexibility vs. Rigid Scavenger Hunt Investigation
3. Flexible is Faster (and more efficient)
4. Review Home Practice

Do: Follow the plan and earn tallies.

Check: How did it go? Did we accomplish our goal?

Remember to check off this step on the GWPDC!

Lightning Round Questions

1. What is one coping strategy you can use when you are feeling like a #5?
2. Two coping strategies that work for me are _____ and _____.
3. One thing that makes me feel like a #4 or #5 is _____ and to get back to a #1 I would use _____ as a coping strategy.

ACTIVITY 1

Flexible vs. Rigid Scavenger Hunt

Activity
~10 minutes

Materials

Not Included

- Whiteboard or chart paper and suitable markers
- At least 2 rigid objects (e.g., ruler, pencil)
- Bag or bin for objects
- At least 2 flexible objects (e.g., straw, string)

Instructions

Reinforce!

Give tallies when students give descriptions of the objects.

Students sometimes have difficulty when another student has the same idea as them. Reinforce students when their "great minds think alike."

1. Write the words Flexible and Rigid on the board. Ask students if they have ever heard or used these words before. Record their descriptions on the board.
2. Tell students you have objects in your bag (include enough objects so each student has a turn) and their job is to select an object and tell you if it is Rigid or Flexible and why.
3. Students select each item one at a time. Ask them if it is Flexible or Rigid and why they think so. Record their answers on the board (Flexible—it bends, it changes shape, it doesn't break; Rigid—stiff, doesn't bend, will break if you try to bend it).
4. Give students a piece of paper and ask them to move around the room and see how many Flexible and Rigid objects they can find and record. Tell them they need to find at least 2 of each kind.

Tips

★ If you anticipate your students will have difficulty finding items on their own, create a list of classroom items, have students locate them and mark if they are Flexible or Rigid.

★ If you think your students are up to the challenge have them work in pairs to locate objects.

Remember to check off this step on the GWPDC!

ACTIVITY 2
Flexible Is Faster (and More Efficient)

Activity
~10 minutes

Materials

Not Included

- Whiteboard or chart paper and suitable markers
- Scrap piece of paper for each student

Instructions

Reinforce!
For trying something hard, like writing with a totally Rigid body!

1. Tell students that you will be conducting a scientific experiment to find out which is faster, more efficient, and easier: a Flexible body or a Rigid one.
2. Tell students they will be asked to write something on the board 3 different ways.

   A. With a Rigid body (you are not allowed to bend any body parts as you write)
   B. With a Rigid body and Flexible fingers (you can bend only your fingers)
   C. With a totally Flexible body (you can bend all of your body parts)

   Ask them to write on a piece of paper which one they predict will be the fastest, easiest, most efficient option (A, B, or C).
3. Bring students up to the board and ask them to write a silly word or short phrase. Start with the rigid body. After each opportunity ask students to describe their experience.
4. Once each child has had the chance to try out all three options ask them to write down which option was the fastest, easiest, most efficient option (A, B, or C).

   Tips

   ★ Try out the Flexible vs. Rigid body experiment in an obstacle course either using equipment in the classroom, in the gym, or on the playground.
   ★ If writing on the board is a challenge for some students, the activity can be adjusted to drawing a picture, building an object out of playdough, or making a peanut butter and jelly sandwich with a rigid or flexible body.

Remember to check off this step on the GWPDC!

CLOSING

Review: Classroom & Home Practice

Wrap-up
~5 minutes

Materials

Not Included

- Pencils (1 per student)
- Group Reinforcement Visual
- Each student's *UOT Notebook*

Included

- Classroom Practice 5
- Home Practice 5

Instructions

Students will review the Home Practice and complete the *check* portion of the Goal, Why Plan, Do, Check.

1. Hand out the Home Practices. Read the goal aloud. Ask students to think about who they will work on their Home Practice (HP) with. Let students know they will each earn a tally for bringing the completed HP with them next time you meet.

   Tip

   ★ Follow the same procedure every day for reviewing and completing HP (e.g., review HP, monitor all students as they put it in their homework folder, monitor all students as they write it in their homework planner).

2. Guide students to file all worksheets in their UOT Notebooks.
3. Read the goal for Lesson 5 aloud to the class. Ask the students if they were able to accomplish the goal. Ask students to identify what helped them accomplish the goal.

   Tip

   ★ During the first few lessons make sure students are able to accomplish the goal so that they feel a sense of success and develop an understanding of how to earn tallies.

4. Review the plan. Ask students if they were able to accomplish the plan. Were there steps that we were not able to accomplish? Did we need to revise the plan in any way?

   Tip

   ★ Sometimes plans have to change: an unexpected fire drill or a great discussion takes too long and you have to alter the plan. Celebrate these changes and let students know that even though the unexpected happened, they were Flexible and made a new plan. This concept will be taught in greater detail in future lessons.

5. Remind students they are working towards a large group prize. Each day you will add their tally marks to a bank. When they reach _____ tallies they will get a group celebration or prize.

   Tips

   ★ Determine what the prize or prize options will be for this ahead of time. See Troubleshooting section for suggestions.

   ★ Monitor the number of tallies students are earning to make sure that you're distributing enough tallies throughout the session.

   ★ Post the tally bank in the front of the classroom so students are constantly reminded of how close they are to their goal (e.g., a thermometer).

6. Distribute the Classroom Practice handout to all instructors who interact with your students and would benefit from supporting students as they work on their new skills.

TOPIC 2

Classroom Practice 5

Session Summary: Students explored how flexible objects are stronger and learned that approaching tasks flexibly is more efficient.

What you can do to support your student's learning and generalization:

1. Identify flexible objects and point out times when flexible is better or stronger. For example:
   - *"It's a good thing this rubber band is **flexible**, or it would have broken!"*
   - *"Wouldn't this be faster if it were **flexible**?"*
2. If you'd like to do more, see who can think of the most flexible things/superheroes/substances, or play "I Spy" Something Flexible the next time your class is waiting in line, waiting for dismissal, or you have a little extra time in class.

TOPIC 2

Home Practice 5

Your child participated in the fifth session of *Unstuck and On Target!* today.

Session Summary: Your child learned today about how flexible objects are stronger and learned that sometimes it is better to be flexible.

What you can do at home:

1. This week's home practice is easy. Just try to use the word "flexible" as often as you can. Identify flexible objects and point out times when flexible is better or stronger. For example:
   - *"It's a good thing this rubber band is **flexible**, or it would have broken!"*
   - *"Wouldn't this be faster if it were **flexible**?"*
2. If you'd like to do more, see who can think of the most flexible things/superheroes/substances, or play "I Spy" Something Flexible the next time you are waiting in line, in the car, or on the bus.

Lesson 6 Flexibility

TOPIC 2

PURPOSE

This lesson forms a bridge from the concept of *Physical Flexibility* to the more abstract concept of *Cognitive Flexibility*. The lesson begins the work of creating a vocabulary of words and concepts that promote a comprehensive understanding of Flexibility. There are two activities in this lesson.

Materials Required for All Activities

Not Included

- Whiteboard or chart paper and suitable markers
- Tape
- 3 pieces of paper (each labeled with a number 1, 2, or 3)
- Dry/wet erase markers or markers
- Fun putty ingredients (see Fun Putty Recipe handout)
- Pencils
- Group Reinforcement Visual
- Each student's *UOT Notebook*

Included

- GWPDC for Lesson 6
- Lightning Round Questions
- Handout: Mystery Word 1
- Educator Guide: Mystery Word 1 Key
- Handout: *Unstuck and On Target!* Dictionary—Flexible
- Handout: Flexible Fun
- Handout: Fun Putty Recipe
- Classroom Practice 6
- Home Practice 6

INTRODUCTION

Preview: GWPDC & Lightning Round

Review & Game
~5 minutes

Materials

Not Included

- Whiteboard or chart paper and suitable markers
- Tape
- 3 pieces of paper (each labeled with a number 1, 2, or 3)

Included

- GWPDC for Lesson 6
- Lightning Round Questions

Instructions

1. Post the GWPDC on the board before the lesson begins.
2. Review the GWPDC with the group.
3. Complete the Lightning Round activity.

**For a complete set of instructions and tips, refer to the GWPDC and Lightning Round instructions (Topic 1, Lesson 2).*

Reinforce!
Encourage students to use their peers for support when they don't know an answer. Reinforce them for working together.

GWPDC

Goal: Figure out what it means to be Flexible with our minds.

Why: When I am Flexible I have more choices. It is so much better to have choices than be stuck with only one option.

Plan:
1. Lightning Round
2. Uncover the Mystery Word 1
3. Are you as Flexible as putty?
4. Review Home Practice

Do: Follow the plan and earn tallies.

Check: How did it go? Did we accomplish our plan? A time when I was Flexible was ________.

Lightning Round Questions

1. When my body is stiff and won't bend it is _____? (Rigid)
2. Name 3 things I can do to help my group earn tallies.
3. Writing on the board was easier when my body was _____? (Flexible)

ACTIVITY 1

Mystery Word—Flexibility

Individual or Group Activity
~10 minutes

Materials

Not Included

- Whiteboard or chart paper and suitable markers

Included

- Handout: Mystery Word 1
- Educator Guide: Mystery Word 1 Key
- Handout: *Unstuck and On Target!* Dictionary—Flexible

Instructions

Students will be presented with one Mystery Word in each lesson of Topic 2. Each new vocabulary word will be presented in a unique, enjoyable way. In the first part of this lesson, you will guide students through the discovery of cognitive flexibility and the beginning of a new vocabulary related to flexibility.

1. Ask students to reflect on the physical flexibility vocabulary and activities from Topic 2, Lesson 5 (flexible/rigid).
2. Distribute Handout: Mystery Word 1 (one per student or one for the group).
3. Once the students have filled in the word *flexibility*, tell them, "We know we can be flexible with our bodies. Raise your hand if you think that you can also be flexible with your mind."
4. Ask students if they have ever been flexible with their minds. They may need some examples to get started. Examples include the following: "The red marker was out of ink, so I used the blue one," or "The book I really wanted wasn't at the library, so I chose a different one." It may be helpful to use examples you have witnessed among your students in recent days.
5. Ask the students to write their examples on the whiteboard. Or write the examples down for them.

Remember to check off this step on the GWPDC!

Mystery Word 1

 + i +  + i + 

__________ + i + __________ + i + __________ = __________

Mystery Word 1 Key

 + i +  + i + 

flex + i + bill + i + tea = Flexibility

Unstuck and On Target! Dictionary

Flexible

Definition:	Examples and Tips:
• Just as we can be flexible with our bodies, we also can be flexible with our minds.	• This means that we can o Change our ideas o Do something different than what we thought we would do o Think something different o Consider new information o Keep an open mind o Identify other flexible mind accomplishments

ACTIVITY 2 *OPTIONAL

As Flexible as Putty

Presentation and Activity
~20 minutes

Materials

Not Included

- Fun Putty ingredients:
  - White glue
  - Water
  - Food coloring (enough so that the students can choose and share)
  - Borax (typically found at the grocery store near the laundry detergent)

Included

- Handout: Flexible Fun
- Handout: Fun Putty Recipe
- Visual: Feelings Chain
- Visual: Feelings Target

Instructions

1. Distribute Handout: Flexible Fun.
2. Tell the students the story of the invention of putty. Use the handout as a guide to your storytelling.
3. Ask the students whether they know what putty can do. (In itself, putty is very Flexible. It can copy newsprint, bounce, and mold. Astronauts used it on Apollo 8 to keep tools in place.)
4. Explain that people need to be Flexible like Peter Hodgson was and in the same way that putty is. When we are not Flexible, we are Rigid, the way that James Wright was.
5. Use the Feelings Chain to chart James' experience vs. Peter's.

James (students will have to make some assumptions about how he must have been feeling)

Event
Putty did not act like rubber

↓

Feeling
Really Angry (4)

↓

Action
Gave up

↓

How Others Feel
Putty did not act like rubber

↓

Consequence
Didn't use the Putty

↓

He Felt
Sad, Disappointed (3/4)

Peter (again, students will have to make some assumptions about how he must have been feeling)

Event
Saw the rubbery substance
Feeling
Hopeful (1)
Action
Came up with lots of uses for the substance
How Others Feel
Excited
Consequence
50 years of fun with the toy
He Felt
Proud (1)

Highlight the positive outcome that resulted from Flexible thinking and actions.

6. Provide the following scenarios for students to consider. Ask students how they would be Flexible with their minds in these situations.
   a. "You go to the playground planning to swing, but all the swings are taken. What could you do if you were being Flexible? What would you do if you were not being Flexible or were being Rigid?"
   b. "What if you think that someone really does not like you and then they offer you a cookie from their lunch and ask you to play a game with them?" Incorporate the word *Rigid* into the scenario. "What would you do if you were not being Flexible or were being Rigid?"
7. Summarize the scenarios as follows: "Being Flexible is not just about bending; it is also about changing an idea, considering new information, or changing what you are doing." Distinguish between *Flexibility* and *giving in.*
8. Distribute Handout: Fun Putty Recipe and the ingredients required to make the Fun Putty (or buy putty if you prefer, instead of making it). Make Fun Putty using the recipe.
9. Post the words Flexible and Rigid and their definitions on the bulletin board.

Remember to check off this step on the GWPDC!

TOPIC 2

Flexible Fun

James Wright was a thinker who worked in a lab. He lived in the 1940s during World War II, when there was a shortage of natural rubber made from trees. Soldiers needed rubber to make boots and tires, so Wright tried to invent a substitute for rubber. Wright invented something that could stretch and bounce and even make perfect copies when he pressed it against a comic strip. But Wright's putty was too gooey for boots or tires, so he gave up on his invention.

Rubber tire

Rubber boots

A few years later, a businessman named Peter Hodgson saw Wright's putty at a party. Just like the goo, Hodgson was flexible. He thought of a new way to use it—put it in a colorful plastic egg, give it a catchy name, and sell it as a toy. Kids have been playing with the stretchy bouncy putty for more than 50 years. It has even been in outer space. Apollo 8 astronauts used it to hold their tools in place when they flew to the moon!

TOPIC 2

Fun Putty Recipe

RECIPE

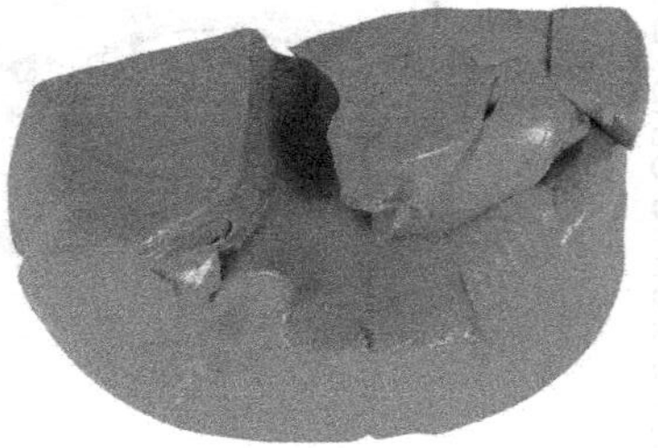

Ingredients:

- 2 cups white glue
- 2 cups water
- Food coloring of choice
- 1 teaspoon Borax

Directions:

1. Mix the white glue, 1½ cups of the water, and the food coloring into a bowl until it is no longer sticky. This will be your glue solution.
2. In a separate bowl, dissolve 1 teaspoon Borax into ½ cup of water.
3. Add the Borax solution to the glue solution.
4. When the two solutions mix, the result will be a very thick clump of slime. Knead the slime with clean hands to get it to mix well. This will take about 10 minutes or so.
5. Enjoy your Fun Putty!

CLOSING

Review: Classroom & Home Practice

Wrap-up
~5 minutes

Materials

Not Included

- Pencils (1 per student)
- Group Reinforcement Visual
- Each student's *UOT Notebook*

Included

- Classroom Practice 6
- Home Practice 6

Instructions

Reinforce…

Remembering the Steps

"You followed all of the steps for putting your Home Practice and worksheet away. You have earned an extra tally."

Students will review the Home Practice and complete the check portion of the Goal, Why, Plan, Do, Check.

1. Hand out the Home Practice sheets. Read the goal aloud. Ask students to think about who they will work on their Home Practice (HP) with. Let students know they will each earn a tally for bringing the completed HP with them next time you meet.

   Tip

   ★ Follow the same procedure every day for reviewing and completing HP (e.g., review HP, monitor all students as they put it in their homework folder, monitor all students as they write it in their homework planner).

2. Guide students to file handouts in their *UOT Notebooks*.
3. Read the goal for Lesson 6 aloud to the class. Ask students if they were able to accomplish the goal. Ask students to identify what helped them accomplish the goal.
4. Review the plan. Ask students if they were able to accomplish the plan. Were there steps that we were not able to accomplish? Did we need to revise the plan in any way?

   Tip

   ★ The putty activity requires lots of interaction between the students and with all of the materials necessary there may be opportunities for practicing reflecting on how the plan needed to shift.

5. Remind students they are working towards a large group celebration/prize. Each day you will add their tally marks to a bank. When they reach _____ tallies they will get a group celebration or prize.

   Tip

   ★ During the lesson if you find students sticking to the plan or following the Code of Conduct remind them what they are working for and reinforce accordingly. ("Great job using respectful words and earning tallies. Our tallies get us closer to our Flexibility party.")

6. Distribute the Classroom Practice handout to all instructors who interact with your students and would benefit from supporting students as they work on their new skills.

TOPIC 2

Classroom Practice 6

Session Summary: Do you remember playing with putty when you were a kid? In group today, students learned the story of putty, which was useless as an alternative to rubber. It was thrown away by the man who created it when it didn't work for that purpose. Someone else came along with an open mind and figured out a way to make it into a toy, showing students that they can also be flexible with their minds and make good things happen.

What you can do to support your student's learning and generalization:

1. Being flexible is not just about bending, it is also about:
   - changing an idea
   - considering new information
   - accepting an unexpected change or event
   - changing what you are doing
2. Distinguish between *flexibility* and *giving in.*
   - *"Being **flexible** helps me get some of what I want."*
3. Identify times when you, characters in books, or figures in history were flexible and good things happened. For example:
   - *"Is there another way to solve this problem? There's more than one way to get the right answer."*
   - *"If Stuart Little had been more **flexible**, he still could have had fun with Harriet even though the canoe didn't work as he had planned."*
   - *"What did Marie Curie do that was **flexible**? How did that work for her?"*

TOPIC 2

Home Practice 6

Your child participated in the sixth session of *Unstuck and On Target!* today.

Session Summary: Do you remember playing with putty when you were a kid? In group today, your child learned the story behind putty, which was useless as an alternative to rubber. It was thrown away by the man who created it when it didn't work for that purpose. Someone else came along with an open mind and figured out a way to make it into a toy, showing students that they can also be flexible with their minds and make good things happen.

What you can do at home:

1. Being flexible is not just about bending, it is also about:
   - changing an idea
   - considering new information
   - accepting an unexpected change or event
   - changing what you are doing
2. Distinguish between *flexibility* and *giving in.*
   - *"Being **flexible** helps me get some of what I want."*
3. Notice times when you or your child were flexible and good things happened. For example:
   - *"Is there another way to solve this problem? There's more than one way to get the right answer."*
   - *"When you did _________, I could tell that you were being **flexible**, and it worked!"*
   - *"Thank you for being **flexible** with _________, it made things much easier."*
4. Talk about times when someone on TV, in the news, or in a book was flexible and good things happened. For example:
   - *"Did you notice how he was **flexible**, and could still get what he wanted?"*
   - *"What if she hadn't been **flexible** then, what would have happened?"*

TOPIC 2

Lesson 7 Getting Stuck

PURPOSE

This lesson extends the concept of *Flexibility* and enables students to compare it with the concept of being *Stuck*. This lesson uses the students' understanding of *Rigid* to link to their conceptualization of *Stuck*. There are two activities in this lesson.

Materials Required for All Activities

Not Included

- Whiteboard or chart paper
- Dry/wet erase markers or markers
- Tape
- 3 pieces of paper (each labeled with a number 1, 2, or 3)
- Craft sticks or tongue depressors
- Putty (or similar substance)
- Pencils
- Group Reinforcement Visual
- Each student's *UOT Notebook*

Included

- GWPDC for Lesson 7
- Lightning Round Questions
- Handout: Mystery Word 2
- Educator Guide: Mystery Word 2 Key
- Handout: *Unstuck and On Target!* Dictionary—Stuck
- Classroom Practice 7
- Home Practice 7

INTRODUCTION
Preview: GWPDC & Lightning Round

Review & Game
~5 minutes

Materials

Not Included

- Whiteboard or chart paper and suitable markers
- Tape
- 3 pieces of paper (each labeled with a number 1, 2, or 3)

Included

- GWPDC for Lesson 7
- Lightning Round Questions

Instructions

1. Post the GWPDC on the board before the lesson begins.
2. Review the GWPDC with the group.
3. Complete the Lightning Round activity.

**For a complete set of instructions and tips, refer to the GWPDC and Lightning Round instructions (Topic 1, Lesson 2).*

Reinforce!

Encourage students to use their peers for support when they don't know an answer. Reinforce them for working together.

GWPDC	
G	**Goal:** Figure out what it means to be Flexible with our minds.
W	**Why:** Being Flexible gives me more choices.
P	**Plan:** 1. Lightning Round 2. Uncover the Mystery Word 2 3. Role Play 4. Review Home Practice
D	**Do:** Follow the plan and earn tallies.
C	**Check:** How did it go? Did we accomplish our plan? A time when I sometimes find myself getting Stuck _____.

Lightning Round Questions

1. Look at the Feelings Target: what number would you rate yourself right now?
2. If you want the green marker but it is being used, what is a Flexible choice you can make?
3. Think about the Feelings Chain. Which step can you control? (I'll give you a hint: the step you control affects how others feel, the consequence, and how you feel in the end.)

ACTIVITY 1

Mystery Word—Stuck

Individual or Group Activity
~10 minutes

Materials

Not Included

- Whiteboard or chart paper and suitable markers

Included

- Handout: Mystery Word 2
- Educator Guide: Mystery Word 2 Key
- Handout: *Unstuck and On Target!* Dictionary—Stuck

Instructions

1. Ask students to reflect on being Flexible with your mind, and the vocabulary and activities from Lesson 6. Ensure that students remember the story of putty.
2. Distribute Handout: Mystery Word 2 (one for each student or one for the group). Ask the students to think about the pictures of people and objects on the handout and determine what they all have in common (they are all Stuck).
3. After students have uncovered the word *Stuck*, explain to the students that when they are Flexible, they never actually get Stuck because they always have a choice. People who are Flexible keep an open mind. This may be the first time students have heard the expression *open mind*. Remind students that when they are Flexible and they keep an open mind they have lots of choices. Continue to incorporate the expression into your conversation with the students.
4. Reiterate to the students that if they choose to be Flexible, they have more choices; however, when they are Stuck, they have only the one choice—being Stuck.
5. Create a flowchart as you review the examples below. See the example below. Use green and red markers to illustrate the difference between *Flexible* and *Stuck*, respectively.
   a. James Wright, who invented putty, got Stuck on the fact that his invention could not be used for the purpose he intended. In contrast, Peter Hodgson was Flexible and saw everything that putty *could* be. Hodgson made many children happy and earned a great deal of money because of his Flexibility.
   b. If two friends are playing and they get Stuck because they want to play different games, they will end up not playing anything; however, if they are both Flexible, they can think of many different games to play.
   c. Add additional examples from familiar situations until you feel that students understand the concept.

Remember to check off this step on the GWPDC!

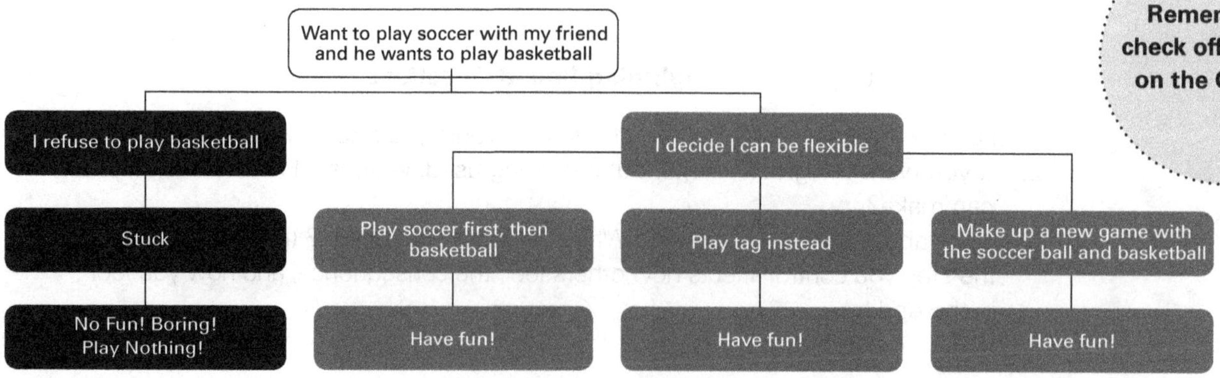

Mystery Word 2

= ____________________

Mystery Word 2 Key

= Stuck

Unstuck and On Target! Dictionary

Stuck	

Definition:
 	
• Just like we can be rigid with our bodies, we also can be rigid with our minds and get stuck.
	Examples and Tips:
	
	• When we are rigid and stuck, we
	  o Do not change our ideas or think differently
	  o Do not do something different than what we thought we would do
	• When we are stuck, we only have one choice: to remain stuck.
	• When we are flexible, we do not get stuck.
	• When we are flexible, we have many choices.

ACTIVITY 2

Flexible/Stuck Role Play

Group Activity
~5–10 minutes

Materials

Not Included

- Whiteboard or chart paper and suitable markers
- Craft sticks or tongue depressors (one for each student)
- Putty (or similar substance; one piece for each student)

Instructions

1. Distribute one craft stick or tongue depressor and one piece of putty to each student.
2. Act out the following scenarios; recruit assistants to help if desired. As they watch, students should decide whether the person in each scenario is being Rigid or Flexible. Following each scenario, ask the students to raise their craft sticks or tongue depressors in the air if the person is being Rigid or their putty if the person is being Flexible.
   a. Look for a particular color of marker that you do not have. When you are unable to find the color you are looking for, abandon writing on the board altogether.
   b. Once again, look for a color of marker that you do not have. When you are unable to find that particular color, decide instead to use a color that you have. On the board, write *I love my students* or something that your students will love to read. Once the students have voted on whether the scenario demonstrated Flexibility or Rigidity, emphasize that the color of marker did not matter but the message did; it was far better to express the message using a non-preferred color of marker than to abandon writing the message altogether.
   c. Act out two additional scenes with contrasting outcomes (e.g., unable to find a preferred article of clothing, unable to find a preferred toy), again highlighting the advantages of Flexibility.
   d. If you have time, ask students to give you examples to act out. You also may ask students to tell you the advantages of Flexibility in the different scenes.
3. Conclude the activity by reiterating the value of Flexibility and the burden of being Stuck. Briefly summarize the vocabulary and activities that have been covered thus far in Topic 2.

Remember to check off this step on the GWPDC!

CLOSING

Review: Classroom & Home Practice

Wrap-up
~5 minutes

Materials

Not Included

- Pencils (one for each student)
- Group Reinforcement Visual
- Each student's *UOT Notebook*

Included

- Classroom Practice 7
- Home Practice 7

Instructions

Students will review the Home Practice and complete the *check* portion of the Goal, Why, Plan, Do, Check.

1. Hand out the Home Practice sheets. Read the goal aloud. Ask students to think about who will work on their Home Practice (HP) with them. Let students know they will each earn a tally for bringing the completed HP with them next time you meet.

   Tip

   ★ Follow the same procedure every day for reviewing and completing HP (e.g., review HP, monitor all students as they put it in their homework folder, monitor all students as they write it in their homework planner).

2. Guide students to file their worksheets in their *UOT Notebooks.*
3. Read the goal for Lesson 7 aloud to the class. Ask students if they were able to accomplish the goal. Ask students to identify what helped them accomplish the goal.
4. Review the plan. Ask students if they were able to accomplish the plan. Were there steps that we were not able to accomplish? Did we need to revise the plan in any way?
5. Remind students they are working towards a large group celebration/prize. Each day you will add their tally marks to a bank. When they reach ____ tallies they will get a group celebration or prize.

   Tip

   ★ During the lesson if you find students sticking to the plan or following the Code of Conduct remind them what they are working for and reinforce accordingly. ("Great job using respectful words and earning tallies. Our tallies get us closer to our flexibility party.")

6. Distribute the Classroom Practice handout to all instructors who interact with your students and would benefit from supporting students as they work on their new skills.

TOPIC 2

Classroom Practice 7

Session Summary: Students learned that when they are *flexible*, they never actually get *stuck* because they always have a choice. People who are flexible *keep an open mind.*

What you can do to support your student's learning and generalization:

1. Remind students that when they are *flexible* and they keep an *open mind* they have lots of choices:

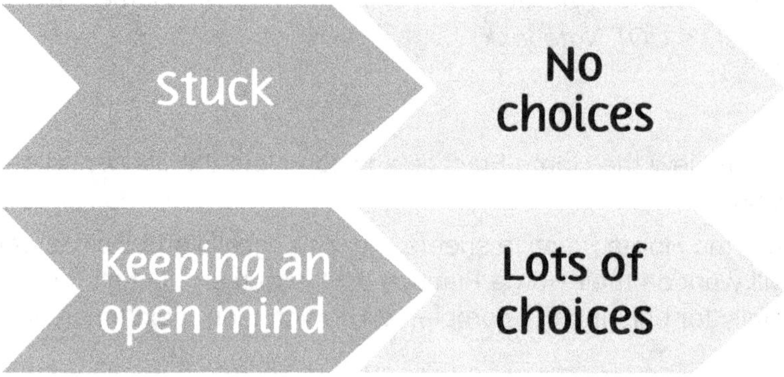

2. Distinguish between *keeping an open mind* and *giving in.*
   - *"I always have more choices when I* ***keep an open mind.*** *Having more choices is not the same as giving in."*
3. Identify times when you, characters in books, or figures in history or politics were *stuck* or didn't *keep an open mind* and bad things happened. For example:
   - *"They both want different things and they are* ***stuck****. Now neither one of them will get what they want. How would it look if they each kept an* ***open mind****?"*
   - *"I got really* ***stuck*** *on finding these shoes to wear to work today, and it took me so long to find them that I was late. What would have happened if I had* ***kept an open mind****?"*

Home Practice 7

Your child participated in the seventh session of *Unstuck and On Target!* today.

Session Summary: Your child learned that when we are *flexible*, we never actually get *stuck* because we always have a choice. People who are flexible *keep an open mind.*

What you can do at home:

1. Remind your child that when he or she is *stuck* on something that can't happen, there are no choices at all, but when he or she keeps an *open mind,* there are lots of choices:

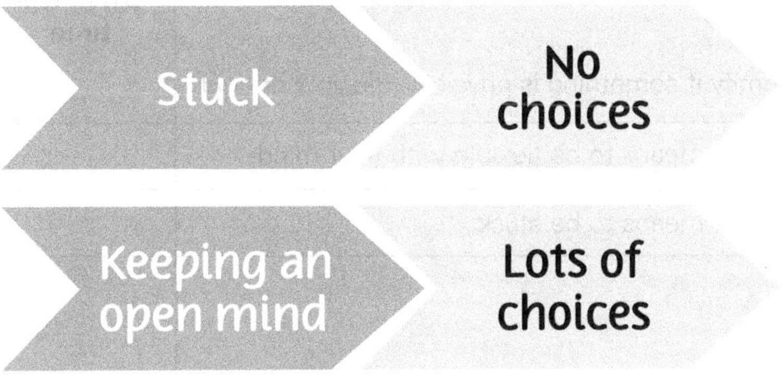

2. Distinguish between *keeping an open mind* and *giving in.*
   - *"I always have more choices when I* **keep an open mind**. *Having more choices is not the same as giving in."*
3. Identify times when you, characters in books or people on TV were *stuck* or didn't *keep an open mind* and bad things happened. For example:
   - *"I got really* ***stuck*** *on having our favorite type of pasta for dinner tonight, so I went to two different stores looking for those noodles because we were out. Now dinner is late. What would have happened if I had* ***kept an open mind****?"*
   - *"I've never eaten that before, and I think I won't like it. Should I keep an* ***open mind*** *and give it a try?"*

Topic 2 Progress Report

Student Name: ______________________ Date: ______________________

Teacher Name: ______________________

Over the last few weeks we have covered the following skills and concepts in Topic 2:

- Physical Flexibility
- Physical Rigidity
- Mental Flexibility
- Stuck

Topic 2 Skills	**All of the time**	**Some of the time**	**None of the time**
1. Is able to define/identify if something is physically flexible or rigid			
2. Is able to define what it means to be flexible with your mind			
3. Is able to define what it means to be stuck			
A success in group:			
Something we will continue to work on:			

X ______________________ (Teacher)

(please detach and return the signed slip, acknowledging you have received the progress report)

- -

I have received the *Unstuck and On Target!* Progress Report

X ______________________ Date: ______________

TOPIC 3

How to Be Flexible

SPECIAL INSTRUCTIONS: The core goal of these lessons is to help students make a habit of using flexibility scripts. To teach the students most effectively, a common vocabulary is vital. The same scripts must be used over and over and be used consistently between home and school. The Big Deal/Little Deal script should not be used to tell a student that something they feel is a Big Deal is really a Little Deal. The Choice/No Choice script is effective only when many more Choice than No Choice situations are identified and No Choice is reserved for true no choice situations (e.g., student has to leave the building during a fire alarm, not student has to write this paragraph right now). The group leader should modify activities as necessary to best meet students' needs.

Summary: The goal of Topic 3 is to teach students five self-regulatory scripts that, combined with the previously introduced GWPDC, give students a set of cognitive routines for regulating their behavior effectively. The five scripts are Plan A → Plan B, Compromise, Big Deal/Little Deal, Choice/No Choice, and Expect the Unexpected. These scripts are practiced repeatedly, reinforced visually, and incorporated into multiple activities at school and at home so that they become automatic for students, teachers, and parents.

Prerequisite skills: Understanding of the meaning of flexibility (Topic 1); familiarity with flexibility vocabulary (Topic 2)

Related skills: Core language comprehension, ability to participate in group discussion and activities

OUTCOME—CRITERIA FOR MASTERY

1. With minimal adult prompts, student applies the Plan A → Plan B and Compromise scripts to develop alternative plans of action when an initial plan fails or is rejected by a partner.
2. With minimal adult prompts, the student applies the Big Deal/Little Deal script to evaluate a situation and respond accordingly.
3. With minimal adult prompts, the student applies the Choice/No Choice script to evaluate a situation and make a choice or accept a requirement.
4. With minimal adult prompts, the student applies the Expect the Unexpected script to do or accept something unusual.

TOPIC BACKGROUND AND RATIONALE

Flexibility is a self-regulation skill. Self-regulation is established through internalized self-talk, and students with executive dysfunction need explicit instruction in self-regulatory self-talk about how to be flexible. Students will not internalize these critical self-regulatory scripts unless the scripts 1) become a habit for teachers and parents in their interactions with students,

2) are practiced repeatedly, and 3) are visually reinforced. The rationale for each of the five scripts is as follows:

- **Plan A → Plan B** is a powerful script that enables the student to regroup when something has not gone according to plan, and instead of blaming others or him- or herself for the failure, recognize that the plan itself was the problem and now there is an opportunity to make a new plan, or even multiple new plans. Many students who are inflexible are actually giddy with excitement at the realization that there are many plans and options (Plans B, C, D, etc.) available to them when things go wrong.
- The **Big Deal/Little Deal** self-regulatory script helps students distinguish what is important from what is not important so that they can be less anxious about situations of lesser importance and take seriously situations of greater importance. It also gives students a strategy for changing a big deal into a little deal when possible. It also empowers the student to decide for himself or herself what is a big vs. a little deal.
- With the **Choice/No Choice** self-regulatory script, students learn to 1) distinguish what is within their power to change and what is not, and 2) break a perseverative mindset and stop trying to influence something they cannot change.
- The **Expect the Unexpected** script gives students a step-by-step approach to adjusting to the unexpected. Children with executive dysfunction rely on very consistent routines and can become upset when change occurs or their expectations are violated. Because they need routine, it is useful to specifically teach them strategies for handling unexpected violations of routine.
- The **Compromise** script gives students a strategy for negotiating with others and avoiding all or nothing solutions. Both people get part of what they want with compromise.

Lesson 8 Plan A → Plan B

PURPOSE

In this lesson, students continue to build a vocabulary foundation for the concept of Flexibility. There are three activities in this lesson.

Materials Required for All Activities

Not Included

- Whiteboard or chart paper
- Dry/wet erase markers or markers
- Tape
- 3 pieces of paper (each labeled with a number 1, 2, or 3)
- Timer
- Pencils
- Group Reinforcement Visual
- Each student's *UOT Notebook*

Included

- GWPDC for Lesson 8
- Lightning Round Questions
- Handout: Mystery Word 3
- Educator Guide: Mystery Word 3 Key
- Handout: *Unstuck and On Target!* Dictionary—Plan A → Plan B
- Handout: Build a Plan A, B, C
- Classroom Practice 8
- Home Practice 8

INTRODUCTION

Preview: GWPDC & Lightning Round

Review & Game
~5 minutes

Materials

Not Included

- Whiteboard or chart paper and suitable markers
- Tape
- 3 pieces of paper (each labeled with a number 1, 2, or 3)

Included

- GWPDC for Lesson 8
- Lightning Round Questions

Instructions

1. Post the GWPDC on the board before the lesson begins.
2. Review the GWPDC with the group.
3. Complete the Lightning Round activity.

**For a complete set of instructions and tips, refer to the GWPDC and Lightning Round instructions (Topic 1, Lesson 2).*

Reinforce...

by Making It Personal

Students love to hear about their teacher's personal experiences. Share times when you have moved up and down the Feelings Target.

G W P D C

Goal: Figure out how to make a Plan B when Plan A doesn't work.

Why: Plan Bs give us a back-up plan.

Plan:

1. Lightning Round
2. Uncover Mystery Word 3 and Dictionary entry
3. Speed B
4. Build a Plan A, B, and C
5. Review Home Practice

Do: Follow the plan and earn tallies.

Check: How did it go? Did we accomplish our plan? Did we need a Plan B?

Lightning Round Questions

1. What is one coping strategy you can use when you are feeling like a #5?
2. Two coping strategies that work for me are ____ and ____.
3. One thing that makes me feel like a #4 or #5 is ____ and to get back to a #1 I would use ____ as a coping strategy.
4. Which gives you more choices: being Stuck or being Flexible?
5. If the tip of your pencil breaks what would you do if you were Stuck? What would you do if you were Flexible? (Come up with 2 options.)
6. Name one thing that makes you upset, and name one thing that makes you happy.

A→B ACTIVITY 1

Mystery Words—Plan A → Plan B

Individual or Group Activity
~10 minutes

Materials

Not Included

- Whiteboard or chart paper
- Dry/wet erase markers or markers

Included

- Handout: Mystery Word 3 (one handout for each student in the group)
- Educator Guide: Mystery Word 3 Key
- Handout: *Unstuck and On Target!* Dictionary—Plan A → Plan B

Instructions

1. Ask students to reflect on the vocabulary they have learned thus far (Flexible, Stuck).
2. Distribute Handout: Mystery Word 3 (one handout for each student or one for the group).
3. After students have uncovered the phrase *Plan A → Plan B*, write the words *Plan A* and *Plan B* on the whiteboard.
4. Explain that people often have a plan for how they want something to go. For example, a student may plan to play outside after school. This is the student's Plan A because it is his or her first plan.
5. Sometimes Plan A does not work out. For example, what if it is raining after school?
   a. Without a Plan B, the student may get mad because he or she did not get what he or she wanted, and the student might be bored because he or she is not doing anything fun.
   b. With a Plan B, the student would have another good plan for backup. For example, the student might go to a friend's house to play a game indoors.
6. Reinforce the idea that when students think of a Plan B at the same time that they think of Plan A, they can make a choice more quickly and avoid getting Stuck.

Remember to check off this step on the GWPDC!

TOPIC 3

Mystery Word 3

Decode these words using the key below.

____	____	____	____	____
16	12	1	14	1

and

____	____	____	____	____
16	12	1	14	2

KEY

A = 1	G = 7	M = 13
B = 2	H = 8	N = 14
C = 3	I = 9	O = 15
D = 4	J = 10	P = 16
E = 5	K = 11	Q = 17
F = 6	L = 12	R = 18
		S = 19

Use your decoded words to fill in the following sentence.

If my ____________________ _____ doesn't work

then I use my ____________________ _____.

I am being FLEXIBLE!!

TOPIC 3

Mystery Word 3 Key

Decode these words using the key below.

P	L	A	N	A
16	12	1	14	1

and

P	L	A	N	B
16	12	1	14	2

KEY

A = 1	G = 7	M = 13
B = 2	H = 8	N = 14
C = 3	I = 9	O = 15
D = 4	J = 10	P = 16
E = 5	K = 11	Q = 17
F = 6	L = 12	R = 18
		S = 19

Use your decoded words to fill in the following sentence.

If my ___Plan___ __A__ doesn't work

then I use my ___Plan___ __B__.

I am being FLEXIBLE!!

Unstuck and On Target! Dictionary

A→B

Plan A → Plan B

Definition:	Examples and Tips:
We all need a plan to help us accomplish our goal. We all have a way that we would like things to go. We start with a *Plan A.* If Plan A doesn't work out, we can always use a *Plan B.*	• Plan A does not always work out, but that is no big deal because I can always make a Plan B to help me accomplish my goal. • With a Plan B, I have another good plan for backup. • I can remember to make a Plan B when I make my Plan A.

A→B

ACTIVITY 2

Speed B

Group Activity

~10 minutes

Materials

Not Included

- Whiteboard or chart paper
- Dry/wet erase markers or markers
- Timer

Included

- Plan B Scenarios (see below)

Instructions

1. Tell students you are going to play a game that will require them to think fast and share their answers. The goal of the game is to listen to the scenario and help come up with as many "Plan Bs" as they can in 30 seconds. For each Plan B they come up with they will get a tally for their group goal. Once the 30 seconds is up, read the next scenario and start the timer again.

   Tips

   ★ You know your kids best, and whether racing the clock can be overwhelming and anxiety provoking for your students instead of motivating. If you think this will be true for your class, don't time them.

   ★ You have to balance the needs of your students. If you have students that process information more slowly or have trouble processing auditory information, adjust the format (e.g., write down the scenario, give all students the same amount of time and add up all of their answers).

   ★ Feel free to adjust the reinforcement (i.e., tallies) for the game to meet the needs of your group.

   ★ If your students have difficulty processing spoken language, write the scenarios on the board.

   ★ If you would like to encourage more peer to peer interaction, have the students brainstorm "Plan Bs" in dyads and then share them with the group.

   ★ Feel free to personalize the scenarios to ones that your students experience at school.

Plan B Scenarios:

1. You wanted to play soccer at recess but the field is too muddy.
2. You wanted to have ice cream for dessert but someone left the freezer open. Now all the ice cream melted.
3. It is raining and you can't go outside for recess.
4. You wanted to be on your friend's baseball team but it is full.
5. You wanted to wear jeans to school but they are in the wash.
6. You were going to have your favorite cereal for breakfast but it is all gone.
7. You wanted to play chess with your friend when he came to your house but you found out he doesn't like chess.

Remember to check off this step on the GWPDC!

ACTIVITY 3

Build a Plan A, B, C

Small or Large Group
~10 minutes

Materials

Not Included

- Whiteboard or chart paper
- Dry/wet erase markers or markers

Included

- Goals (see below)
- Handout: Build a Plan A, B, C

Set-up

Prepare copies of the Build a Plan A, B, C worksheet (you will need enough for each dyad to have a copy). Before you hand out the worksheets, write a goal on each one (see the list of goals below).

Instructions

1. Explain to students that sometimes you need more than a Plan B to accomplish your goal. Sometimes you need a Plan B, C, D, E, etc. Tell them that today they get to write their own Plan A, B, and C to accomplish a goal.
2. Before dividing the students into groups of two, demonstrate the activity as a large group. Read the goal (to have a fun playdate). As a group come up with a Plan A, Plan B, and Plan C that would help you accomplish your goal.
3. Divide students in to groups of two. Explain that they are in charge of writing a Plan A, Plan B, and Plan C for their goal.

Tips

★ If you feel that your students are not ready to work in dyads, this can be run as a large group activity.

★ Customize the goals to be ones that will be meaningful to your students.

Group Example:

GOAL	To have a fun time hanging out with my friend
WHY	If we will have fun I will have a good time and my friend will want to come back.
PLAN A	Play outside
PLAN B	Play video games
PLAN C	Watch a movie

Goals: (Feel free to create your own goals, or update the language to appeal to your group.)

- To have fun at recess
- To have a delicious dinner
- To get a good grade on my quiz
- To relax after school
- To go to a baseball game

Remember to check off this step on the GWPDC!

TOPIC 3

Build a Plan A, B, C

A→B

GOAL	
WHY	
PLAN A	
PLAN B	
PLAN C	

CLOSING
Review: Classroom & Home Practice

Wrap-up
~5 minutes

Materials

Not Included

- Pencils (1 per student)
- Group Reinforcement Visual
- Each student's *UOT Notebook*

Included

- Classroom Practice 8
- Home Practice 8

Instructions

Students will review the Home Practice and complete the check portion of the Goal, Why, Plan, Do, Check.

1. Hand out the Home Practice sheets. Read the goal aloud. Ask students to think about who will work on their Home Practice (HP) with them. Let students know they will each earn a tally for bringing the completed HP with them next time you meet.

   Tip

   ★ Follow the same procedure every day for reviewing and completing HP (e.g., review HP, monitor all students as they put it in their homework folder, monitor all students as they write it in their homework planner).
2. Guide students to file all worksheets in their *UOT Notebook.*
3. Read the goal for Lesson 8 aloud to the class. Ask students if they were able to accomplish the goal. Ask students to identify what helped them accomplish the goal.
4. Review the plan. Ask students if they were able to accomplish the plan. Were there steps that we were not able to accomplish? Did we need to revise the plan in any way?
5. Remind students they are working towards a large group prize. Each day you will add their tally marks to a bank. When they reach ____ tallies they will get a group celebration or prize.

   Tip

   ★ During the lesson if you find students sticking to the plan or following the Code of Conduct remind them what they are working for and reinforce accordingly. ("Great job using respectful words and earning tallies. Our tallies get us closer to our Flexibility party.")
6. Distribute the Classroom Practice handout to all instructors who interact with your students and would benefit from supporting students as they work on their new skills.

Classroom Practice 8

Session Summary: Students learned a new script today, *Plan A → Plan B*. It is a powerful script that enables the student to regroup when something has not gone according to plan, and stop blaming others or him- or herself for the failure. Instead *Plan B* allows the student to recognize that the plan itself was the problem and now there is an opportunity to make a new plan or even multiple new plans. Many inflexible students are actually giddy with excitement at the realization that there are many plans and options (*Plans B, C, D, etc.*) available to them when things go wrong.

What you can do to support your student's learning and generalization:

1. If a student's approach to solving a math problem, making a friend, or any other situation is not producing good results, ask the student if he or she has a *Plan B.* Students may need support creating a Plan B.
   - *"If your **Plan A** isn't working, what is your **Plan B**?"*
   - *"What is our **Plan B**? Do we need to have a **Plan C**?"*
2. Pay particular attention to your own actions as the educator, and narrate aloud. For example, tell students when you are trying to come up with a *Plan B.*
   - *"We were going to do our math facts now, but the worksheets aren't done yet. My **Plan B** is to do our math investigation, and we'll do the math facts later."*
3. Praise and reinforce all of your students for keeping an open mind, being flexible, or coming up with a *Plan B.*
   - *"I love the way you **kept an open mind** and came up with a **Plan B**!"*
   - *"You were so **flexible**, you came up with a **Plan C**!"*
4. If you'd like to do more, try the "Plan Z" game.
   - Come up with a situation, and then take turns coming up with new, funny, and increasingly outrageous plans. For example:
     - (you) Plan A: Play *Around the World* during Math today
     - (student) Plan B: Make flash cards during math
     - (you) Plan C: Sing math facts to the tune of Yankee Doodle
     - (student) Plan D: Do math on the playground
     - (you) Plan E: Do math sitting under our desks
     - (student) Plan F: Do math while tossing bean bag
     - (you) Plan G: Say math facts in a fake British accent
     - And so on, for as long as you can keep it up.
   - They don't have to be good plans, the point is to really show how many choices we have when we keep an open mind and don't get stuck with our Plan A.

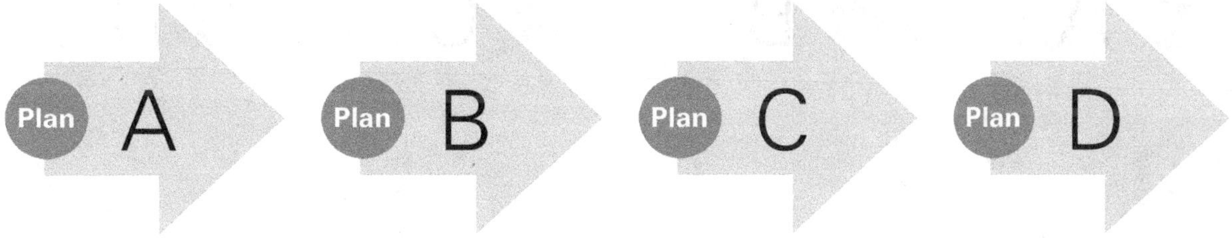

TOPIC 3

Home Practice 8

A→B

Your child participated in the eighth session of *Unstuck and On Target!* today.

Session Summary: Your child learned new Unstuck vocabulary today, *Plan A → Plan B.* It is a powerful script that can help when something has not gone according to plan. Instead of blaming others or him- or herself for the failure, your child can recognize that the plan itself was the problem and now there is an opportunity to make a new plan, or even multiple new plans. There are many plans and options (*Plans B, C, D, etc.*) when things don't go according to plan.

What you can try at home:

1. The next time you have to come up with a *Plan B,* share your thoughts with your child out loud. For example:
   - *"I planned to wear my red sweater today, but it is in the wash. I chose this one for my Plan B."*
2. Ask your child to help you come up with a *Plan B* when you can:
   - *"This milk is spoiled. I need a Plan B for breakfast! What should my Plan B be?"*
3. Praise your child for keeping an open mind, being *flexible,* or coming up with a *Plan B.*
   - *"I love the way you **kept an open mind** and came up with a **Plan B**!"*
   - *"You were SO **flexible**, you came up with a **Plan C**!"*
4. If you'd like to do more, try the "Plan Z" game.
   - Come up with a situation, and then take turns coming up with new, funny, and increasingly outrageous plans. For example:
     - (you) Plan A: Have pizza for dinner
     - (your child) Plan B: Have spaghetti for dinner
     - (you) Plan C: Skip dinner, and keep the house awake all night with my rumbling stomach
     - (your child) Plan D: Eat dinner in our pajamas in bed
     - (you) Plan E: Only eat things that are blue
     - (your child) Plan F: Eat everything in the fridge for dinner
     - (you) Plan G: Eat dinner upside down

     And so on, for as long as you can keep it up.
   - They don't have to be good plans, the point is to really show how many choices we have when we *keep an open mind* and don't get *stuck* with our *Plan A.*

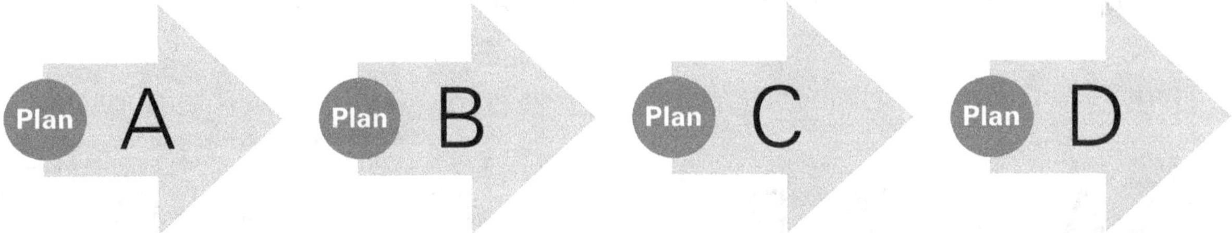

Lesson 9 Compromise

TOPIC 3

PURPOSE

In this lesson, students continue to build a vocabulary foundation for *Flexibility*, adding the term *Compromise*. There are two activities in this lesson.

Materials Required for All Activities

Not Included

- Whiteboard or chart paper
- Dry/wet erase markers or markers
- Tape
- 3 pieces of paper (each labeled with a number 1, 2, or 3)
- Pencils
- Group Reinforcement Visual
- Each student's *UOT Notebook*

Included

- GWPDC for Lesson 9
- Lightning Round Questions
- Handout: Mystery Word 4
- Educator Guide: Mystery Word 4 Key
- Handout: *Unstuck and On Target!* Dictionary—Compromise
- Materials: Compromise Game Cards
- Classroom Practice 9
- Home Practice 9

INTRODUCTION

Preview: GWPDC & Lightning Round

Review & Game
~5 minutes

Materials

Not Included

- Whiteboard or chart paper and suitable markers
- Tape
- 3 pieces of paper (each labeled with a number 1, 2, or 3)

Included

- GWPDC for Lesson 9
- Lightning Round Questions

Instructions

1. Post the GWPDC on the board before the lesson begins.
2. Review the GWPDC with the group.
3. Complete the Lightning Round activity.

**For a complete set of instructions and tips, refer to the GWPDC and Lightning Round instructions (Topic 1, Lesson 2).*

Reinforce...
Memory
"Great job remembering that from our last group, I can tell you were really paying attention."

Goal: Learn how to Compromise.

Why: Compromise helps me get some of what I want, which is better than nothing.

Plan:
1. Lightning Round
2. Uncover Mystery Word 4 and Dictionary entry
3. Play the Compromise Game
4. Review Home Practice

Do: Follow the plan and earn tallies.

Check: How did it go? Did we accomplish our plan? How would you rate yourself on our Feelings Target?

Lightning Round Questions

1. What is one thing you would do if you were feeling like a #4 or #5 to get back to just-right, #1?
2. What do we need if Plan A doesn't work?
3. What is a Plan B you could use if it is raining and you can't go out for recess?

ACTIVITY 1

Mystery Word—Compromise

Individual or Group Activity

~10 minutes

Materials

Not Included

- Whiteboard or chart paper
- Dry/wet erase markers or markers

Included

- Handout: Mystery Word 4 (one for each student or group)
- Educator Guide: Mystery Word 4 Key
- Handout: *Unstuck and On Target!* Dictionary—Compromise

Instructions

1. Begin by reviewing the previous vocabulary words. Review what it means to be Flexible and to keep an open mind. Revisit the word *Stuck*; highlight that when a person is Stuck, there are no choices but to be Stuck. Ask students what they can do when they are Stuck or when their Plan A does not work (make a Plan B). Tell students that today they will be learning another way to avoid getting Stuck.
2. Distribute Handout: Mystery Word 4 (one for each student or one for the group).
3. Once the students have uncovered the word *Compromise*, write the word on the whiteboard. Point out common strategies for Compromising: each person *gets part* of what he or she wants, *takes turns*, and *picks something new* that both people like.
   a. Give the students examples of Compromise:
      - Each get part: "I want a cupcake and my husband wants ice cream for dessert; we Compromise and have mini cupcakes with a little bit of ice cream."
      - Pick something new: "If you want to throw the baseball and your brother wants to shoot baskets, you can Compromise and play catch with a football."
      - Take turns: "If you want to play Connect 4 for recess and your friend wants to go outside, you can Compromise by going outside for half of the time and playing Connect 4 for the other half of the time."

   b. Provide additional examples, and ask students to come up with ways the people in the example could make a Compromise. Discuss that Compromise is different from giving in, which means that you do not get anything that you want. Give examples of giving in, and discuss what a Compromise solution might have been.

TOPIC 3

Mystery Word 4

comp +  + 

+ 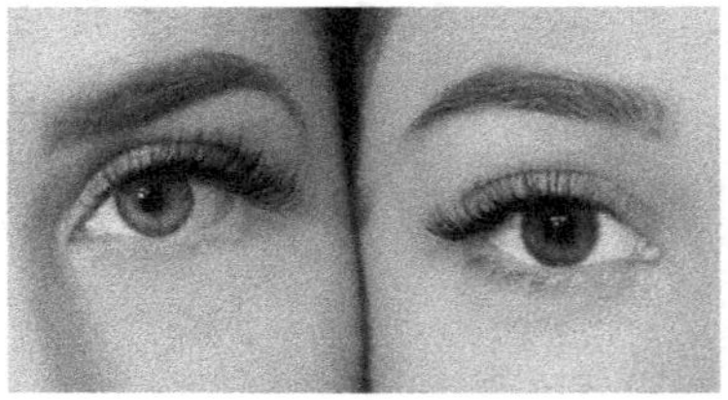

__________ + __________ + __________ + __________ = ______________

TOPIC 3

Mystery Word 4 Key

comp +  +  + 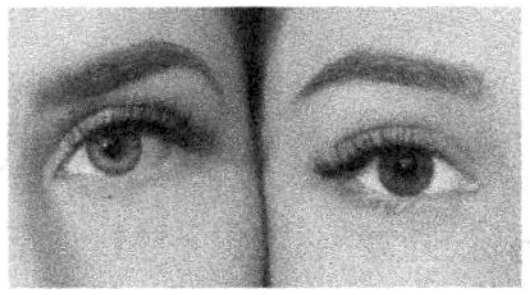

comp + row + m + eyes = Compromise

Unstuck and On Target! Dictionary

Compromise

Definition:	Examples and Tips
When two or more people each want something different, Compromise is a way for everyone to get a little bit of what they want. There are 3 ways to Compromise.	3 Ways to Compromise: 1. **Each Person Gets Part:** Since we both have different ideas, we will combine our ideas so we each get part of what we like. 2. **Pick Something New:** Since we both have different ideas, we will pick something new that we both like. 3. **Take Turns:** Since we both have different ideas, we will take turns with our ideas—we will do your idea, then my idea.

ACTIVITY 2

Compromise Game

Game

~10 minutes

Materials

Not Included

- Dry erase board/markers

Included

- Game scenarios (see below)
- Materials: Compromise Game Cards

Set up

Cut out the game cards, lay them face down on the table.

Instructions

1. Remind students that Compromising can mean that both people get some of what they want, or that you choose something new to make both people happy. Write the words Plan A, Plan B, Compromise, both get part of what we want, and something new and Stuck on the board (see below for example).

	Plan A	Plan B		
		Compromise		**Stuck**
		Part	Something new	
Cupcakes	Vanilla (1)	Choc. Cake/ Vanilla Icing (2)	Strawberry (2)	No Cupcakes (4)
Game	Soccer (1)	10 soccer/10 basketball (1/2)	Swings (1)	No one to play with (5)

Share several examples to illustrate the point.

Example: I want chocolate cupcakes, you want vanilla. We can have chocolate cupcakes with vanilla icing, or we can choose strawberry cupcakes instead because we both like those. If I decide I will only have chocolate and refuse vanilla, we won't be allowed to have any.

Look at the Feelings Target. Ask students to describe and give a number to how they would feel with each of the Compromise and Stuck options. Record the answers on the board. See numbers in parentheses in the example chart above.

Example: I want to play soccer and you want to play basketball. We can play soccer for 10 minutes and basketball for 10 minutes, or we can play on the swings instead. Use the feelings chart numbers again to add in how each option makes them feel.

2. Game: 1 player comes up to the front of the room. Read them a scenario (below). The player picks one card from the pile. The cards say "Compromise" or "Stuck". If they draw "Compromise: Choose Something New" they have to give an example of a possible Compromise where they do something new. If they draw "Compromise Part of What You Want" they have to give an example of a possible Compromise where they each get

part of what they want. If they draw "Stuck" they have to give an example of what would happen if they were Stuck. They then have to use the Feelings Target to decide how the Compromise or being Stuck would make them feel. The student gets a tally towards the group goal for working together and coming up with an answer.

Game Scenarios:

1. I want to play chess and you want to play checkers.
2. I want pizza for dinner and you want macaroni and cheese.
3. We want to play together but you want to swing and I want to play tag.
4. I would like to watch a TV show and you want to watch a movie.
5. I want to go outside for recess and you want to stay inside.
6. We are allowed to have one dessert. I want chocolate chip cookies and you want oatmeal.

Compromise: Part of what you want	**Stuck**	**Compromise:** Choose something new
Compromise: Part of what you want	**Stuck**	**Compromise:** Choose something new
Compromise: Part of what you want	**Stuck**	**Compromise:** Choose something new
Compromise: Part of what you want	**Stuck**	**Compromise:** Choose something new
Compromise: Part of what you want	**Stuck**	**Compromise:** Choose something new

CLOSING

Review: Classroom & Home Practice

Wrap-up
~5 minutes

Materials

Not Included

- Pencils (1 per student)
- Group Reinforcement Visual
- Each student's *UOT Notebook*

Included

- Classroom Practice 9
- Home Practice 9

Instructions

Students will review the Home Practice and complete the *check* portion of the Goal, Why, Plan, Do, Check.

1. Hand out the Home Practice sheets. Read the goal aloud. Ask students to think about who they will work on their Home Practice (HP) with. Let students know they will each earn a tally for bringing the completed HP with them next time you meet.

   Tip

   ★ Follow the same procedure every day for reviewing and completing HP (e.g., review HP, monitor all students as they put it in their homework folder, monitor all students as they write it in their homework planner).
2. Guide students to file all worksheets in their *UOT Notebook.*
3. Read the goal for Lesson 9 aloud to the class. Ask students if they were able to accomplish the goal. Ask students to identify what helped them accomplish the goal.
4. Review the plan. Ask students if they were able to accomplish the plan. Were there steps that we were not able to accomplish? Did we need to revise the plan in any way?
5 Remind students they are working towards a large group prize. Each day you will add their tally marks to a bank. When they reach ____ tallies they will get a group celebration or prize.

   Tip

   ★ During the lesson if you find students sticking to the plan or following the Code of Conduct remind them what they are working for and reinforce accordingly. ("Great job using respectful words and earning tallies. Our tallies get us closer to our flexibility party.")
6. Distribute the Classroom Practice handout to all instructors who interact with your students and would benefit from supporting students as they work on their new skills.

Classroom Practice 9

Session Summary: Students learned that if people *compromise* when they want different things, then they each get something that they want, and something is better than nothing. Students learned three ways to *compromise* today:

Each person gets part:	• Since we both have different ideas, we will combine our ideas so we each get part of what we want.
Pick something new:	• Since we both have different ideas, we will pick something new that we both like.
Take turns:	• Since we both have different ideas, we will take turns with our ideas—we will do your idea, then my idea.

What you can do to support your student's learning and generalization:

1. If two or more students want different things, help them develop a compromise. Or, better yet, you come to a *compromise* with your students.
   - *"I need to make sure you know these vocabulary words, so I plan to give you homework. I know you don't want homework. I can compromise, though. If you pass the pretest, I won't give you the homework. How does that sound?"*
2. Praise and reinforce all of your students for keeping an open mind, being flexible, coming up with a Plan B, or *compromising.*
   - *"You and Sami did a great job **compromising** today."*
   - *"Sometimes our **Plan B** needs to be a **compromise**. Can you think of a compromise so you can both get some of what you want?"*

TOPIC 3

Home Practice 9

Your child participated in the ninth session of *Unstuck and On Target!* today.

Session Summary: Your child learned that if people *compromise* when they want different things, then they each get something that they want, and something is better than nothing. Your child learned three ways to *compromise* today:

Each person gets part:	• **Since we both have different ideas, we will combine our ideas so we each get part of what we want.**
For example:	• Your child wants to play catch, but his friend wants to play on the slide. They could play catch on the slide.
Pick something new:	• **Since we both have different ideas, we will pick something that we both like.**
For example:	• They both like hide and seek, so they decide to play that instead.
Take turns:	• **Since we both have different ideas, we will take turns with our ideas—we will do your idea, then my idea.**
For example:	• First they play on the slide, then they play catch.

What you can try at home:

1. Try to come to a reasonable *compromise* with your child.
   - *"I need to go to the grocery and the drugstore. I know you don't like going to the grocery or the drugstore. I can compromise, though. If you are good in the grocery, we will skip the drugstore and I'll play a game with you when we get home. How does that sound?"*

2. Praise your child for keeping an open mind, being flexible, coming up with a Plan B, or *compromising*.
   - *"You and Sami did a great job **compromising** today."*
   - *"Sometimes our **Plan B** needs to be a **compromise**. Can you think of a compromise so you can both get some of what you want?"*

Lesson 10 Big Deal/Little Deal

TOPIC 3

PURPOSE

Students, teachers, and parents learn the Big Deal/Little Deal script and incorporate it into their daily conversation. There are three activities in this lesson.

Materials Required for All Activities

Not Included

- Whiteboard or chart paper
- Dry/wet erase markers or markers
- Tape
- 3 pieces of paper (each labeled with a number 1, 2, or 3)
- Masking tape
- Pencils
- Group Reinforcement Visual
- Each student's *UOT Notebook*

Included

- GWPDC for Lession 10
- Lightning Round Questions
- Handout: Mystery Word 5
- Educator Guide: Mystery Word 5 Key
- Handout: *Unstuck and On Target!* Dictionary—Big Deal/Little Deal
- Materials: Big Deal/Little Deal Cards
- Visual: Big Deal/Little Deal 1–5 Scale
- Classroom Practice 10
- Home Practice 10

INTRODUCTION

Preview: GWPDC & Lightning Round

Review & Game
~5 minutes

Materials

Not Included

- Whiteboard or chart paper and suitable markers
- Tape
- 3 pieces of paper (each labeled with a number 1, 2, or 3)

Included

- GWPDC for Lesson 10
- Lightning Round Questions

Instructions

1. Post the GWPDC on the board before the lesson begins.
2. Review the GWPDC with the group.
3. Complete the Lightning Round activity.

**For a complete set of instructions and tips, refer to the GWPDC and Lightning Round instructions (Topic 1, Lesson 2).*

G W P D C	**Goal:** Figure out the difference between Big Deal and Little Deal and how to turn a Big Deal into a Little Deal. **Why:** Knowing how to turn a Big Deal into a Little Deal helps me feel better. **Plan:** 1. Lightning Round 2. Mystery Word 5 and Dictionary entry 3. Big Deal/Little Deal practice 4. Converting Big Deals to Little Deals 5. Review Home Practice **Do:** Follow the plan and earn tallies. **Check:** How did it go? Did we accomplish our plan? If we weren't able to finish our plan would that be a Big Deal or Little Deal? Why?

Lightning Round Questions

1. True or False: Compromise can help me get part of what I want.
2. True or False: Sometimes all of what I want is not possible.
3. True or False: When I am Stuck I have many choices.

Reinforce...

Collaboration

"I like the way you worked together to come up with an answer."

Tips

★ The purpose of the Lightning Round is to prepare students for the lesson, to establish a hook and routine to start each group, and to provide an opporunity to review concepts and skills learned in previous lessons and provide you with an assessment of what the students have learned and retained. Please feel free to alter/adjust the questions and format provided to better meet these goals.

★ If you would like each student to answer a question each day, you can create additional questions.

★ This should be a very quick activity and take no more than 5 minutes.

★ Reinforce students working together to answer a question and for good effort.

★ If students have difficulty not being called on first, leave it up to chance—write everyone's name on a popsicle stick and put them in a jar. Randomly select a stick and call on that student.

ACTIVITY 1

Mystery Words—Big Deal/Little Deal

Individual or Group Activity

~10 minutes

Materials

Not Included

- Whiteboard or chart paper
- Dry and/or wet erase markers or markers

Included

- Handout: Mystery Word 5
- Educator Guide: Mystery Word 5 Key
- Handout: *Unstuck and On Target!* Dictionary—Big Deal/Little Deal

Instructions

The Mystery phrase for this lesson is Big Deal/Little Deal

1. Begin by reviewing the previous vocabulary words (Flexibility, Stuck, Compromise). Ask students to pull out their UOT dictionary. Review what it means to be Flexible and to keep an open mind. Revisit the word Stuck; highlight that when a person is Stuck, there are no choices but to be Stuck. Remind students that Compromising is one way to avoid getting Stuck and today they will be learning another way to avoid getting Stuck.
2. Hand out Mystery Word 5. To figure out the rest of the phrase students are going to need to listen closely to your directions.

   Follow the script to help students uncover the words:

   1. Next to #1, write the word "DOG."
   2. Change the first middle letter to the first letter in the words ICE CREAM. (I)
   3. What is the new word? (DIG)
   4. Now, change the first letter to the second letter in the alphabet. (B)
   5. What is the new word? (BIG)
   6. Read the 2 words together. (BIG DEAL)
   7. Next to #2, write the word LIT.
   8. Double the last letter. (TT)
   9. What do you have written now? (LITT)
   10. At the end of the word add the first letter in the word LOVE. (LITTL)
   11. Eggplant, Elephant, Everyone, Egg all begin with what letter? (E)
   12. Write that at the end of your word.
   13. What is the word now? (LITTLE)
   14. Read the 2 words together. (LITTLE DEAL)
   15. Who can read aloud today's Mystery Phrase? (BIG DEAL/LITTLE DEAL)
3. Once the students have uncovered the phrase "Big Deal/Little Deal," write the phrase on the whiteboard.
4. Hand out the Big Deal/Little Deal Dictionary page and review.

Remember to check off this step on the GWPDC!

Mystery Word 5

1. ______________________________ DEAL

2. ______________________________ DEAL

Mystery Word 5 Key

Big Deal

DOG → DIG → BIG

Little Deal

LIT → LITT→ LITTL → LITTLE

Unstuck and On Target! Dictionary

Big Deal/Little Deal

Definition:	Tips and Examples
A Little Deal is something that is a small problem, can be fixed quickly, and doesn't take many people to solve. A Big Deal is a large problem, takes a long time to fix, and usually takes a lot of people to solve.	It is ok if something feels like a Big Deal. My job is to figure out how to turn it into a Little Deal. I have strategies I can use to turn a Big Deal into a Little Deal. If I have a Big Deal problem I can always ask for help.

D OR d

ACTIVITY 2

Big Deal/Little Deal Practice

Group Activity
~15 minutes

Materials

Not Included

- Whiteboard or chart paper
- Dry/wet erase markers or markers

Included

- Materials: Big Deal/Little Deal Cards (print double-sided on card stock) or make your own response cards using index cards or something similar

Instructions

In this activity, students practice applying their new knowledge.

1. Give each student one Big Deal/Little Card. One side of the card should say "Big Deal," and the other should say "Little Deal." Or use two separate stacks of cards—one "Big Deal" the other "Little Deal" if that is easier.
2. Read the following scenarios, and ask students to vote on each one using one of the cards. Is it a Big Deal or a Little Deal? *Adjust scenario to meet the needs/interests of your students.*
   a. You break your leg.
   b. There is nothing at all to eat in your house for a week.
   c. You are not picked to be first in line for an activity.
   d. You cannot sit where you want during lunch.
   e. The lunch menu changes at the last minute.
   f. P.E. is canceled because the teacher is sick.
   g. Your pet dies.
   h. Your friend gets ahead of you in line, and you get so upset that you hit him.
   i. Your teacher asks you to revise an essay that you wrote.
   j. You fail a subject because you refuse to revise your work.
   k. Your friend believes in the Loch Ness Monster, but you do not.
   l. Your classmate supported a presidential candidate that you oppose.
3. Keep a tally of votes on the whiteboard, and discuss disagreements.
4. Generate additional examples from your experiences with students, and invite students to offer scenarios. Review at least 10 scenarios.

   Tip

   ★ Active student responding, or having students "do" something to demonstrate they are engaged in the lesson is a simple and easy way to make sure everyone is participating, check for understanding, and help students maintain attention during the lesson. Using index cards to indicate Big Deal/Little Deal is an example of an active student responding strategy. Feel free to use this strategy whenever you want to increase active participation.

LITTLE DEAL	LITTLE DEAL
LITTLE DEAL	LITTLE DEAL
LITTLE DEAL	LITTLE DEAL
LITTLE DEAL	LITTLE DEAL
LITTLE DEAL	LITTLE DEAL

BIG DEAL	BIG DEAL
BIG DEAL	BIG DEAL
BIG DEAL	BIG DEAL
BIG DEAL	BIG DEAL
BIG DEAL	BIG DEAL

D OR d

ACTIVITY 3

Converting Big Deals to Little Deals

Group Activity

~15 minutes

Materials

Not Included

- Marker
- Masking tape

Included

- Visual: Big Deal/Little Deal 1–5 Scale

Instructions: (select examples that are relevant and meaningful to your students)

1. Introduce the idea that some things that are a Big Deal can be changed into a Little Deal but some cannot. The death of a student's pet is a Big Deal that cannot be turned into a Little Deal; a student needs time and the support of family and school to get over this type of situation.
2. But some Big Deals can be turned into Little Deals. For example, if a student works really hard on an essay and even adds pictures, and then the essay gets stepped on by mistake and torn, that feels like a Big Deal to the student. But if a teacher can help the student print out a new copy of the essay, the Big Deal can be turned into a Little Deal.
3. Place a long piece of masking tape on the floor in an area with plenty of space. Write the numbers 1–5 along the tape, indicating 5 is a Big Deal and 1 is a Little Deal.
4. Post Visual Big Deal/Little Deal 1–5 Scale so all students can see it. Read the following scenarios one at a time, and ask students to stand on the number on the masking tape that shows how big a deal each scenario is to them. (Explain ahead of time that these are personal opinions; situations feel different to every person.)
   a. You lose your homework.
   b. You break your pencil.
   c. You cannot go outside for recess because it is raining.
   d. Your pet dies.
   e. You stub your toe.
   f. You have a fight with your friend.
   g. You cannot have dessert.
   h. You lose $20.
   i. You trip and fall down the stairs.
   j. You get a C on your science test.
   k. The computer crashes before you can save your work.
5. After you have read several scenarios, ask students to identify how they would make each Big Deal into a Little Deal. Provide suggestions. Then, have them move to the number that represents this Little Deal.

Tips

★ You can keep the 1–5 Big Deal/Little Deal visual posted prominently in your classroom. We suggest you keep it close to your Feelings Target as the two are closely linked. As a child reflects on the "size of the deal," ask them to identify how they feel on the target. As they move from feeling like it is a Big Deal to a Little Deal, ask them to identify how their feelings on the target change.

★ Make sure to adjust the scenarios to meet the needs and interests of your students.

Reinforce...

Students for thinking thoughtfully about their answer and feeling confident to make a rating that is different from what their peers have chosen.

"I can tell you really thought about that answer, tally mark for that thoughtful answer."

Remember to check off this step on the GWPDC!

Big Deal/Little Deal Scale

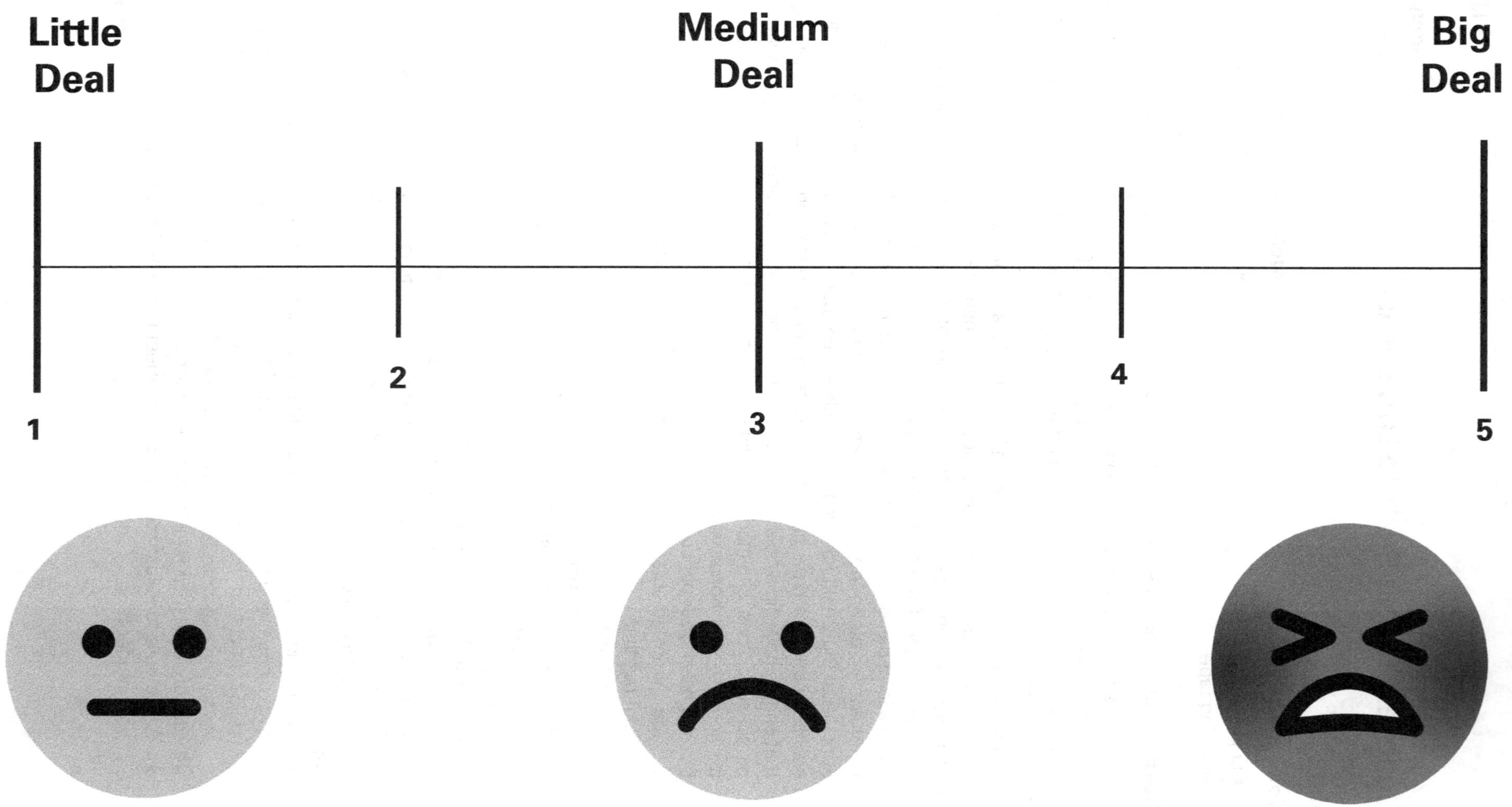

CLOSING

Review: Classroom & Home Practice

Wrap-up
~5 minutes

Materials

Not Included

- Pencils (1 per student)
- Group Reinforcement Visual
- Each student's *UOT Notebook*

Included

- Classroom Practice 10
- Home Practice 10

Instructions

Students will review the Home Practice and complete the *check* portion of the Goal, Why, Plan, Do, Check.

1. Hand out the Home Practice sheets. Read the goal aloud. Ask students to think about who will work on their Home Practice (HP) with them. Let students know they will each earn a tally for bringing the completed HP with them next time you meet.

   Tip

   ★ Follow the same procedure every day for reviewing and completing HP (e.g., review HP, monitor all students as they put it in their homework folder, monitor all students as they write it in their homework planner).
2. Guide students to file all worksheets in their *UOT Notebook.*
3. Read the goal for Lesson 10 aloud to the class. Ask students if they were able to accomplish the goal. Ask students to identify what helped them accomplish the goal.
4. Review the plan. Ask students if they were able to accomplish the plan. Were there steps that we were not able to accomplish? Did we need to revise the plan in any way?
5. Remind students they are working towards a large group prize. Each day you will add their tally marks to a bank. When they reach ____ tallies they will get a group celebration or prize.
6. Distribute the Classroom Practice handout to all instructors who interact with your students and would benefit from supporting students as they work on their new skills.

TOPIC 3

Classroom Practice 10

D OR d

Session Summary: Students learned the Big Deal/Little Deal self-regulatory script, which helps them distinguish what is important from what is not important so that they can be less anxious or upset about situations of lesser importance and take situations of greater importance seriously. It also gives students a strategy for changing a Big Deal into a Little Deal when possible. Finally, it empowers the student to decide for him- or herself what is a Big Deal vs. a Little Deal.

What you can do to support your student's learning and generalization:

1. Keep in mind that whether or not something is a **Big Deal** is very personal!
   - Just because something is a **Big Deal** to you, does not automatically mean that it will be a **Big Deal** to your student.
     i. For example, it might be a **Big Deal** to you for the whole class to pass their spelling test, but spelling tests are a **Little Deal** for your student. Or maybe it is the other way around, where your student feels he or she has to get every answer correct, while you think a "B" on a spelling test is a **Little Deal**.

2. It won't work if you just try to tell your students something is no **Big Deal**. Instead, try saying something like this:
   - *"It is ok if something feels like a **Big Deal.** I'll help you figure out how to turn it into a **Little Deal.**"*
   - *"If you have a **Big Deal.** problem you can always ask for help. We all need help with a **Big Deal.**"*

3. Praise your students for asking for help with a **Big Deal**, or for being able to recognize when something is a **Little Deal**.
   - *"Is this a **Big Deal.** or a **Little Deal** to you?"*
   - *"You are right, this does feel like a **Big Deal.** Let's figure out who else to ask for help."*

Home Practice 10

Your child participated in the tenth session of *Unstuck and On Target!* today.

Session Summary: Your child learned about the difference between a Big Deal and a Little Deal today in group. A Big Deal is a large problem, takes a long time to fix, and usually takes a lot of people to solve. A Little Deal is something that is a small problem, can be fixed quickly, and doesn't take many people to solve.

Little Deal **Big Deal**

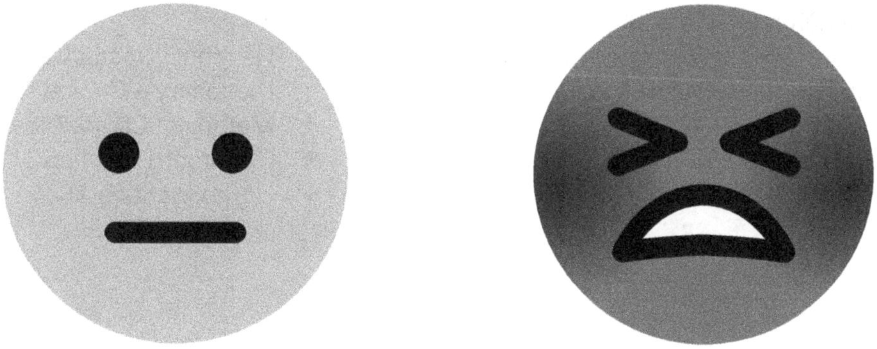

What you can try at home:

1 Keep in mind that whether or not something is a **Big Deal** is very personal.

- Just because something is a **Big Deal** to you, does not automatically mean that it will be a **Big Deal** to your child.
    - i. For example, it might be a **Big Deal** to you for the family to eat together on Sundays, but it is a **Little Deal** for your child. Or maybe it is the other way around.
    - ii. Maybe it is a **Big Deal** for your child that they are always on time, but you feel like being 5 minutes late is no **Big Deal**. Or maybe it is the other way around.

2. Don't tell your child something is not a **Big Deal.** Instead, try saying something like this:
    - *"It is ok if something feels like a **Big Deal**. I'll help you figure out how to turn it into a **Little Deal.**"*
    - *"If you have a **Big Deal** problem you can always ask for help. We all need help with a **Big Deal**."*

3. Praise your child for asking for help with a **Big Deal**, or for being able to recognize when something is a **Little Deal.**
    - *"Is this a **Big Deal** or a **Little Deal** to you?"*
    - *"You are right, this does feel like a **Big Deal**. Let's figure out who to ask for help."*

Lesson 11 Choice/No Choice

PURPOSE

Students, teachers, and parents learn the Choice/No Choice script and incorporate it into their daily conversation. There are two activities in this lesson.

Materials Required for All Activities

Not Included

- Whiteboard or chart paper
- Dry/wet erase markers or markers
- Tape
- 3 pieces of paper (each labeled with a number 1, 2, or 3)
- Pencils
- Group Reinforcement Visual
- Each student's *UOT Notebook*

Included

- GWPDC for Lesson 11
- Lightning Round Questions
- Handout: Mystery Word 6
- Educator Guide: Mystery Word 6 Key
- Handout: *Unstuck and On Target!* Dictionary—Choice/No Choice
- Materials: Choice/No Choice Cards
- Classroom Practice 11
- Home Practice 11

INTRODUCTION

Preview: GWPDC & Lightning Round

Review & Game
~5 minutes

Materials

Not Included

- Whiteboard or chart paper and suitable markers
- Tape
- 3 pieces of paper (each labeled with a number 1, 2, or 3)

Included

- GWPDC for Lesson 11
- Lightning Round Questions

Instructions

1. Post the GWPDC on the board before the lesson begins.
2. Review the GWPDC with the group.
3. Complete the Lightning Round activity.

**For a complete set of instructions and tips, refer to the GWPDC and Lightning Round instructions (Topic 1, Lesson 2).*

Reinforce…
Staying on Task
"This is supposed to be a quick game, thank you for staying on task and keeping the game moving."

G W P D C

Goal: Figure out what it means to have a Choice vs. No Choice.

Why: Usually I have choices but sometimes there are No Choice situations. I need to know how not to get Stuck on them. That will save me time and help me get more of what I want.

Plan:
1. Lightning Round
2. Mystery Word 6 and Dictionary entry
3. Choice/No Choice practice
4. Review Home Practice

Do: Follow the plan and earn tallies.

Check: How did it go? Did we accomplish our plan?

Lightning Round Questions

1. When something feels like a Big Deal, one way to make it a Little Deal is to ____?
2. If I want a chocolate cupcake and my friend wants vanilla we could compromise by ____?
3. What would happen if my pencil broke and because it felt like a Big Deal, I started to scream and cry?

Don't forget to check off this step on the GWPDC!

C ?

ACTIVITY 1

Mystery Words—Choice/No Choice

Group Activity
~5 minutes

Materials

Not Included

- Whiteboard or chart paper
- Dry and/or wet erase markers or markers

Included

- Handout: Mystery Word 6
- Educator Guide: Mystery Word 6 Key
- Handout: *Unstuck and On Target!* Dictionary—Choice/No Choice

Instructions

In this lesson students will be introduced to the Mystery phrase, Choice/No Choice.

1. Begin by reviewing the previous vocabulary words: Flexible, Stuck, Compromise, Big Deal/ Little Deal. Ask students to pull out their UOT dictionary. Review what it means to be Flexible and to keep an open mind. Revisit the word Stuck; highlight that when a person is Stuck, there are no choices but to be Stuck. Tell students that today they will be learning another way to avoid getting Stuck.
2. Distribute Handout: Mystery Word 6 (one per student or one for the group).
3. Students will uncover the words "Choice/No Choice" by following the flashlight to track the letters and build the words.
4. On the 8 pieces of white paper write the letters C-H-O-I-C-E N-O
5. Tape the letters to the ceiling or around the room.
6. Turn off the lights. Use the flashlights to highlight each letter in order.
7. Each time you highlight a letter your students should record it on their Mystery Word 6 sheet.
8. Once the students have uncovered the phrase "Choice/No Choice", write the phrase on the whiteboard
9. Review the Choice/No Choice Dictionary page.

Don't forget to check off this step on the GWPDC!

Mystery Word 6

___ ___ ___ ___ ___ ___

___ ___   ___ ___ ___ ___ ___   ___

Mystery Word 6 Key

C H O I C E

N O C H O I C E

Unstuck and On Target! Dictionary

C ?

Choice/No Choice

Definition:	Tips and Examples:
A *Choice* is possible when there is more than one way to solve a problem. A *No Choice* situation occurs when there is only one possible way to do something.	• Most of the time I have a Choice, and there is more than one way to solve a problem. • If it is a No Choice situation, there are no other options, and I just have to go with it. • Getting Stuck can make a situation more difficult, so going with it is better for me. *What do you think?*

ACTIVITY 2

Choice/No Choice Practice

Group Activity
~15 minutes

Materials

Not Included

- Whiteboard or chart paper
- Dry/wet erase markers or markers

Included

- Materials: Choice/No Choice Cards (print double-sided on card stock)

Instructions

In this activity, students practice applying their new knowledge.

1. Print the Choice/No Choice Cards double-sided on card stock. Cards say "Choice" on one side and "No Choice" on the other side. You should have a total of 10 cards. Give each student a Choice/No Choice card. Or make 2 sets of one-sided cards if that is easier, and give each student one of each.
2. Read the following scenarios, and ask students to vote on each one using the card. Is it a Choice or No Choice situation?
   a. You are trying to decide whether to order pizza or fried chicken for lunch.
   b. You need to use the restroom.
   c. You have a new language arts teacher.
   d. You and a classmate have free time.
   e. The fire drill goes off.
   f. You are trying to decide whether to wear your red shirt or your blue one.
   g. The stoplight for walkers says Don't Walk.
   h. Students have to learn to read.
   i. You want to buy a candy bar, and the cashier asks for $1.09.
   j. You are trying to decide who to invite over to your house.
   k. Your dad tells you that it is time to go to the doctor's office.
3. Keep a tally of votes on the whiteboard, and discuss disagreements.
4. Generate additional examples from your experiences with students, and invite students to offer scenarios. Review at least 10 scenarios.

Don't forget to check off this step on the GWPDC!

CHOICE	CHOICE
CHOICE	CHOICE
CHOICE	CHOICE
CHOICE	CHOICE
CHOICE	CHOICE

NO CHOICE	NO CHOICE
NO CHOICE	NO CHOICE
NO CHOICE	NO CHOICE
NO CHOICE	NO CHOICE
NO CHOICE	NO CHOICE

CLOSING

Review: Classroom & Home Practice

Wrap-up
~5 minutes

Materials

Not Included

- Pencils (1 per student)
- Group Reinforcement Visual
- Each student's *UOT Notebook*

Included

- Classroom Practice 11
- Home Practice 11

Instructions

Students will review the Home Practice and complete the *check* portion of the Goal, Why, Plan, Do, Check.

1. Hand out the Home Practices. Read the goal aloud. Ask students to think about who will work on their Home Practice (HP) with them. Let students know they will each earn a tally for bringing the completed HP with them next time you meet.

   Tip

   ★ Follow the same procedure every day for reviewing and completing HP (e.g., review HP, monitor all students as they put it in their homework folder, monitor all students as they write it in their homework planner).
2. Guide students to file all worksheets in their *UOT Notebook.*
3. Read the goal for Lesson 11 aloud to the class. Ask students if they were able to accomplish the goal. Ask students to identify what helped them accomplish the goal.
4. Review the plan. Ask students if they were able to accomplish the plan. Were there steps that we were not able to accomplish? Did we need to revise the plan in any way?
5. Remind students they are working towards a large group prize. Each day you will add their tally marks to a bank. When they reach ____ tallies they will get a group celebration or prize.
6. Distribute the Classroom Practice handout to all instructors who interact with your students and would benefit from supporting students as they work on their new skills.

TOPIC 3

Classroom Practice 11

C ?

Session Summary: Your student learned about the difference between having a choice and having no choice. With the Choice/No Choice self-regulatory script, students learn to

1) distinguish what is within their power to change and what is not, and

2) break a perseverative mindset and stop trying to influence something they cannot change.

What you can do to support your student's learning and generalization:

1. Use **"No Choice"** sparingly with students! Things that are **No Choice** situations are usually a matter of law or safety. Remember that bad choices are still choices. A **No Choice** situation is coming to school, leaving the building during a fire drill, or going to the doctor, but writing a paragraph on a president is not a **No Choice** situation. Students love to hear of your **No Choice** situations:
   - *"It's tax day, I don't like paying taxes, but it is a **No Choice** situation for me."*
   - *"You will have a substitute tomorrow because I have no choice, I have to go to the dentist."*

2. Most of the time we all have **choices**, and there is more than one way to solve a problem. Try to focus on **choices** most of the time. For example, you might say:
   - *"We still have many **choices** here; should we come up with a Plan B?"*
   - *"This is definitely not a **No Choice** situation. Let's look at our **choices**."*

3. If your student is having a hard time in a **No Choice** situation, try saying something like:
   - *"If it is a **No Choice** situation, there are no other options, and I just have to go with it."*
   - *"Getting stuck can make a situation more difficult, so going along with it is better for me. What do you think?"*

Home Practice 11

Your child participated in the eleventh session of *Unstuck and On Target!* today.

Session Summary: Your child learned about the difference between having a Choice and having No Choice. A Choice is possible when there is more than one way to solve a problem. A No Choice situation occurs when there is only one possible way to do something.

What you can try at home:

1. Use **No Choice** sparingly! Things that are **No Choice** situations are usually a matter of law or safety. Remember that bad choices are still choices. Some examples of **No Choice** situations are:
   - Attending school
   - Getting vaccinations
   - Paying taxes
   - Needing to sleep every day
2. Most of the time we all have **choices**, and there is more than one way to solve a problem. Try to focus on **choices** most of the time. For example, you might say:
   - *"We still have many **choices** here, should we come up with a Plan B?"*
   - *"This is definitely not a **No Choice** situation. Let's look at our **choices**."*
3. If your child is having a hard time in a **No Choice** situation, try saying something like:
   - *"If it is a **No Choice** situation, there are no other options, and I just have to go with it."*
   - *"Getting stuck can make a situation more difficult, so going along with it is better for me. What do you think?"*

TOPIC 3

Lesson 12 Expect the Unexpected

PURPOSE

Students, teachers, and parents learn the Expect the Unexpected script and incorporate it into their toolkit for accepting change. There are two activities in this lesson.

Materials Required for All Activities

Not Included

- Whiteboard or chart paper
- Dry/wet erase markers or markers
- Tape
- 3 pieces of paper (each labeled with a number 1, 2, or 3)
- Game tokens
- Die
- Pencils
- Group Reinforcement Visual
- Each student's *UOT Notebook*

Included

- GWPDC for Lesson 12
- Lightning Round Questions
- Educator Guide: Handling the Unexpected Game Rules
- Materials: Handling the Unexpected Game Board
- Materials: Handling the Unexpected Game Cards
- Visual: Big Deal/Little Deal 1–5 Scale (from Lesson 10)
- Classroom Practice 12
- Home Practice 12

INTRODUCTION

Preview: GWPDC & Lightning Round

Review & Game
~5 minutes

Materials

Not Included

- Whiteboard or chart paper and suitable markers
- Tape
- 3 pieces of paper (each labeled with a number 1, 2, or 3)

Included

- GWPDC for Lesson 12
- Lightning Round Questions

Instructions

1. Post the GWPDC on the board before the lesson begins.
2. Review the GWPDC with the group.
3. Complete the Lightning Round activity.

**For a complete set of instructions and tips, refer to the GWPDC and Lightning Round instructions (Topic 1, Lesson 2).*

Reinforce...
Memory
"Great job remembering that from our last group, I can tell you were really paying attention. Here is a tally for the group."

G W P D C

Goal: Figure out how to expect, or handle, the unexpected.

Why: Sometimes things happen that I don't expect. I have to figure out a way to handle that without getting upset or stuck. If I can do this I usually avoid feeling bad.

Plan:
1. Lightning Round
2. Discuss Expect the Unexpected
3. Play Handling the Unexpected Game
4. Review Home Practice

Do: Follow the plan and earn tallies.

Check: How did it go? Did we accomplish our plan?

Lightning Round Questions

1. Do teachers and parents have No Choice situations?
2. Name 2 times when you have Choices.
3. Is going to school a Choice or No Choice situation?

Don't forget to check off this step on the GWPDC!

ACTIVITY 1

Expect the Unexpected Introduction

Presentation
~10 minutes

Materials

Not Included

- Whiteboard or chart paper
- Dry/wet erase markers or markers

Instructions

In this activity, students receive a basic introduction to Expecting the Unexpected.

1. Ask your students: "Has anyone ever been mad or upset because things did not go as expected—for example, when there was a substitute teacher or you don't get picked for a sports team even though you are a really good player? That can feel like a really big deal, right?"
2. Have students offer examples, and record the main ideas on the whiteboard. Provide additional examples (e.g., Once a field trip to the zoo was canceled because of bad weather and I was really upset; I was so mad when I got sick the day before I was supposed to go to the amusement park and the trip had to be canceled).
3. Ask students what helps handle the unexpected. Write their ideas on the whiteboard. Add your own ideas, too. Following are some examples:
   a. Being told in advance about the change
   b. Getting a 5-minute warning that you will have to stop doing something when you're having fun
   c. Taking a deep breath and remembering that you can be Flexible
   d. Asking questions so you can learn exactly what will change and what will stay the same
   e. Knowing when the change will be over
   f. Knowing that there is a good reason for the unexpected event
4. Keep this list.

ACTIVITY 2

Handling the Unexpected Exploration

Group Activity
~15–20 minutes

Materials

Not Included

- Game tokens
- Die

Included

- Educator Guide: Handling the Unexpected Game Rules
- Materials: Handling the Unexpected Game Board
- Materials: Handling the Unexpected Game Cards (cut out ahead of time)
- Visual: Big Deal/Little Deal 1–5 Scale (from Lesson 10)

Instructions

1. Follow Educator Guide: Handling the Unexpected Game Rules to play the Handling the Unexpected Game. This game is designed to help students practice the scripts and skills they have learned in Topic 3.
2. There are extra blank cards in Handling the Unexpected Game Cards so you or your students can add relevant scenarios if desired.

Don't forget to check off this step on the GWPDC!

TOPIC 3

Handling the Unexpected Game Rules

Goal: For each player to reach the end of the game board.

How to Play the Game

1. Each player places a game token on Start.
2. Players take turns rolling the die and move the corresponding number of spaces.
3. Players take a game card, read the scenario, and follow the directions for the color they have landed on (see Game Card Key).

Game Card Key

	Turn it back!		Rate the situation on the 1–5 scale then discuss the strategy you would use to turn it back into a Little Deal.
	Super friend to the rescue!		Read the scenario and give advice to the group for how to handle the unexpected event.
	Make a list!		Read the scenario about the unexpected event. List two things that will stay the same and two things that will be different.
	Act it out!		Read the scenario about the unexpected event. Act out a stuck way to handle the unexpected event. Act out a flexible way to handle this unexpected event.

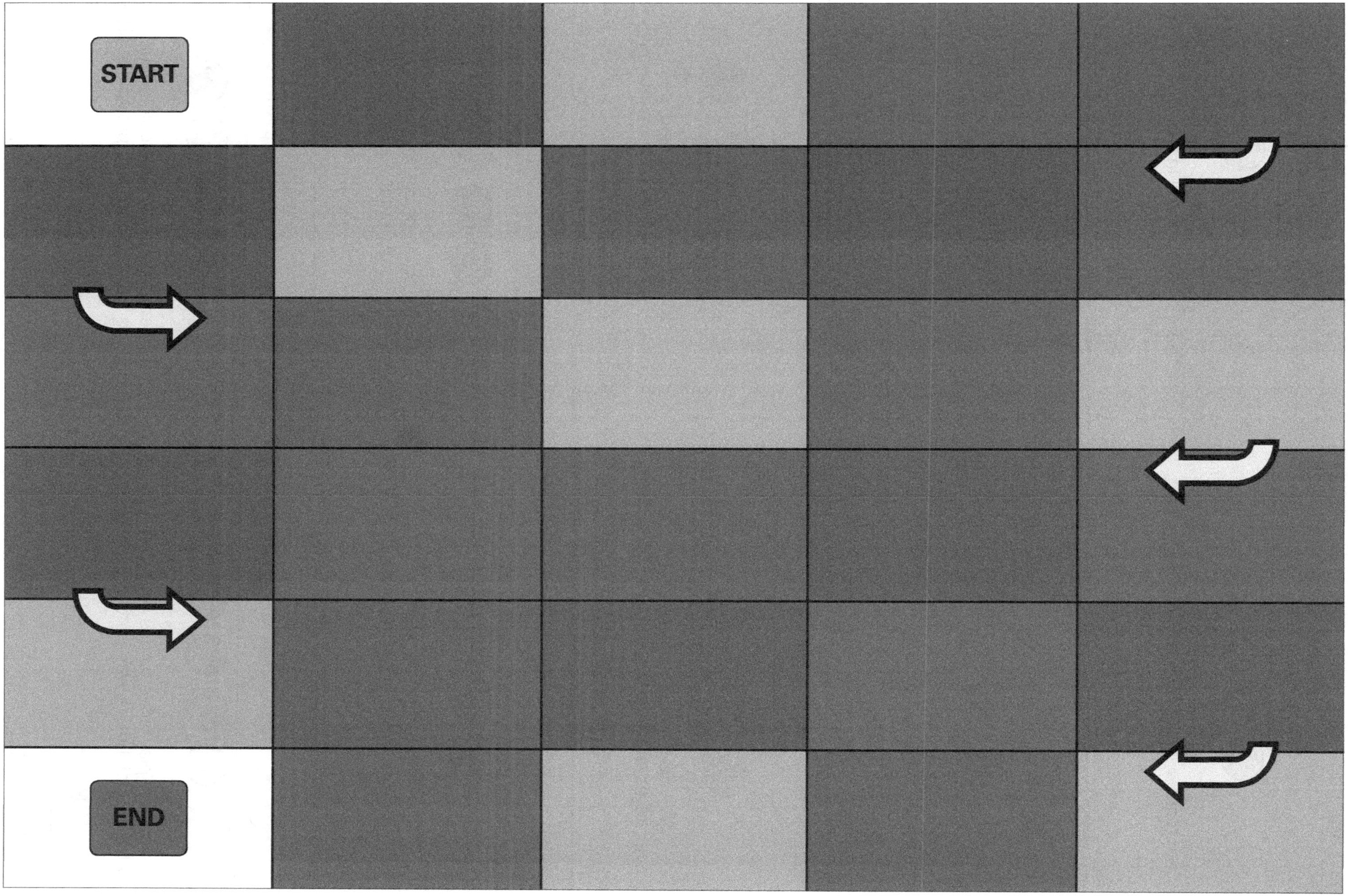
START
END

My teacher is sick, so we have a substitute.

There was a fire drill in the middle of recess.

It snowed all day, and I couldn't go to my friend's house.

The seat I wanted in the cafeteria was taken.

We have a guest speaker in our class, and we have to rearrange our daily schedule.

My mom's phone died, and I didn't save the game I was playing.

The teacher moved us to all new desks in the classroom.

I planned to check out my favorite comic book from the library, but it was already checked out.

I planned to play video games with my brother after school, but he was watching a movie.

The teacher said we would not have time to finish our science projects in class.

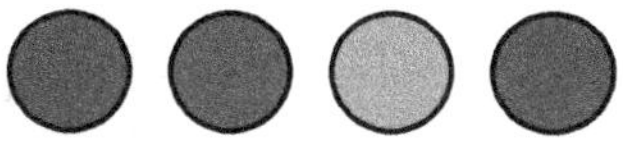

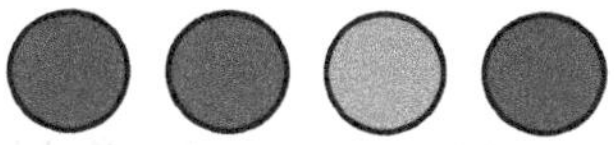

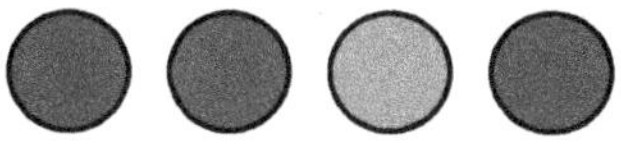

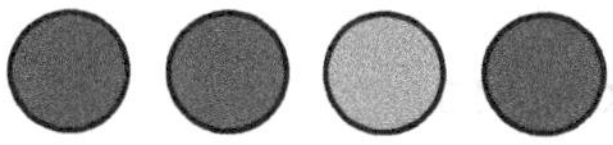

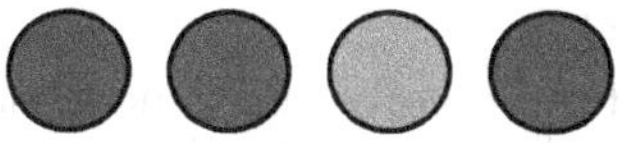

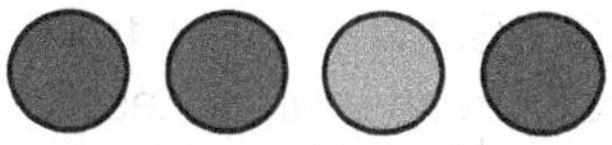

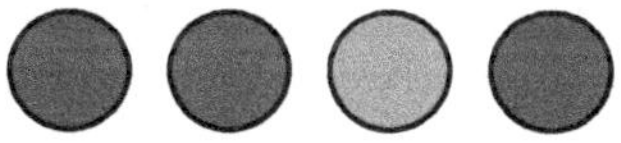

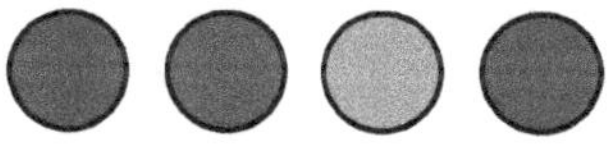

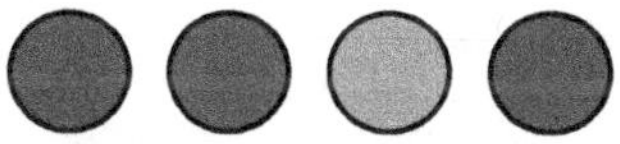

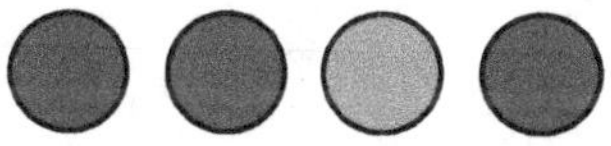

CLOSING

Review: Classroom & Home Practice

Wrap-up
~5 minutes

Materials

Not Included

- Pencils (1 per student)
- Group Reinforcement Visual
- Each student's *UOT Notebook*

Included

- Classroom Practice 12
- Home Practice 12

Instructions

Students will review the Home Practice and complete the *check* portion of the Goal, Why, Plan, Do, Check.

1. Hand out the Home Practices. Read the goal aloud. Ask students to think about who will work on their Home Practice (HP) with them. Let students know they will each earn a tally for bringing the completed HP with them next time you meet.

   Tip

   ★ Follow the same procedure every day for reviewing and completing HP (e.g., review HP, monitor all students as they put it in their homework folder, monitor all students as they write it in their homework planner).
2. Guide students to file all worksheets in their *UOT Notebook.*
3. Read goal for Lesson 12 aloud to the class. Ask students if they were able to accomplish the goal. Ask students to identify what helped them accomplish the goal.
4. Review the plan. Ask students if they were able to accomplish the plan. Were there steps that we were not able to accomplish? Did we need to revise the plan in any way?
5. Remind students they are working towards a large group prize. Each day you will add their tally marks to a bank. When they reach ____ tallies they will get a group celebration or prize.
6. Distribute the Classroom Practice handout to all instructors who interact with your students and would benefit from supporting students as they work on their new skills.

TOPIC 3

Classroom Practice 12

Session Summary: Your student learned how to **Expect, or Handle, the Unexpected,** to help them adjust to the unexpected. Children with executive dysfunction rely on very consistent routines and can become upset when change occurs or their expectations are violated. Because they need routine, it is useful to specifically teach them strategies for handling unexpected violations of routine.

What you can do to support your student's learning and generalization:

1. Many of us adults have a hard time **handling the unexpected,** especially if the unexpected event includes disappointment. But we all know a few people who don't even like nice surprises, like surprise parties in their honor. Be empathic with your students who really depend on routine; try to respect and maintain routines as much as possible, and gently support your students when something happens that is unexpected.

2. Students made a list of possible strategies for them to use when they need to **handle the unexpected**. Some examples of possible strategies that you can try, or help them try, are:
   - **Give warnings!**
     - Inform students in advance about any upcoming changes
     - Give a 5-minute warning that your students will have to stop doing something when they're having fun
   - **Be clear!**
     - Allow your students to ask questions so they can know exactly what will change and what will stay the same
     - Let your students know when the change will be over
     - If there is a good reason for the unexpected event, share that with the students

3. Give lots of praise when your students show that they can **handle the unexpected**. This is really hard work for them!
   - *"You were super flexible when we had to make that change!"*
   - *"You really knew how to **expect the unexpected**! How did you do it!?"*

TOPIC 3

Home Practice 12

Your child participated in the twelfth session of *Unstuck and On Target!* today.

Session Summary: Your child learned how to **Expect, or Handle, the Unexpected.** Your child may need very consistent routines and become upset when change occurs or their expectations are violated. Because your child likes it better when everything goes as they expect it to, it is useful for them to know how to handle unexpected changes.

What you can try at home:

1. Many of us grown-ups have a hard time **handling the unexpected**, especially if the change includes disappointment. And, we all know a few people who don't even like nice surprises, like surprise parties in their honor. If this can be a problem for grown-ups, just imagine how hard it is for your child who loves routine. Be understanding with your child; try to keep things according to routine when you can. Gently support your child when something happens that is unexpected.

2. Your child made a list of possible strategies to use to **handle the unexpected**. Some examples of things you can try at home are:

    - **Give warnings!**
        - Tell your child in advance about any upcoming changes
        - Give a 5-minute warning before any shift from one activity to another
        - Give a 10-minute and then a 5-minute warning if your child will have to stop doing something fun (like stop watching TV to go to bed)
        - Sometimes you may need to count down on your fingers, holding them up so your child can see them. Start at 10, with all of your fingers up, and count down slowly until you get to 0.
    - **Be clear!**
        - Allow your child to ask lots of questions to know exactly what will change and what will stay the same
        - Let your child know when the change will be over
        - If there is a good reason for the change, share that with your child

3. Give lots of praise when your child shows that they can **handle the unexpected**. This is really hard work for them!
    - *"You were super flexible when we had to make that change!"*
    - *"You really knew how to* ***expect the unexpected****! How did you do it!?"*

TOPIC 3

Topic 3 Progress Report

Student Name: ______________________ Date: ______________________

Teacher Name: ____

Over the last few weeks we have covered the following skills and concepts in Topic 3:

- Plan A → Plan B
- Compromise
- Big Deal/Little Deal
- Choice/No Choice
- Expect the Unexpected

Topic 3 Skills	**All of the time**	**Some of the time**	**None of the time**
1. Is able to create a Plan A and Plan B before an event			
2. Is able to create a Plan B in the moment (i.e., during an event when Plan A fails)			
3. Is able to define Compromise or provide examples of a Compromise			
4. Is able to create a Compromise in a moment			
5. Using hypothetical situations is able to identify ways to change a Big Deal into a Little Deal			
6. Is able to use strategies to change a Big Deal into a Little Deal in the moment			
7. Is able to identify something that is a Choice and something that is not a Choice			
8. Is able to identify a strategy to use to help them manage when something Unexpected happens			
A success in group:			
Something we will continue to work on:			

X ______________________________ (Teacher)

(please detach and return the signed slip, acknowledging you have received the progress report)

- -

I have received the *Unstuck and On Target!* Progress Report

X ______________________________ Date:______________

TOPIC 4

Why Be Flexible?

SPECIAL INSTRUCTIONS: The core goal of these lessons is to help students establish intrinsic motivation for being flexible. Although it is important to implement each component of this topic, the group leader can modify the activities as necessary to better meet students' needs. This is especially important regarding motivation to change. *Every student has something that motivates them, but what is motivating can vary from student to student.* The group leader may have to individualize the lessons to make sure they are motivating to each student. When implementing the lessons, use examples from students' experiences whenever possible.

Summary: This topic stresses intrinsic motivation for helping students to be flexible. In these two lessons, students explore how flexibility creates positive feelings and puts them in charge of outcomes. This topic includes explicit instruction, continued use of critical flexibility vocabulary, and an opportunity to examine outcomes that are possible when students are flexible and when they are not.

Prerequisite skills: Understanding of the meaning of flexibility (Topic 1), familiarity with flexibility vocabulary (Topic 2) and flexibility scripts (Topic 3)

Related skills: Intrinsic motivation, self-concept, goal setting

OUTCOME—CRITERIA FOR MASTERY

1. The student identifies the positive feelings that result from being flexible.
2. The student identifies the outcomes that will occur when he or she is flexible.

TOPIC BACKGROUND AND RATIONALE

Like all individuals, students with executive dysfunction respond best when their motivation level is high. However, implicit social or accomplishment-based motivation (i.e., the knowledge that a teacher is happy when the student does well or that by developing the reputation of being a flexible goal directed student, the teacher would be happier with the student and/or more likely to grant privileges) is not consistently available to the student with executive dysfunction. Therefore, it is important to explicitly teach the advantages of flexibility for achieving concrete goals that are meaningful to the individual student. Finding the right incentives to support learning is one of the crucial first steps in teaching students new skills. To effect behavioral change over time, it is important to establish and explicitly demonstrate how flexibility gives students more control and results in positive outcomes.

TOPIC 4

Lesson 13 The Advantages of Being Flexible

PURPOSE

This lesson will help students establish intrinsic motivation for being Flexible by exploring, through concrete experiences, how being Flexible can get them what they want and give them more independence. This lesson includes two activities.

Materials Required for All Activities

Not Included

- Whiteboard or chart paper
- Dry/wet erase markers or markers
- Tape
- 3 pieces of paper (each labeled with a number 1, 2, or 3)
- Video clip of a student reacting negatively to being Stuck (optional)
- Game tokens (e.g., Bingo chips, coins)
- Die
- Pencils
- Group Reinforcement Visual
- Each student's *UOT Notebook*

Included

- GWPDC for Lesson 13
- Lightning Round Questions
- Handout: What to Do When What I Want Is Impossible
- Handout: My Two Choices
- Educator Script: My Two Choices
- Visual: Group Flexibility Chant
- Educator Guide: Flexibility Freeway Game Rules
- Materials: Flexibility Freeway Game Board
- Materials: Flexibility Freeway Game Cards
- Classroom Practice 13
- Home Practice 13

INTRODUCTION

Preview: GWPDC & Lightning Round

Review & Game
~5 minutes

Materials

Not Included

- Whiteboard or chart paper
- Dry/wet erase markers or markers
- Tape
- 3 pieces of paper (each labeled with a number 1, 2, 3)

Included

- GWPDC for Lesson 13
- Lightning Round Questions

Instructions

1. Post the GWPDC on the board before the lesson begins.
2. Review the GWPDC with the group.
3. Complete the Lightning Round activity.

**For a complete set of instructions and tips, refer to the GWPDC and Lightning Round instructions (Topic 1, Lesson 2)*

G W P D C

Goal: Learn to be Flexible when what I want is impossible.

Why: Learning how to be Flexible gets me more of what I want and gives me more control of how things end up.

Plan:
1. Lightning Round
2. What to Do When What I Want Is Impossible
3. My 2 Choices Worksheet
4. Play Flexibility Freeway (optional)
5. Review Home Practice and Classroom Practice

Do: Follow the plan and earn tallies

Check: How did it go? Did we accomplish our plan? What should I do when something I want is impossible?

Lightning Round Questions

1. What can I do if I feel like a #3 or a #4 and I want to get back to feeling just right or like a #1?
2. If I want cake for dessert and my sibling wants brownies, how can we compromise?
3. How many options do we have when we are stuck?

ACTIVITY 1

What to Do When What I Want Is Impossible

Group Activity
~10–15 minutes

Materials

Not Included

- Whiteboard or chart paper
- Dry/wet erase markers or markers

Included

- Visual: Feelings Target
- Handout: My Two Choices

Instructions

1. Explain that students are going to learn more about how being Flexible is helpful to them. Explain that there are certain things in life that are always true, and these are sometimes called *facts of life*. One fact of life is that what we want is not always possible.
2. Ask the students, "Has there ever been anything that you wanted that you could not get?" Be prepared to share your own examples to help students think on their own. Student examples might include not being able to have the snack they wanted; not being able to do something in the order they wanted to do it in; not being able to play the game they wanted to play. Not sitting in a preferred seat; or hanging out with a certain friend. Write a list of these examples on the side of the board.
3. Write the following on the board: Sometimes what I want is impossible. Tell the students that every time there is something they want that is not possible to have, they have 2 choices and they are in charge of those choices. We are going to create a flow chart to illustrate this point.
4. Choose one example from the list of "times students did not get what they wanted".
5. Identify the first choice "stuck". Ask students to identify what happens if they get stuck. Ask students to recall how it feels to be stuck (use the Feelings Target to guide this discussion). Record these answers on the board.
6. Identify the second choice. Ask students to identify what they can do instead (i.e. Plan B). Ask students to recall how it would feel to choose the other option (use the Feelings Target to guide this discussion). Record the answers on the board.

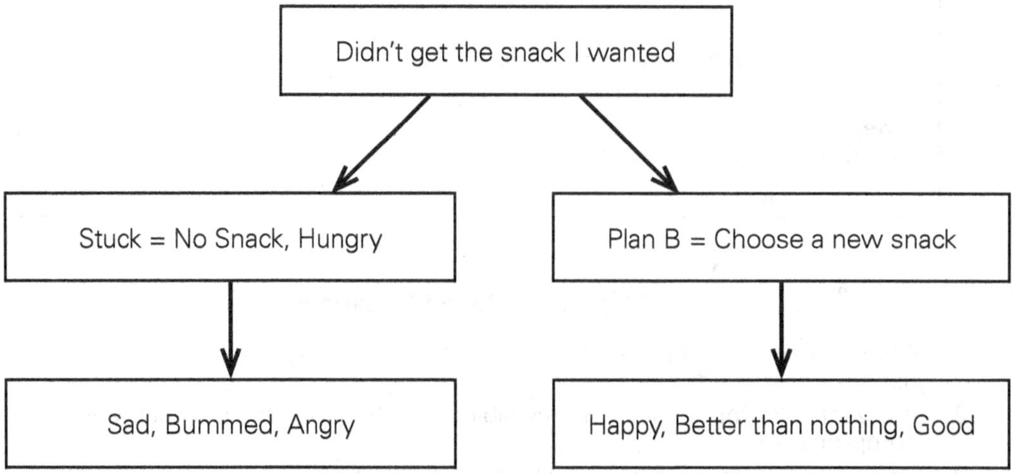

7. If you feel your students would benefit from additional practice repeat the process with additional examples before beginning the next activity.
8. Divide the students into dyads. Give each pair a "My 2 Choices" worksheet. Hand out scenario cards to each group; students should use these scenarios to complete the worksheet (feel free to create scenarios that would be applicable to your group). Challenge each group to come up with as many alternatives as they can. To increase motivation, have each new suggestion equal a tally mark. Students should present their scenario to the group.

TOPIC 4

My Two Choices

I really wanted to play Connect 4, but the game is broken.	I really wanted French fries, but they are sold out.	I really wanted to sit in the front row at the movie, but all of the seats in the front row are taken.
I really wanted to go outside for recess, but it is raining.	I really wanted vanilla ice cream for dessert, but it melted.	I really wanted cheese crackers for my snack, but they are all gone.
I really wanted to use the green marker, but it is dried up.	I really wanted to watch a movie, but the DVD is missing.	I really wanted to sit with my best friend at lunch, but all of the seats are taken.

TOPIC 4

Group Flexibility Chant

When I'm Flexible I'll get part…

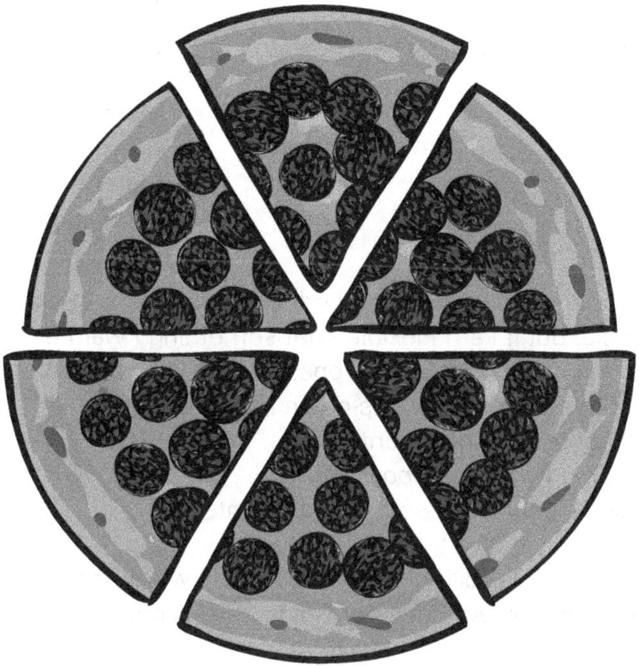

and I'll feel good in my heart.

ACTIVITY 2 *OPTIONAL

Flexibility Freeway Game

Group Activity
~10–15 minutes

Materials

Not Included

- Game tokens (e.g., Bingo chips, coins)
- Die

Included

- Educator Guide: Flexibility Freeway Game Rules
- Materials: Flexibility Freeway Game Board
- Materials: Flexibility Freeway Game Cards (cut out ahead of time)

Instructions

1. Summarize what the students have learned, and reiterate the following: Sometimes what I want is impossible, but if I am Flexible I get something I want and feel good.
2. State the following phrases. After each one, have students give you a thumbs-up if they agree with the statement or a thumbs-down if they disagree.
   a. I can always get everything I want.
   b. Sometimes what I want is *impossible*.
   c. Being Flexible helps me get something I want.
   d. Being Flexible feels better than being Stuck.
3. Have students play the Flexibility Freeway Game, in which they have the chance to make flexible choices. Review Educator Guide: Flexibility Freeway Game Rules before beginning

Remember to check off this step on the GWPDC!

Flexibility Freeway Game Rules

Goal

For each player to reach End of the Freeway at space 50 on the board.

Directions

1. Everyone starts at Space 1 on the game board.

2. Take turns rolling the die and moving the corresponding number of spaces.

3. If you land on a mud puddle with a bridge, pick up a bridge card. Read the scenario. If you can identify a plan for how to be flexible and continue to work toward the goal on the card, you can go over the bridge and to the next space. If you cannot come up with a flexible solution, you are "stuck in the mud" until your next turn. You may move on your next turn.

4. If you land on a mud puddle with a detour sign, pick up a detour card. Read the scenario. If you recognize that you can't always get what you want but can identify a plan for how to be flexible and work toward a new goal that you feel good about, you can follow the detour sign to a new space. If you cannot come up with a flexible solution, you are "stuck in the mud" until your next turn. You may move on your next turn.

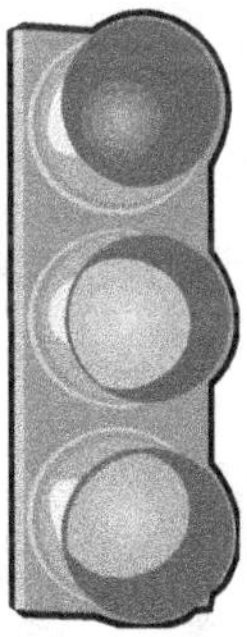

5. If you land on a stoplight, pick up a stoplight card. Read the scenario. If you answer the question correctly, you can move ahead to the next space. If you do not answer the question correctly, stay where you are until your next turn.

FLEXIBILITY FREEWAY GAME BOARD

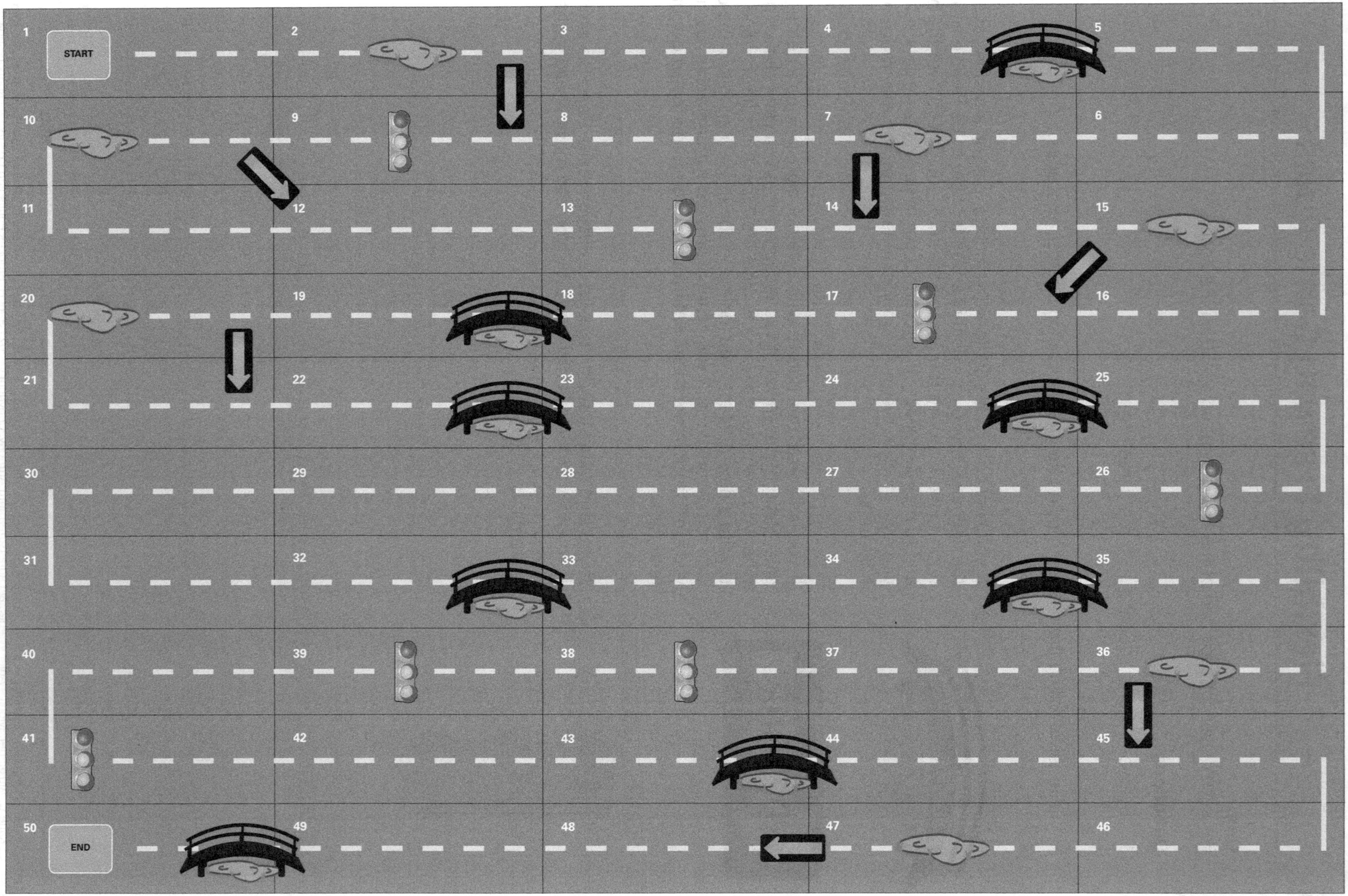

STUCK IN THE MUD!

I would love some chicken nuggets. McDonald's is closed until 3:00 P.M. How can I be Flexible and still reach my goal to eat chicken nuggets?

STUCK IN THE MUD!

I want to write, but the point on my favorite pencil is broken. How can I be Flexible and still reach my goal to use my favorite pencil?

STUCK IN THE MUD!

I want to play with Sam. He is playing with John. How can I be Flexible and still reach my goal to play with Sam?

STUCK IN THE MUD!

I really want to swing on the swings. Right now all of the swings are taken. How can I be Flexible and still reach my goal to swing on the swings?

STUCK IN THE MUD!

I want to talk about video games, but my friends want to talk about dinosaurs. How can I be Flexible and still reach my goal to talk about video games?

STUCK IN THE MUD!

I want to watch SpongeBob SquarePants, but my mom wants me to clean my room. How can I be Flexible and still reach my goal to watch SpongeBob?

STUCK IN THE MUD!

I want to play outside, but I have to do my homework. How can I be Flexible and still reach my goal to play outside?

STUCK IN THE MUD!

I want to go first in the board game, but my friend rolled the higher number. How can I be Flexible and still reach my goal to go first in a game?

STUCK IN THE MUD!

I want to play baseball, but my friends are already playing basketball. How can I be Flexible and still reach my goal to play baseball?

STUCK IN THE MUD!

I want to play with blocks, but my friends are playing a board game. How can I be Flexible and still reach my goal to play with blocks?

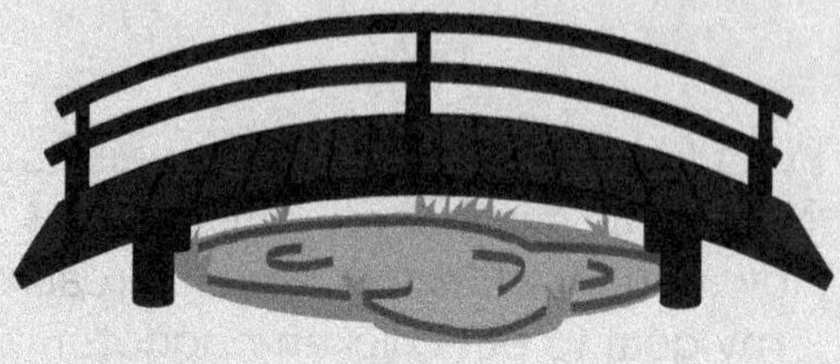

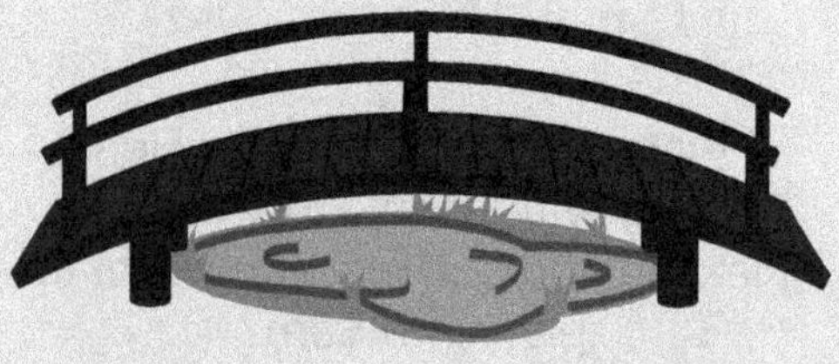

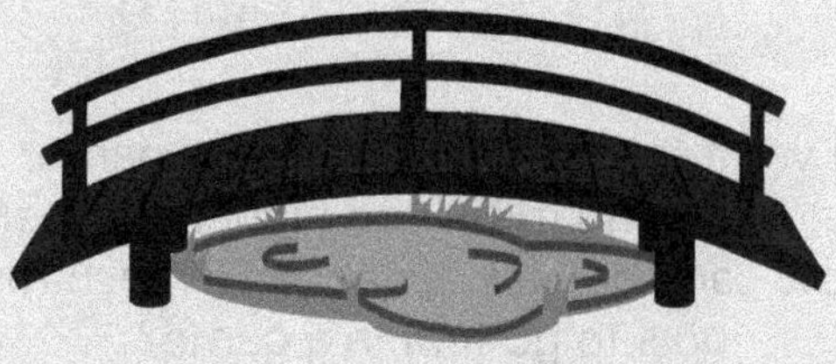

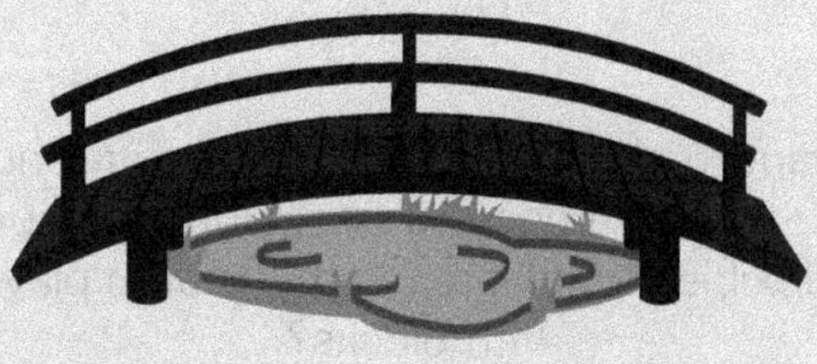

DETOUR!

I wanted a hot dog for lunch, but there are none left. Since I can't always get what I want, how can I be Flexible and get something else I can feel good about?

DETOUR!

I wanted to play on the computer, but they are all being used. Since I can't always get what I want, how can I be Flexible and get something else I can feel good about?

DETOUR!

I wanted to talk about airplanes, but my friend doesn't. Since I can't always get what I want, how can I be Flexible and talk about something else I can feel good about?

DETOUR!

I wanted to watch a movie, but it is time for bed. Since I can't always get what I want, how can I be Flexible and get something else I can feel good about?

DETOUR!

I wanted to go first in the game of Tag. Since I can't always get what I want, how can I be Flexible and get something else I can feel good about?

DETOUR!

I wanted to play video games, but it is time to do my homework. Since I can't always get what I want, how can I be Flexible and get something else I can feel good about?

DETOUR!

I wanted a vanilla ice cream cone, but the store is out of vanilla. Since I can't always get what I want, how can I be Flexible and get something else I can feel good about?

DETOUR!

I wanted to read the soccer book, but my friend is looking at it. Since I can't always get what I want, how can I be Flexible and get something else I can feel good about?

DETOUR!

I wanted to play outside for recess, but it is too cold. Since I can't always get what I want, how can I be Flexible and get something else I can feel good about?

DETOUR!

I wanted to answer the teacher's question, but she called on my classmate first. Since I can't always get what I want, how can I be Flexible and get something else I can feel good about?

DETOUR

DETOUR

DETOUR

DETOUR

DETOUR

DETOUR

DETOUR

DETOUR

DETOUR

DETOUR

STOPLIGHT!

TRUE OR FALSE?

If I have a temper tantrum when I don't get what I want, people will want to help me come up with a plan to help me get something else I can feel good about.

STOPLIGHT!

TRUE OR FALSE?

I can always get everything I want.

STOPLIGHT!

TRUE OR FALSE?

I am in charge of my choice to be stuck in the mud or be Flexible.

STOPLIGHT!

TRUE OR FALSE?

If I am stuck in the mud, I will not get anything I can feel good about.

STOPLIGHT!

TRUE OR FALSE?

Sometimes what I want is not possible.

STOPLIGHT!

TRUE OR FALSE?

Even if the thing I want is not available, it feels better to get something else I want than to be stuck in the mud and get nothing at all.

STOPLIGHT!

TRUE OR FALSE?

Being Flexible helps me get something I want.

STOPLIGHT!

TRUE OR FALSE?

When I can't get what I want, I should yell and cry. If false, what should I do instead?

STOPLIGHT!

TRUE OR FALSE?

Being Flexible feels better than being Stuck.

STOPLIGHT!

When I can't get what I want, I have two choices. What are they?

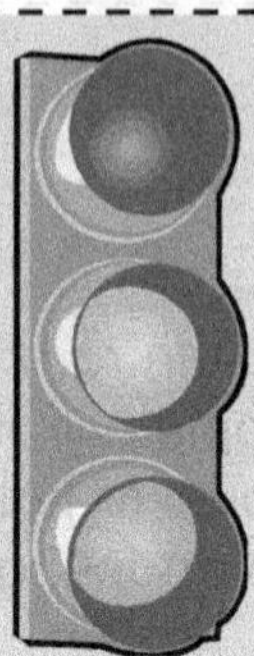

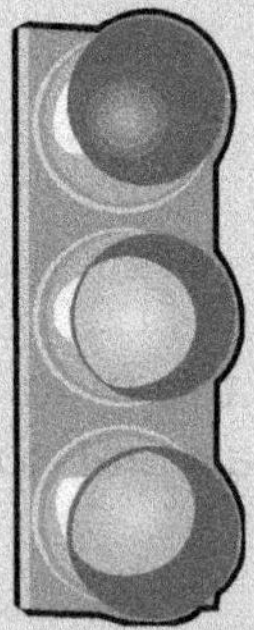

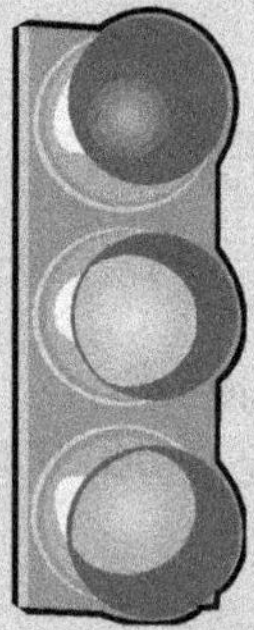

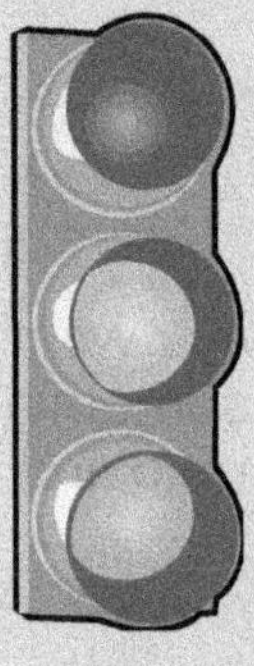

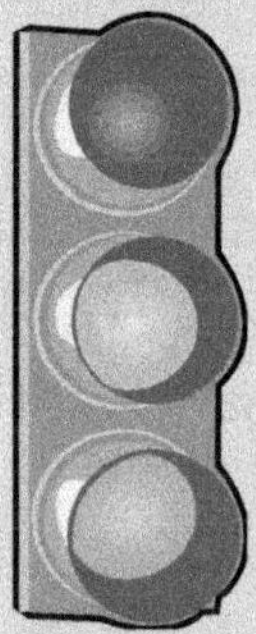

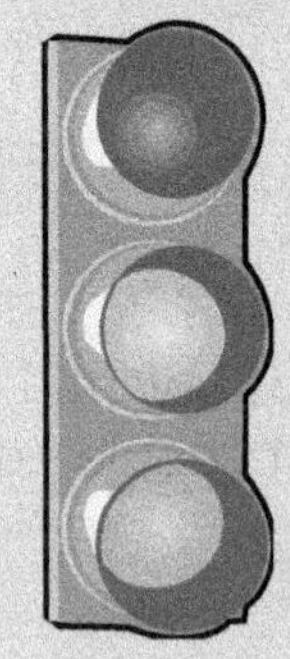

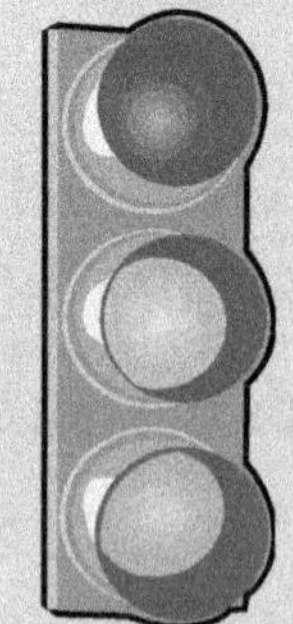

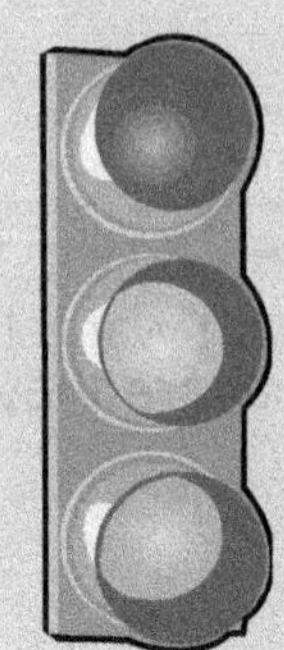

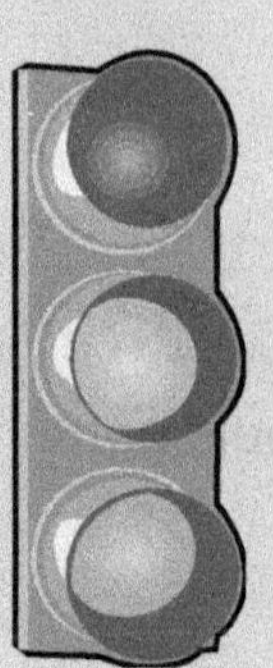

CLOSING

Review: Classroom & Home Practice

Wrap-up
~5 minutes

Materials

Not Included

- Pencils (1 per student)
- Group Reinforcement Visual
- Each student's *UOT Notebook*

Included

- Classroom Practice 13
- Home Practice 13

Instructions

Reinforce!

During the lesson if you find students sticking to the plan or following the Code of Conduct, remind them what they are working for and reinforce accordingly.

"Remember when we use respectful words with one another we earn tallies, and our tallies get us closer to our flexibility party."

Students will review the Home Practice and complete the *check* portion of the Goal, Why, Plan, Do, Check.

1. Hand out the Home Practice sheets. Read the goal aloud. Ask students to think about who they will work on their Home Practice (HP) with. Let students know they will each earn a tally for bringing the completed HP with them next time you meet.

   Tip

   ★ Follow the same procedure every day for reviewing and completing HP (e.g., review HP, monitor all students as they put it in their homework folder, monitor all students as they write it in their homework planner).
2. Guide students to file all worksheets in their *UOT Notebook.*
3. Read the goal for Lesson 13 aloud to the class. Ask students if they were able to accomplish the goal. Ask students to identify what helped them accomplish the goal.
4. Review the plan. Ask students if they were able to accomplish the plan. Were there steps that we were not able to accomplish? Did we need to revise the plan in any way?
5. Remind students they are working towards a large group prize. Each day you will add their tally marks to a bank. When they reach ____ tallies they will get a group celebration or prize.
6. Distribute the Classroom Practice handout to all instructors who interact with your students and would benefit from supporting students as they work on their new skills.

Remember to check off this step on the GWPDC!

TOPIC 4

Classroom Practice 13

Session Summary: Your student learned about how being flexible is helpful to them (they will feel better and get more of what they want when they are flexible). They learned that one of the facts of life is that what we want is not always possible. Students then examined how they would feel and what happens when they are flexible vs. when they get stuck, when what they want is impossible.

What you can do to support your student's learning and generalization:

Teacher self-assessment:

This is a good time to evaluate how much progress you feel you and your student(s) are making in becoming more flexible. Make sure that you are doing everything you can to support these new skills in your student by taking the self-quiz below:

✓ How often do I specifically praise my students for showing good flexibility skills? (Remember, praise should be specific, true, and immediate.)

- ❑ Daily
- ❑ Sometimes
- ❑ Never

✓ Am I praising more than I correct my students? (Try to praise at least 4 times more often than you correct your students.)

- ❑ I praise more than I correct
- ❑ I praise and correct about the same
- ❑ I correct more than I praise

✓ Am I showing my students how to be flexible by being flexible myself? Flexibility is contagious!

- ❑ I am flexible every chance I get
- ❑ I am trying to be more flexible
- ❑ I really need to work on this

✓ How often do I use the flexibility vocabulary?

- ❑ Daily
- ❑ Sometimes
- ❑ Never

Note: If your scores aren't where you want them or you aren't seeing much progress in your student, check in with the *Unstuck and On Target!* group leader to figure out how to make things work better.

TOPIC 4

Home Practice 13

Your child participated in the thirteenth session of *Unstuck and On Target!* today.

Session Summary: Your child learned about how being flexible is helpful to them (they will feel better and get more of what they want when they are flexible). Your child learned that one of the "facts of life" is that what we want is not always possible. Your child then examined how they would feel and what happens when they are flexible vs. when they get stuck, when what they want is impossible.

What you can try at home:

1. Try to use this week's vocabulary whenever you or your child wants something that is not possible (your favorite shirt is dirty, so it isn't possible to wear it; someone is already on the swing in the park, so it isn't possible to use it right now; etc.):
    - ***"Sometimes what we want just isn't possible."***
    - *"How are we going to **feel** if we get **stuck** on something that isn't possible?"*
    - *"How are we going to **feel** if we are **flexible** when something we wanted isn't possible?"*

2. Parent self-assessment:

    This is a good time to evaluate how much progress you feel you and your child are making in becoming more flexible. Make sure that you are doing everything you can to support these new skills by taking the self-quiz below. Note: If your scores aren't where you want them or you aren't seeing much progress in your child, check in with your *Unstuck and On Target!* group leader to figure out how to make things work better.

    ✓ How often do I specifically praise my child for showing good flexibility skills? (Remember, praise should be specific, true, and immediate.)

    ❑ Daily
    ❑ Sometimes
    ❑ Never

    ✓ Am I praising more than I correct my child? (Try to praise at least 4 times more often than you correct your child.)

    ❑ I praise more than I correct
    ❑ I praise and correct about the same
    ❑ I correct more than I praise

    ✓ Am I showing my child how to be flexible by being flexible myself? Flexibility is contagious!

    ❑ I am flexible every chance I get
    ❑ I am trying to be more flexible
    ❑ I really need to work on this

    ✓ How often do I use the flexibility vocabulary?

    ❑ Daily
    ❑ Sometimes
    ❑ Never

TOPIC 4

Lesson 14 Being Flexible Can Make Good Things Happen

PURPOSE

The purpose of this lesson is to illustrate that when students are Flexible, they gain power and increase the likelihood that other people will recognize their Flexibility. As a direct result, students are more likely to earn preferred, positive experiences. In other words, Flexibility increases the likelihood of positive outcomes, such as increased privileges. The students apply this concept to the creation of a video game that follows the same principles. There are two activities in this lesson.

Materials Required for All Activities

Not Included

- Whiteboard or chart paper
- Dry/wet erase markers or markers
- Tape
- 3 pieces of paper (each labeled with a number 1, 2, or 3)
- Marbles (or similar objects (e.g., cheese balls, Bingo chips for each student)
- Jar or other container to hold marbles, preferably something transparent
- Chart paper
- Markers
- Pencils
- Group Reinforcement Visual
- Each student's *UOT Notebook*

Included

- GWPDC for Lesson 14
- Lightning Round Questions
- Educator Script: Flexibility Gives You Power Scenarios
- Educator Script: Marble Jar: Flexible Reputation Scenarios
- Classroom Practice 14
- Home Practice 14

INTRODUCTION

Preview: GWPDC & Lightning Round

Review & Game
~5 minutes

Materials

Not Included

- Whiteboard or chart paper and suitable markers
- Tape
- 3 pieces of paper (each labeled with a number 1, 2, or 3)

Included

- GWPDC for Lesson 14
- Lightning Round Questions

Instructions

1. Post the GWPDC on the board before the lesson begins.
2. Review the GWPDC with the group.
3. Complete the Lightning Round activity.

**For a complete set of instructions and tips, refer to the GWPDC and Lightning Round instructions (Topic 1, Lesson 2).*

Think outside of the box...
There is more than 1 right answer to each question. Encourage multiple students to share an answer for each question.

G W P D C

Goal: To learn about how being Flexible can increase our "powers" and the importance of repeatedly being Flexible.

Why: Being repeatedly Flexible helps me build a reputation for being Flexible, which leads to more "powers" and helps me get more of what I want.

Plan:
1. Lightning Round
2. Flexibility Powers
3. My Flexible Reputation
4. Review Home Practice

Do: Follow the plan and earn tallies.

Check: How did it go? Did we accomplish our plan? Why is your reputation important?

Lightning Round Questions

1. How does it feel to be Stuck?
2. Why does choosing to be Flexible feel better?
3. If I can't have the pizza I want for dinner, what would I say if I were Stuck? What would I say if I am being Flexible?

Remember to check off this step on the GWPDC!

ACTIVITY 1

Flexibility Powers

Group Activity
~5–10 minutes

Materials

Not Included

- Whiteboard or chart paper
- Dry/wet erase markers or markers

Included

- Educator Script: Flexibility Gives You Power Scenarios

Instructions

Reinforce!
Provide tallies for participation
"Excellent participation! You are all showing me that you understand this important fact of life—that sometimes what you want is impossible, and you still have choices."

1. Ask students to think of a video game that has a quest, journey, or challenge that has to be met (e.g., Super Mario Brothers). Make sure each child can think of an example, and ask one student to describe a game. Ask additional questions about the game: What is the name of the game? What is the object of the game? What happens as the characters pass through the different levels? Are there special powers or abilities that help the characters reach their goals? How do the characters get those powers? Are there bonus points or special prizes in the game? Tell the students that being Flexible can help them gain "powers," or privileges, just like the characters in a video game gain powers.
2. Ask: "What powers do you think you earn from being Flexible?" (Answers may include earning more privileges, having more independence, earning greater trust from teachers and parents, having classmates enjoy being around them, and making a choice for themselves instead of having an adult tell them what to do.)
3. Read aloud the scenarios in Educator Script: Flexibility Gives You Power Scenarios. After reading each one, ask students what powers the students in the scenarios might gain from being Flexible. Record their answers on the whiteboard.

Remember to check off this step on the GWPDC!

TOPIC 4

Flexibility Gives You Power Scenarios

Scenario 1

Jimmy loves pizza. He would like to eat pizza every night. His parents decided that the family would have special pizza night every Friday.

Another tradition in Jimmy's family is that whoever has a birthday gets to pick his or her favorite meal to have for dinner. This Friday is Jimmy's sister's birthday. Jimmy recognized how special his sister's birthday was and decided to be flexible and not get upset about missing "Pizza Friday."

What are some powers Jimmy might gain from his parents for being so flexible?

Scenario 2

Sarah went to see the new *Transformers* movie with her mom and her friend Ben. When they got to the theater, they found out that the movie was sold out. Sarah was disappointed that she couldn't see *Transformers*, but she didn't want her fun time with her friend to end just because their first plan didn't work out. Sarah decided that she would be flexible and select another movie.

What are some powers Sarah might gain from her parents for being so flexible?

ACTIVITY 2

Flexible Reputation

Group Activity
~20 minutes

Materials

Not Included

- Marbles (or similar objects (e.g., cheese balls, Bingo chips for each student)
- Jar or other container to hold marbles, preferably something transparent (one for each student)
- Chart paper
- Markers

Included

- Educator Script: Marble Jar: Flexible Reputation Scenarios

Instructions

The idea for students to understand in this lesson is that when they are repeatedly Flexible, they develop a Flexible reputation. People start to think of them as Flexible and are then more likely to give them privileges ("powers") based on the repeated Flexibility.

1. Have students brainstorm situations in which they have had to be Flexible. (You may use prompts to elicit answers, such as dinner, dessert, video game, computer game, waiting in line, playing a certain position on a sports team, order of playing a game, or selecting a game.) Record their answers on chart paper.
2. Tell students that when they are repeatedly Flexible over a period of time, they develop a reputation for being Flexible. Make sure students understand the meaning of reputation: "Your behavior gives people certain thoughts about you—it forms your reputation. When you have a certain reputation, people start to treat you in a certain way." Give some examples: 1) someone who always says please and thank you—polite; 2) someone who loves to run around, constantly moving—energetic; and 3) someone who likes to talk with people and play games with others—friendly.
3. Help students make the connection between reputation and how people treat them. Record these thoughts visually to support student comprehension. For example,
   a. Friendly reputation = people want to be around you and play games with you.
4. Ask students to brainstorm how people will treat them differently if they have a Flexible reputation. Use examples that are meaningful to your students. For example,
   a. Was Flexible when dessert was not available = an extra treat the following day
   b. Went to bed at bedtime instead of watching my favorite movie = able to stay up late the next day
   c. Let a classmate go first in line = teacher puts me first next time
5. Remind students that reputations develop over time. As they follow the scenarios you are going to read, they will watch a Flexible reputation develop.
6. Hand out a small container and a handful of marbles to each student. Marbles represent flexible acts. The accumulation of marbles represents a growing Flexible reputation.
7. Read the scenarios aloud from the Educator Script: Marble Jar: Flexible Reputation Scenarios. If the fictional student was Flexible, have students place a marble in their container. If the fictional student was not Flexible, no marble goes in the container. Pause as indicated on Educator Script: Marble Jar: Flexible Reputation Scenarios to probe students' understanding of Flexibility, reputation, and when it is okay to choose not to be Flexible.

Reinforce!
Provide tallies for participation
"Excellent participation! You are all showing me that you understand how being flexible gives you more powers!"

Reinforce!

Provide tallies for sharing personal examples and stories

"Thank you for helping all of us learn by sharing your story/example."

8. Repeat this activity as many times as necessary to ensure student comprehension.
   a. If students are forthcoming with personal examples, you can use those as scenarios.
   b. Create a fictional student who chooses not to be Flexible more often than to be Flexible. What type of reputation is this student developing?
9. At the end of the activity, review how the reputation was developed. What privileges did the student likely earn as a result of his or her Flexible reputation? When is it okay not to be Flexible?

Remember to check off this step on the GWPDC!

TOPIC 4

Marble Jar: Flexible Reputation Scenarios

Students place one marble in their jar for each flexible act. Pause at the italicized text to reflect on how the student's behavior is helping to develop reputation.

1. My favorite ice cream was sold out, so I had to order pie.
2. The swings were taken on the playground, so I went on the slide.
3. The computer was out of batteries, so I played a board game.
4. I knew my friend loved to be first in line, so I went second.
5. Both my friend and I wanted to be pitcher in the baseball game, so I let her pitch and I was catcher.

How does your jar look now? Based on how full your jar is, what type of a reputation does this student have? Why?

6. My sister was watching a movie, so I used the computer instead.
7. I was going to have toast, but we were out so I chose to have cereal instead.
8. I wanted to read the new Harry Potter book, but it was checked out of the library so I chose a science fiction book.
9. My friend didn't want me to play with one of my classmates. I told him I didn't want to leave my classmate out and included my classmate anyway.

Was the student flexible here? Why not? Do you think it was okay for him to choose not to be flexible? (Yes, sometimes you need to stand up for what you believe in.) What did this do to his reputation? (His jar is still very full, so he still has a flexible reputation.)

10. I wanted a chocolate bar, but only Skittles were available. I chose to eat the Skittles even though they're not my favorite.
11. I was going to go outside to play, but it started raining. I told my teacher that I had wanted to play outside, and I got Stuck thinking about how much I had wanted to play outside. My teacher tried to help me get unstuck, but it was too hard. I was so Stuck that I couldn't do a Plan B and missed playing inside during recess time. Then, I was Stuck because I didn't get to play, and I felt so upset that my teacher suggested that I take a break. After my break, I felt a little better, but it was harder to do my work. So I have more homework than usual from my science class.
12. I wanted the chair closest to the door, but when I got in the room, my classmate had already taken it. I sat in another chair.

How does your jar look now? Highlight that even though this student got really stuck and didn't get his work done that his overall reputation is preserved. This is a good opportunity to reiterate that we all make mistakes, and that it is okay and we can learn from those mistakes. Based on how full your jar is, what type of a reputation does this student have? Why? What sorts of privileges (powers) do you think the student might get because he has such a flexible reputation?

13. My favorite teacher was absent today, so I did math with the substitute.

(continued)

TOPIC 4

Marble Jar: Flexible Reputation Scenarios

14. I play a board game every afternoon with my friend. He has gone first in the game for the last six days. He wanted to go first today. I told him I thought it would be fair if I was allowed to go first today.
15. My friend promised me that he would bring my favorite comic book back to school with him today, but he forgot it. I got so stuck thinking about how much I had wanted to read it today that I told my teacher I wasn't going to do any of my morning work. My teacher helped me, but I didn't have time to do my math work this morning because it took me so long to get unstuck.

How does your jar look now? Again highlight that even though this student had a difficult time that his overall reputation is still one of being a flexible student. Based on how full your jar is, what type of a reputation does this student have? Why? What sorts of privileges (powers) do you think the student might get because he has such a flexible reputation?

16. A new student joined my classroom, so I had to change math groups.
17. My teacher wanted to rearrange the seats in the classroom. She put my desk in the last row. I told her I could not see the board from there, and asked if it would be possible to keep my old seat up front.
18. I was looking forward to doing our classroom presentations on traveling in communities in the United States. I had prepared a great presentation on light rail transportation in large cities. Right before it was my turn, our teacher told us that we had run out of time and we would finish our presentations the next day. I got so stuck thinking about how I had wanted to do my presentation today that I yelled out that I hate running out of time. I also yelled at my friend who had just pre-sented because it felt like it was her fault. My teacher reminded me of the classroom rules, so I apologized. I still wish that I could have given my presentation on the first day.

How does your jar look now? Based on how full your jar is, what type of a reputation does this student have? Why? What sorts of privileges (powers) do you think the student might get because he has such a flexible reputation?

19. We had a 2-hour delay at school because of snow, and we were not able to have music, my favorite class. I felt really upset about that and yelled out that I was so mad at the snow storm and the delay in school. My teacher reminded me that I should keep a calm voice. I asked her if we could come up with a Plan B. She reminded me that we would have music next week, and she promised me that we could listen to music during our indoor recess.

Continue with examples until you think the students understand the development and positive consequences of a Flexible reputation. They should also understand the importance and validity of standing their ground in some cases and that in the end this rigidity does not negatively affect a Flexible reputation.

CLOSING

Review: Classroom & Home Practice

Wrap-up
~5 minutes

Materials

Not Included

- Pencils (1 per student)
- Group Reinforcement Visual
- Each student's *UOT Notebook*

Included

- Classroom Practice 14
- Home Practice 14

Instructions

Reinforce!

During the lesson if you find students sticking to the plan or following the Code of Conduct, remind them what they are working for and reinforce accordingly.

"Remember when we use respectful words with one another we earn tallies, and our tallies get us closer to our flexibility party."

Students will review the Home Practice and complete the *check* portion of the Goal, Why, Plan, Do, Check.

1. Hand out the Home Practice sheets. Read the goal aloud. Ask students to think about who they will work on their Home Practice (HP) with. Let students know they will each earn a tally for bringing the completed HP with them next time you meet.

   Tip

   ★ Follow the same procedure every day for reviewing and completing HP (e.g., review HP, monitor all students as they put it in their homework folder, monitor all students as they write it in their homework planner).
2. Guide students to file all worksheets in their *UOT Notebook.*
3. Read the goal for Lesson 14 aloud to the class. Ask students if they were able to accomplish the goal. Ask students to identify what helped them accomplish the goal.
4. Review the plan. Ask students if they were able to accomplish the plan. Were there steps that we were not able to accomplish? Did we need to revise the plan in any way?
5. Remind students they are working towards a large group prize. Each day you will add their tally marks to a bank. When they reach ____ tallies they will get a group celebration or prize.
6. Distribute the Classroom Practice handout to all instructors who interact with your students and would benefit from supporting students as they work on their new skills.

Don't forget to check off this step on the GWPDC!

Classroom Practice 14

Session Summary: Today, your student learned about how being flexible can help you get more of what you want, such as earning more privileges, having more independence, earning greater trust from teachers and parents, having classmates enjoy being around you, and making a choice for yourself instead of having an adult tell you what to do. Once they develop a **flexible reputation**, more of these privileges will come to you.

What you can do to support your student's learning and generalization:

Try to help your student see the benefits of being more **flexible**:

Benefits of being flexible:

- You get more of what you want
- You feel better
- Others give you more choices when you build a "flexible reputation"

Costs of being stuck:

- You get nothing
- You feel bad
- You have fewer choices

Home Practice 14

Your child participated in the fourteenth session of *Unstuck and On Target!* today.

Session Summary: Today, your child learned about how being flexible can help you get more of what you want, such as earning more privileges, having more freedom, earning greater trust from teachers and parents, having kids like you better, and having more choices for yourself. Once you develop a **flexible reputation,** more of these privileges will come to you.

What you can try at home:

Try to help your child see the benefits of being more **flexible**:

Benefits of being flexible:

- You get more of what you want
- You feel better
- Others give you more choices when you build a "flexible reputation"

Costs of being stuck:

- You get nothing
- You feel bad
- You have fewer choices

TOPIC 4

Topic 4 Progress Report

Student Name: ______________________ Date: ______________________

Teacher Name: ______________________

Over the last few weeks we have covered the following skills and concepts in Topic 4:

- Sometimes what I want is *impossible*
- Flexible Reputation
- Stuck = no choices
- Flexible = choice

Topic 4 Skills	**All of the time**	**Some of the time**	**None of the time**
1. Is able to identify how it feels to be stuck			
2. Is able to identify that being stuck= no choices/options			
3. Is able to identify that being flexible = choices			
4. Is able to identify the benefits of a flexible reputation			
A success in group:			
Something we will continue to work on:			

X ______________________ (Teacher)

(please detach and return the signed slip, acknowledging you have received the progress report)

- -

I have received the *Unstuck and On Target!* Progress Report

X ______________________ Date: ____________

TOPIC 5

Your Goals

Getting What You Want

SPECIAL INSTRUCTIONS: The core goal of these lessons is to help students identify what goals are and how to set and achieve goals. Although it is important to introduce the concept of goals and reinforce the Goal, Why, Plan, Do, Check (GWPDC) script, please modify the activities as necessary to better meet the needs of your students.

Summary: In this topic, students learn how to establish a goal and how to make a plan for obtaining a goal. This topic allows students to practice the empirically supported script and routine Goal, Why, Plan, Do, Check (GWPDC).

Prerequisite skills: Understanding of the meaning of flexibility; familiarity with flexibility vocabulary; understanding of the value of flexibility

Related skills: Core language comprehension, ability to identify concrete goals

OUTCOME—CRITERIA FOR MASTERY

1. The student defines *goal.*
2. The student identifies a goal.
3. With minimal prompts, the student applies the GWPDC script to structure a multiple-step task.

TOPIC BACKGROUND AND RATIONALE

This topic practices and reinforces a fundamental script that underlies many of the activities in *Unstuck and On Target!* It is a generic and widely applicable self-regulatory/problem-solving script that provides a template for approaching a problem, situation, or project. The first part of this script is the introduction of the concept of a goal. Making the definition of goal explicit is a very important step for students on the autism spectrum or with ADHD because they can easily over-focus on details and lose sight of the main reason for, or goal of, their activity. In this topic, students practice a standard operating procedure for reaching goals known as the GWPDC. Students are encouraged to try things out (their plan), then check on the success of the plan and whether they were able to accomplish their goal. This provides a prompt for the self-monitoring that is often difficult for them. An additional virtue of this approach is that the focus is on the plan, not on the student's difficulties; therefore, a breakdown in the situation can be blamed on an unhelpful plan rather than on the student.

TOPIC 5

Lesson 15 Setting and Achieving Goals Using GWPDC

PURPOSE

In these lessons students expand their understanding of Goal, Why, Plan, Do, Check (GWPDC). Students will learn that more than one plan is often needed and that when a plan does not work, it is okay. What is needed is simply a different plan. Students apply their Compromising strategies, practice asking for help, and learn about possible distractors as they work to create plans to accomplish their goals. There is one activity in this lesson.

Materials Required for All Activities

Not Included

- Whiteboard or chart paper
- Dry/wet erase markers or markers
- Tape
- 3 pieces of paper (each labeled with a number 1, 2, or 3)
- Video clip: Pink Panther, "Think Before You Pink"
- Pencils
- Group Reinforcement Visual
- Each student's *UOT Notebook*

Included

- GWPDC for Lesson 15
- Lightning Round Questions
- Handout: Think Pink—GWPDC
- Classroom Practice 15
- Home Practice 15

INTRODUCTION

Preview: GWPDC & Lightning Round

Review & Game
~5 minutes

Materials

Not Included

- Whiteboard or chart paper and suitable markers
- Tape
- 3 pieces of paper (each labeled with a number 1, 2, or 3)

Included

- GWPDC for Lesson 15
- Lightning Round Questions

Instructions

1. Post the GWPDC on the board before the lesson begins.
2. Review the GWPDC with the group.
3. Complete the Lightning Round activity.

**For a complete set of instructions and tips, refer to the GWPDC and Lightning Round instructions (Topic 1, Lesson 2).*

Reinforce...
Following the Code of Conduct
Give a tally each time a student follows the Code of Conduct.

G W P D C

Goal: Write a Goal, Why, Plan, Do, Check for Pink Panther.

Why: Sometimes I will need multiple plans to reach my goals and make sure I am able to get what I want or need.

Plan:
1. Lightning Round
2. Watch *Think Pink*
3. Watch *Think Pink* (again) and fill out the GWPDC
4. Review Home Practice

Do: Follow the plan and earn tallies.

Check: How did it go? Did we accomplish our plan?

Remember to check off this step on the GWPDC!

Lightning Round Questions

1. What is a reputation?
2. Name 2 things you are likely to do if you have a Flexible reputation.
3. Name 2 things you are likely to do if you have a reputation as someone who is not Flexible, or who gets Stuck all of the time.

ACTIVITY 1
Think Pink—GWPDC

Video and Discussion
~15 minutes

Materials

Not Included

- Whiteboard or chart paper
- Dry/wet erase markers or markers
- Video clip: Pink Panther, "Think Before You Pink" (6 minutes, 30 seconds)

Included

- Handout: Think Pink—GWPDC

Instructions

1. Ahead of time, search the Internet for the Pink Panther video clip "Think Before You Pink." Once you have located the video, please watch it the entire way through, as we cannot vouch for the many versions that may be available for public viewing.
2. Explain to students that once they decide what they want to do (their goal) and *why* they want to achieve that goal (their motivation), they must decide *how* they are going to do it (their plan). Write the following on the whiteboard or chart paper. Use a different color for the goal, the why, and the plan, colors that you will use consistently throughout this topic.
   a. *Goal: what you want to do*
   b. *Why: why you want to do it*
   c. *Plan: how you will do it*
3. Inform students that they are about to watch a video of the Pink Panther trying to meet his goal. Show the video clip. As they watch, have students try to figure out Pink Panther's goal as well as the number of plans he attempts.
4. At the conclusion of the video, ask the following questions:
   a. What was the Pink Panther's goal? (To cross the street.)
   b. Why did he want to cross the street? (To get to the other side, of course!)
   c. Did the Pink Panther use one plan or more than one plan? (More than one.)
   d. Can anyone tell how many plans the Pink Panther used? (There were 12 attempts!)
   e. Can anyone name some of the Pink Panther's plans? (Discuss a few.)
5. Explain that it is not enough to have just one plan—Plan A. Students need to have at least one other plan—Plan B. In fact, they may need many plans.
6. Write the following on the board:
   a. *Start with a Plan A and a Plan B.*
   b. *You may need many plans.*
7. Distribute Handout: Think Pink—GWPDC. As a group fill out the Goal (to cross the street) and Why (to get to the other side). Let students know you are going to show the video a second time. Their job this time is to record each plan Pink Panther attempts (in the plan section), and rate how it went (in the check section). Reflect on how many plans it took Pink Panther to accomplish his goal. What would have happened if he had given up after plan C or D?

   Tip

   ★ There is a lot of text on this worksheet. If students are visually overwhelmed you can cut it into strips, have them uncover only the item they are working on, or work on it as a group.
8. Emphasize that it is not enough to have just one plan, you may need many plans.

Reinforce!
Provide tallies for participation
"Excellent participation! You are all showing me that you understand this important fact of life—that sometimes what you want is impossible, and you still have choices."

Remember to check off this step on the GWPDC!

TOPIC 5

Think Pink—GWPDC

GOAL		
WHY		
PLAN(S)	**A**	**CHECK:** **Did he accomplish his goal?** Yes No **How did it go?** Not Well Ok Good
	B	**CHECK:** **Did he accomplish his goal?** Yes No **How did it go?** Not Well Ok Good
	C	**CHECK:** **Did he accomplish his goal?** Yes No **How did it go?** Not Well Ok Good
	D	**CHECK:** **Did he accomplish his goal?** Yes No **How did it go?** Not Well Ok Good
	E	**CHECK:** **Did he accomplish his goal?** Yes No **How did it go?** Not Well Ok Good
	F	**CHECK:** **Did he accomplish his goal?** Yes No **How did it go?** Not Well Ok Good
	G	**CHECK:** **Did he accomplish his goal?** Yes No **How did it go?** Not Well Ok Good
	H	**CHECK:** **Did he accomplish his goal?** Yes No **How did it go?** Not Well Ok Good
	I	**CHECK:** **Did he accomplish his goal?** Yes No **How did it go?** Not Well Ok Good
	J	**CHECK:** **Did he accomplish his goal?** Yes No **How did it go?** Not Well Ok Good
	K	**CHECK:** **Did he accomplish his goal?** Yes No **How did it go?** Not Well Ok Good
	L	**CHECK:** **Did he accomplish his goal?** Yes No **How did it go?** Not Well Ok Good

CLOSING

Review: Classroom & Home Practice

Wrap-up
~5 minutes

Materials

Not Included

- Pencils (1 per student)
- Group Reinforcement Visual
- Each student's *UOT Notebook*

Included

- Classroom Practice 15
- Home Practice 15

Instructions

Students will review the Home Practice and complete the *check* portion of the Goal, Why, Plan, Do, Check.

1. Hand out the Home Practice sheets. Read the goal aloud. Ask students to think about who will work on their Home Practice (HP) with them. Let students know they will each earn a tally for bringing the completed HP with them next time you meet.

   Tip

   ★ Follow the same procedure every day for reviewing and completing HP (e.g., review HP, monitor all students as they put it in their homework folder, monitor all students as they write it in their homework planner).
2. Guide students to file all worksheets in their *UOT Notebook*.
3. Read the goal for Lesson 15 aloud to the class. Ask students if they were able to accomplish the goal. Ask students to identify what helped them accomplish the goal.
4. Review the plan. Ask students if they were able to accomplish the plan. Were there steps that we were not able to accomplish? Did we need to revise the plan in any way?
5. Remind students they are working towards a large group prize. Each day you will add their tally marks to a bank. When they reach ____ tallies they will get a group celebration or prize.
6. Distribute the Classroom Practice handout to all instructors who interact with your students and would benefit from supporting students as they work on their new skills.

Remember to check off this step on the GWPDC!

TOPIC 5

Classroom Practice 15

Session Summary: Today, your student's *Unstuck and On Target!* group switched topics and started to build new goal setting and planning skills. These new skills will build on the foundation of all of the flexibility skills learned so far. They also build on the introduction to goal setting and planning from Lesson 2.

What you can do to support your student's learning and generalization:

1. Try to help your students see how setting their own goals and making plans will benefit them:
   - ***If you set your <u>own</u> goals, you will get more of what you want!***

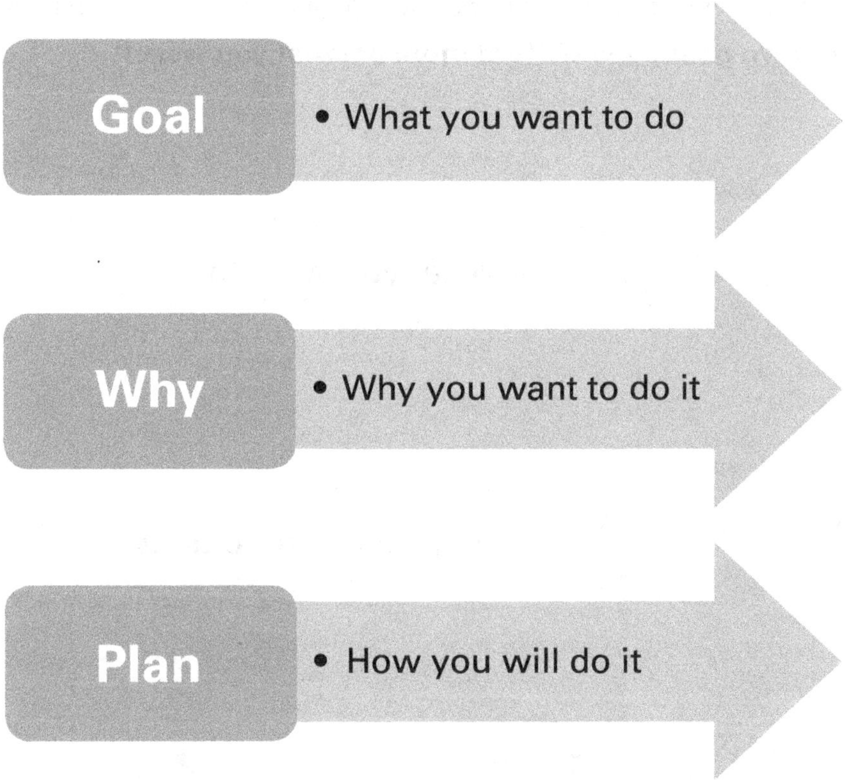

2. Your student watched a Pink Panther video called "Think Before You Pink," where Pink Panther makes 12 different plans to cross a busy street. If your student hits an obstacle, ask him or her, "What would Pink Panther do right now?" (He'd come up with another plan!)
3. If you need more examples of using goal setting in your class, re-review Classroom Practice 2, which introduced the Goal, Why, Plan, Do, Check vocabulary.

TOPIC 5

Home Practice 15

Your child participated in the fifteenth session of *Unstuck and On Target!* today.

Session Summary: Today, your child's *Unstuck and On Target!* group switched topics and started to build new goal setting and planning skills. These new skills will build on the foundation of all of the flexibility skills they have learned so far. They also build on the introduction to goal setting and planning from Lesson 2.

What you can try at home:

1. Review the Home Practice 2 about Goal, Why, Plan, Do, Check.
2. Try to help your child see how setting his or her own goals and making plans will benefit him or her:
   - ***If you set your <u>own</u> goals, you will get more of what you want!***

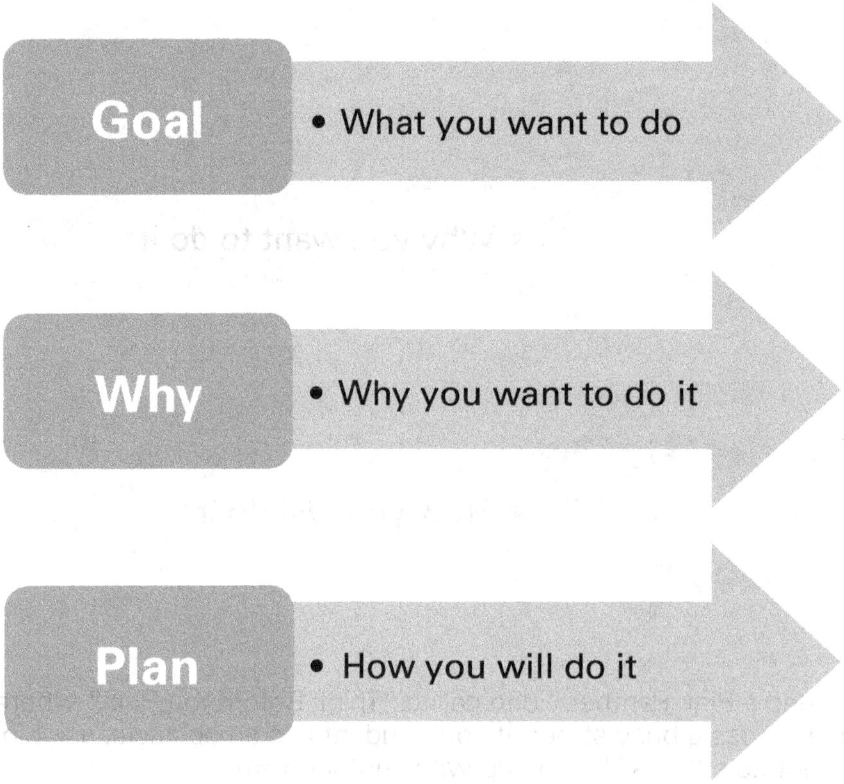

3. Your child watched a Pink Panther video in group today called "Think Before You Pink," where Pink Panther makes 12 different plans to cross a busy street.
   - See if you can find this video by searching on the Internet and watch the video with your child (it's only 6 minutes long). Talk about how Pink Panther doesn't give up.
   - If your child hits an obstacle, ask him or her, "What would Pink Panther do right now?" (He'd come up with another plan!)

Lesson 16 GWPDC Application and Practice

PURPOSE

Students practice using Goal, Why, Plan, Do, Check (GWPDC) to solve problems and obtain goals that are meaningful to them. This guided practice is critical to fostering the routine use of GWPDC. In addition to guided practice, it is essential that teachers embed GWPDC language in every routine of the day. There is one activity and two additional/optional activities in this lesson.

Materials Required for All Activities

Not Included

- Whiteboard or chart paper
- Dry/wet erase markers
- Tape
- 3 pieces of paper (each labeled with a number 1, 2, or 3)
- Cereal
- Milk
- Bowl
- Spoon
- Paper towels
- Video clip: Pink Panther, "In the Pink of the Night"
- Pencils
- Group Reinforcement Visual
- Each student's *UOT Notebook*

Included

- GWPDC for Lesson 16
- Lightning Round Questions
- Classroom Practice 16
- Home Practice 16

INTRODUCTION

Preview: GWPDC & Lightning Round

Review & Game
~5 minutes

Materials

Not Included

- Whiteboard or chart paper and suitable markers
- Tape
- 3 pieces of paper (each labeled with a number 1, 2, or 3)

Included

- GWPDC for Lesson 16
- Lightning Round Questions

Instructions

1. Post the GWPDC on the board before the lesson begins.
2. Review the GWPDC with the group.
3. Complete the Lightning Round activity.

**For a complete set of instructions and tips, refer to the GWPDC and Lightning Round instructions (Topic 1, Lesson 2).*

Check for understanding...
Ask the students to restate the "why" in their own words.

Reinforce
Provide positive feedback when students say they don't know an answer and ask for help.

G W P D C

Goal: Create a Goal, Why, Plan, Do, Check.

Why: There are always things I want or need (these are my goals). To make sure I get what I want or need, I need to create a Plan A, and sometimes a Plan B.

Plan:
1. Lightning Round
2. Group GWPDC
3. Learn about Target Goals
4. Review Home Practice

Do: Follow the plan and earn tallies.

Check: How did it go? Did we accomplish our goal? How did Plan B help us today?

Lightning Round Questions

1. What is a goal?
2. What do we need to create to help us accomplish our goal?
3. What do we do if Plan A doesn't work?

Remember to check off this step on the GWPDC!

ACTIVITY 1 *OPTIONAL

Cereal

Group Activity
~30 minutes

Materials

Not Included

- Whiteboard or chart paper
- Dry/wet erase markers or markers
- Dry/wet erase markers or markers
- Cereal
- Milk
- Bowl
- Spoon
- Paper towels (in case of a milk spill)

Tip

★ Read through the activity and consider your students. If your group has strong food preferences, allergies, or the materials will be too hard to acquire, please modify the activity. Select an activity that the students would be engaged with and for which they desire to see the outcome. Examples of alternative activities include having your students tell you how to brush your teeth, drawing something while your students describe it, playing catch with a beach ball, or building something like LEGOs or blocks.

Instructions

This is intended as a playful way to try GWPDC and refine the students' approach to problem solving.

1. Briefly review GWPDC. Introduce this activity by stating, "Today we will practice using Goal, Why, Plan, Do, Check to make a bowl of cereal." Ask how many students know how to make cereal.
2. Show the students all of the ingredients.
3. Ask them to tell you what the goal is. Write it on the board.
4. Ask them to tell you what they think the first step in the plan should be. Write the step on the board. Have them continue giving you the steps, and record them in order on the board.
5. When they believe they have given you all the steps, explain that you are now going to do their plan. Follow the steps on the board *exactly*. If the step says to put the cereal in the bowl, put the box of cereal in the bowl (without opening it).
6. Continue carrying out the plan until you have done all the steps.
7. Ask students to *check*—decide how their plan worked. Have them use the following scale.

1	2	3	4	5	6	7	8	9	10
Did not go well				Some of the plan worked				It worked!	

8. Ask them whether any part of the plan needs to be fixed. Next to the original plan, write *Plan B*. Tell them that sometimes when checking, they might decide that they need a Plan B, which will bring them back to the plan stage.

9. Go through each step again, rewriting the steps that worked and amending the steps that need to be changed.
10. Do the new plan by following the steps on the board. This time it should work.
11. Then *check*—have students use the scale and discuss how the new plan went.

1	2	3	4	5	6	7	8	9	10
Did not go well				Some of the plan worked				It worked!	

12. To summarize the activity, highlight the students' Flexibility in generating another plan and their expertise at plan making.

ADDITIONAL ACTIVITY *OPTIONAL

What is a Target Goal?

Presentation

~5 minutes

Materials

Not Included

- Whiteboard or chart paper
- Dry/wet erase markers or markers

Instructions

In this lesson, students review the basic definition of *goal* and learn the definition of *Target Goal.*

1. Explain that a Target Goal is something that you want or need to do that is more important than anything else you may want to do at the same time.
2. Explain that there is often much happening at the same time, so it is important to focus on the most important goal—the Target Goal—at any point in time.
3. Provide examples to illustrate this point.
   - My target goal is to finish my work before recess. What are some of the distractor goals that could get in the way and prevent me from achieving my target goal?
     - Talking to my friend
     - Reading the book I brought from home
   - Ask students to help you think of a way to continue to work towards your target goal but come up with a plan to accomplish the distractor goal as well.
     - Finish my work, and make a plan to talk to my friend at recess.
     - Read my book if I finish my work.
   - My target goal is to finish my homework. What are some of the distractor goals that could get in the way and prevent me from achieving my target goal?
     - Playing video games
     - Taking a nap
     - Talking on the phone
   - Ask students to help you think of a way to continue to work towards your target goal but come up with a plan to accomplish the distractor goal as well.
     - Finish my homework and play video games when I am finished.
     - Set my alarm, take a 10-minute nap, then finish my homework.

ADDITIONAL ACTIVITY

Target Goal Example

Video and Discussion

~20 minutes

Materials

Not Included

- Whiteboard or chart paper
- Dry/wet erase markers or markers
- Video clip: Pink Panther, "In the Pink of the Night" (6 minutes, 7 seconds)

Instructions

1. Ahead of time, search the Internet for the Pink Panther video clip "In the Pink of the Night." Once you have located the video, please watch it the entire way through, as we cannot vouch for the many versions that may be available for public viewing.
2. Inform the students that they are about to watch a video of the Pink Panther. He has a Target Goal (TG), but other goals keeping getting in the way. Ask students to think about what the Pink Panther's TG might be.
3. Have students watch the video.
4. At the conclusion of the video, ask the following questions and write the students' answers on the whiteboard:
   a. What was the Pink Panther's TG? (He wanted to catch the train on time, so he needed to get out of bed.)
   b. What were some of his other goals? (Possible answers include staying asleep, keeping the alarms quiet, silencing the bird, and eating breakfast.) Respond to students' answers.
5. Summarize for students that it can be really hard to balance a TG with other goals that also reflect something they want. In the video, the Pink Panther wanted more sleep, but he was really upset when he missed the train. Explain that the class will continue to work together to learn how to set a TG and achieve it even when other goals are desirable too.

CLOSING

Review: Classroom & Home Practice

Wrap-up
~5 minutes

Materials

Not Included

- Pencils (1 per student)
- Group Reinforcement Visual
- Each student's *UOT Notebook*

Included

- Classroom Practice 16
- Home Practice 16

Instructions

Reinforce...

Sticking to the Plan and following the Code of Conduct

"Remember when we use respectful words with one another we earn tallies, and our tallies get us closer to our flexibility party."

Students will review the Home Practice and complete the *check* portion of the Goal, Why, Plan, Do, Check.

1. Hand out the Home Practice sheets. Read the goal aloud. Ask students to think about who they will work on their Home Practice (HP) with. Let students know they will each earn a tally for bringing the completed HP with them next time you meet.

   Tip

   ★ Follow the same procedure every day for reviewing and completing HP (e.g., review HP, monitor all students as they put it in their homework folder, monitor all students as they write it in their homework planner).
2. Guide students to file all worksheets in their *UOT Notebook.*
3. Read the goal for Lesson 16 aloud to the class. Ask students if they were able to accomplish the goal. Ask students to identify what helped them accomplish the goal.
4. Review the plan. Ask students if they were able to accomplish the plan. Were there steps that we were not able to accomplish? Did we need to revise the plan in any way?

   Tip

   ★ The cereal activity requires many mistakes, and possibly mess, providing many opportunities for practicing reflecting on how the plan needed to shift.
5. Remind students they are working towards a large group prize. Each day you will add their tally marks to a bank. When they reach ____ tallies they will get a group celebration or prize.
6. Distribute the Classroom Practice handout to all instructors who interact with your students and would benefit from supporting students as they work on their new skills.

Remember to check off this step on the GWPDC!

TOPIC 5

Classroom Practice 16

Session Summary: Today, your students learned how to check to see how their plan worked. This self-evaluation process is crucial for students' success in reaching their own goals.

What you can do to support your student's learning and generalization:

1. There are two barriers your students may face when they try to reach their goals.
   - First, the **plan** may not work. Students can **check** on how well their plan worked, just like they can check their work in math, or like you check to make sure you have completed all the steps of a recipe. Sometimes parts of a plan might work, important steps might be left out, or a new plan would work better.
     - *"Let's **check** and see how our **plan** worked."*
     - *"Do we need to change our **plan**?"*
     - *"Looks like we may need a Plan B."*
   - Second, your student may encounter **distractors**. Once they get distracted, it becomes impossible to reach their goal since they aren't carrying out their plan.
     - *"Did we stick to our **plan**, or did we get **distracted**?"*
     - *"Are we **on target** to reach our **goal**?"*
     - *"Let's focus on the next step of our plan so we can reach our **goal**."*

TOPIC 5

Home Practice 16

Your child participated in the sixteenth session of *Unstuck and On Target!* today.

Session Summary: Today, your child learned how to check to see how a plan worked. This self-evaluation process is crucial for your child to be successful in reaching his or her own goals.

What you can try at home:

1. There are two problems your child may face when trying to reach goals.
   - First, the **plan** may not work. Your child can learn to **check** on how well his or her plan worked, just like he or she can double check their work in math, or you check to make sure you have completed all the steps of a recipe. Sometimes parts of a plan might work, important steps might be left out, or a new plan would work better.
     - *"Let's **check** and see how our **plan** worked."*
     - *"Do we need to change our **plan**?"*
     - *"Let's check our Plan A and see if we need a Plan B."*
   - Second, your child may face **distractors** that tempt them. Once your child gets distracted, it becomes impossible to reach their goal since they aren't carrying out their plan.
     - *"Did we stick to our **plan**, or did we get **distracted**?"*
     - *"Are we **on target** to reach our **goal**?"*
     - *"I think we may be getting **distracted** and **off target**. Do we still want to reach our **goal**?"*

Lessons 17 & 18 GWPDC Stations

PURPOSE

Students practice using Plan B to solve problems related to asking for help, compromising, and resisting a distractor. In addition, Lesson 18 provides multiple opportunities to practice Goal, Why, Plan, Do, Check (GWPDC) across a variety of situations as well as additional practice with generating a Plan B, Plan C, Plan D, and so on. This guided practice is critical to promoting an adaptive use of GWPDC in daily life. In addition to guided practice, it is essential that teachers embed GWPDC language in every routine of the day. There are two activities in this lesson.

Important Educator Notes:

1. This lesson will require 2 days to complete.
2. This lesson requires more set-up than what is typical for *UOT* activities.

Materials Required for All Activities

Not Included

- Whiteboard or chart paper
- Dry/wet erase markers
- Tape
- 3 pieces of paper (each labeled with a number 1, 2, or 3)
- Books/games
- Game for Station 1 (see Activity 2)
- A piece of paper
- Pencils
- Group Reinforcement Visual
- Each student's *UOT Notebook*

Included

- GWPDC for Lessons 17 & 18
- Lightning Round Questions
- Handout: GWPDC Station 1
- Handout: Compromise Station 2
- Handout: GWPDC Station 3
- Materials: Distractor Game Cards Station 4
- Materials: Distractor Game Tracking Sheet Station 4
- Materials: Distractor Game Cards Answer Key Station 4
- Handout: GWPDC Station 5
- Handout: GWPDC Station 5 Scenarios
- Classroom Practice 17 & 18
- Home Practice 17 & 18

INTRODUCTION

Preview: GWPDC & Lightning Round

Review & Game

~5 minutes

Materials

Not Included

- Whiteboard or chart paper and suitable markers
- Tape
- 3 pieces of paper (each labeled with a number 1, 2, or 3)

Included

- GWPDC for Lessons 17 & 18
- Lightning Round Questions

Instructions

1. Post the GWPDC on the board before the lesson begins.
2. Review the GWPDC with the group.
3. Complete the Lightning Round activity.

**For a complete set of instructions and tips, refer to the GWPDC and Lightning Round instructions (Topic 1, Lesson 2).*

Reinforce!
Any time a student uses GWPDC language mark a tally up on the board!

G W P D C

Goal: Create GWPDCs to accomplish our goal.

✓ Ask for help
✓ Make a Compromise ✐✐
✓ Make a Plan B ✐✐
✓ Resist a distractor

Why: There are always things I want or need (these are my goals). I need lots of tools I can use to make sure I can get what I want or need.

Plan:
1. Lightning Round
2. Plan B Strategies
3. GWPDC Stations
4. Review Home Practice

Do: Follow the plan and earn tallies.

Check: How did it go? Did we accomplish our plan? What was hard about the stations? What was easy about the stations?

Remember to check off this step on the GWPDC!

Lightning Round Questions

1. What does GWPDC stand for?
2. Name 2 goals you have during the day.
3. What happens if your Plan A doesn't work and you refuse to create a Plan B?

A→B ACTIVITY 1

Plan B Strategies

Discussion
~5 minutes

Materials

Not Included

- Whiteboard or chart paper
- Dry/wet erase markers or markers
- Books/games (props for "Ask for Help" scenario)

Instructions

1. Write *Goal, Why, Plan A, Plan B, Do, Check* on the board.
2. Remind students that whenever a Plan A doesn't work, we always have the option to make a Plan B. Highlight that there are millions of ways to create a Plan B, but that today you are going to talk about a couple useful strategies that may work when your Plan A fails.

   In a big circle on the board write, *Plan B strategies: ask for help, resist a distractor,* and *Compromise*. Review each of the Plan B strategies.

Strategy #1—Asking for Help

3. (For this next activity you will attempt to carry a very large load across the classroom, you will act as though it is too much to carry and drop some items.)

   On the board, next to goal, write *Move books and games across the classroom.* Next to Plan A, write *1. Pick up books and games. 2. Carry books and games across classroom. 3. Put books away.* Attempt the task, struggle, drop books, and eventually give up. Go to the board and as a group reflect on how it went. Next to check write, *could not carry books by myself. Plan A didn't work.* Ask kids for a suggestion for Plan B. Ask students to look at the strategies listed on the board and select one that might be a good Plan B (asking for help). Role play asking for help. After you have completed the task, reflect on how it went. Next to check write, *Plan B worked, moved books and games to new location.*

   Ask students if they can think of other plan Bs that would have worked (take one book at a time, etc.).

Reinforce!
Students for coming up with alternative Plan Bs.

Strategy #2—Compromise

4. Read the following scenario aloud.

   > John and Bobby want to have fun at recess and play together. John wants to play soccer, Bobby wants to play basketball. What can we do so that both people are able to accomplish their goals?

   Ask students to look at the board and select one strategy that might be a good plan B (Compromise).

Write *Goal 1, Goal 2, Compromise, Plan, Do, Check* on the board (Compromise framework from Topic 2).

Fill in the Goal 1 (to have fun at recess)/Plan A (to play basketball) and Goal 2 (to have fun at recess)/ Plan A (to play soccer) based on the scenario. Ask students to help you come up with a Compromise and a Plan B.

5. **Strategy #3—Resist a Distractor**
Remind students that we set goals all day long. Sometimes things, people, or events might get or try to get in the way of us accomplishing our goals. These are called *distractors*. The way we resist a distractor is to always think about our goal and what we need to do to accomplish our goal.

Ask students to think about how they might resist this distractor.

Write *Goal, Why, Plan, Do, Check* on the board.

> You really want to get a good grade on tomorrow's math test. You are planning on studying when you get home from school.

Fill in the GWPDC with what you know (Goal=to get a good grade on the test; Why=because you want to get a good grade on your report card; Plan=study tonight). Continue the scenario.

> On the way home your friend asks if he can come over and finish playing the video game you started yesterday. This is your favorite video game and you are really sure you can win.

Ask students to identify what might distract them from accomplishing their goal (playing the video game). Ask students if both things are important (yes). Can they think of a way that they could prevent the distractor from ruining their goal but that they could make both things happen? (Play video game for 20 minutes then study, study for 1 hour then call friend to come over, ask friend to come over the following day, etc.)

Remember to check off this step on the GWPDC!

ACTIVITY 2 *OPTIONAL

GWPDC Stations

Stations
~2 sessions

Materials

Not Included

- Whiteboard or chart paper
- Dry/wet erase markers or markers
- Game for Station 1—remove game pieces (make sure to select a game that can be played quickly and that all students are familiar with)
- A piece of paper (Station 3)

Included

- Handout: GWPDC Station 1
- Handout: Compromise Station 2
- Handout: GWPDC Station 3
- Materials: Distractor Game Cards Station 4
- Materials: Distractor Game Cards Answer Key Station 4
- Materials: Distractor Game Tracking Sheet Station 4
- Handout: GWPDC Station 5
- Handout: GWPDC Station 5 Scenarios

Instructions

Make the reinforcement meaningful and immediate

Give each student an index card, as you move around the classroom give students tally marks for following the Code of Conduct and each step of the GWPDC they complete.

1. Divide students into groups of two.
2. Tell the students that over the next two classes they will be competing in the Goal, Why, Plan, Do, Check (GWPDC) challenge. At each station, they will be responsible for uncovering the strategy they need to use to complete the GWPDC.
   Let students know that as they move through the stations there will be incredible opportunities to earn tallies.
   - For each step of the GWPDC they complete they will earn a tally towards the group goal.
   - They will earn tallies for following the Code of Conduct.

   Tip

   ★ This is a great time to go over the Code of Conduct and ask students to think about what each item means and what it will look like when they are working with a partner. (e.g., "If you are being respectful, what might it sound like if you have a different idea from your partner?")
3. Point to the "Plan B Strategies" on the board from Activity 1. Read them and remind students that they might be necessary as they solve their challenges. Walk around the room and briefly explain the instructions at each station.

   Station 1: Your goal is to play the game. Your job is to accomplish the goal. When you sit down, you and your partner will write a plan for how you are going to accomplish that goal. If for some reason your Plan A doesn't work out, you will need a Plan B.

   Station set-up: GWPDC Station 1 worksheet, a game students are familiar with and can be played quickly, with a key piece removed (e.g., Connect 4 with red pieces removed), pencils. After students complete the GWPDC, they will complete a Feelings Chain to reflect on their experience.

Station 2: Read the first scenario on your worksheet. Make a Plan A choice and write it on your worksheet. If your Plan As are different from one another you might need to come up with a Compromise.

Station set-up: Compromise Station 2 worksheet, pencils

Station 3: Your goal is to make a paper airplane. You will write a plan to accomplish this goal. Follow the plan, and if your plan doesn't work, make sure to check your strategies and write a Plan B.

Station set-up: A piece of paper for the airplane, GWPDC worksheet

Station 4: At this station, students will play the Distractor Game. The goal is to earn 50 points and reach the top of the chart. Each student selects a card from the pile. The student reads the card aloud and thinks of a plan for how they can achieve their distractor goal as well as their target goal. Each time they come up with a plan to achieve both, they can color in a 5-point box. Students should take turns until they reach 50.

Station set-up: Distractor Game Tracking Sheet, Distractor Game Cards (12), Distractor Game Cards Answer Key.

Station 5: Plan Challenge. At this station your goal is to not only create a Plan B, Plan C, Plan D, but to create as many plans as you can to accomplish your goal. See if you can get to Z!

Station set-up: GWPDC Station 5 worksheet, scenario card, pencils

Tips

★ If writing is a laborious or difficult task for your students, you can modify the activity by writing answers on strips of paper so students can select, order, and glue them onto the worksheet; you can encourage students to write only 1 word answers or you can fill out the majority of the worksheet, leaving key sections blank.

★ If working in pairs is too difficult for your students these activities can be done as whole group activities.

★ Create direction cards as cheat sheets for what to do at each station.

Remember to check off this step on the GWPDC!

GWPDC Station 1

	GWPDC	
GOAL		
WHY		
PLAN(S)	**A**	**B**
DO		
CHECK	Did I accomplish my goal? How did it go? 1 2 3 4 5 No, not so good / Part, OK / Yes, great	

(continued)

GWPDC Station 1

Think about how you felt when something unexpected happened and how you felt when you solved the problem. Fill in this Feelings Chain.

Event

Feeling

Feelings word: Number:

Pause Pause

Action

How Others Feel

Consequence

I Feel

Feelings word: Number:

TOPIC 5

Compromise Station 2

Name____

Compromise Station

Pick Something New	• Pick something new that you both like. • For example: I want gummy bears, you want chocolate, let's have Twizzlers instead.
Combine Ideas	• Put your ideas together. • For example: I like chocolate cupcakes, you like vanilla, let's have chocolate cupcakes with vanilla icing.
Take Turns	• Each person gets a chance to do what they like. • For example: I want to play basketball, you want to play soccer. Let's play soccer first, then basketball.

You are in charge of picking a special treat for the class to have during the upcoming party.

Choose a treat.

Did you and your partner choose the same thing? Yes No

Do you need a Compromise? Try combining ideas. What did you come up with?

____

It is recess time. The class is going to play a game together. What game should the class play?

Choose a game.

Did you and your partner choose the same thing? Yes No

Do you need a Compromise? Try taking turns. What is your plan?

____

The class gets to watch a movie today. What movie do you think the class should watch?

Choose a movie.

Did you and your partner choose the same thing? Yes No

Do you need a Compromise? Try something new. What is your plan?

____

(continued)

TOPIC 5

Compromise Station 2

How do you think it would feel to solve a problem by compromising?

Pick one of your compromises and complete this Feelings Chain.

Event

Feeling

Feelings word: Number:

Pause Pause

Action

How Others Feel

Consequence

I Feel

Feelings word: Number:

GWPDC Station 3

	GWPDC	
GOAL		
WHY		
PLAN(S)	**A**	**B**
DO		
CHECK	Did I accomplish my goal? How did it go? 1 2 3 4 5 No, not so good / Part, OK / Yes, great	

My goal is to get good grades. I really want to play video games, but I have homework. I made a plan so that I can do both. My plan is . . .	My goal is to eat healthy. It is my friend's birthday, and I would like to have a cupcake and candy. I made a plan to have the cupcake but still work toward my Target Goal. My plan is . . .
My name is Batman. My goal is to protect Gotham City from evil. I am feeling really tired and need a nap. I made a plan, so I can get some rest and still save the city. My plan is . . .	I am SpongeBob SquarePants. My goal is to be the best fry cook in the ocean. Patrick wants me to come over for his birthday. I made a plan, so I can still work at the Krusty Krab but see my buddy as well. My plan is . . .
My name is Obi-Wan Kenobi, and my goal is to train the Jedi Knights. I found a new light saber that I want to try out. I found a way to try the new light saber without missing training time. My plan is . . .	My goal is to be a good friend. I really want to play basketball, but my friend really likes soccer. I made a plan to help me work toward my goal. My plan is . . .
My goal is to be a good friend. I really want to watch a Harry Potter movie, but my friend is not allowed to see it. I made a plan to help me work toward my goal. My plan is . . .	My goal is to be a flexible friend. My friend wants to play tag at recess, and I would like to swing. I made a plan to help me work toward my goal. My plan is . . .
My goal is to be a good student, so I can get a good job. I wanted to go to my friend's birthday party instead of doing my book report. I made a plan to help me work toward my goal. My plan is . . .	My goal is to follow directions in class. I really want to talk about my new video game during math class. I made a plan to help me work toward my goal. My plan is . . .

My goal is to get good grades. I really want to play video games, but I have homework. I made a plan so that I can do both.
My plan is ______________________.
Answer: A plan that combines a time to play video games and time to study.

My goal is to eat healthy. It is my friend's birthday, and I would like to have a cupcake and candy. I made a plan to have the cupcake but still work toward my Target Goal.
My plan is ______________________.
Answer: A plan that combines having a small amount of the treat and continuing to eat healthy.

My name is Batman. My goal is to protect Gotham City from evil. I am feeling really tired and need a nap. I made a plan, so I can get some rest and still save the city.
My plan is ______________________.
Answer: A plan that gives Batman a chance to take a rest then go back to saving the city.

I am SpongeBob SquarePants. My goal is to be the best fry cook in the ocean. Patrick wants me to come over for his birthday. I made a plan, so I can still work at the Krusty Krab but see my buddy as well.
My plan is ______________________.
Answer: A plan that combines going to the party, then getting back to work at the Krab.

My name is Obi-Wan Kenobi, and my goal is to train the Jedi Knights. I found a new light saber that I want to try out. I found a way to try the new light saber without missing training time.
My plan is ______________________.
Answer: A plan that combines using the light saber and finding time for training.

My goal is to be a good friend. I really want to play basketball, but my friend really likes soccer. I made a plan to help me work toward my goal.
My plan is ______________________.
Answer: A plan that involves playing both sports.

My goal is to be a good friend. I really want to watch a Harry Potter movie, but my friend is not allowed to see it. I made a plan to help me work toward my goal.
My plan is ______________________.
Answer: A plan where I see what my friend is allowed to see and a chance to see Harry Potter later.

My goal is to be a flexible friend. My friend wants to play tag at recess, and I would like to swing. I made a plan to help me work toward my goal.
My plan is ______________________.
Answer: A plan that combines swinging and tag.

My goal is to be a good student, so I can get a good job. I wanted to go to my friend's birthday party instead of doing my book report. I made a plan to help me work toward my goal.
My plan is ______________________.
Answer: A plan where I can go to the birthday party and set aside time to work on my book report the following day.

My goal is to follow directions in class. I really want to talk about my new video game during math class. I made a plan to help me work toward my goal.
My plan is ______________________.
Answer: A plan to finish my math work and talk to my friend about my video game at lunch.

TOPIC 5

Distractor Game Tracking Sheet Station 4

50
45
40
35
30
25
20
15
10
5

TOPIC 5

GWPDC Station 5

	Try to think of as many plans as you can to achieve your goal.
GOAL	To have fun at recess
WHY	Recess is a great time of day.
PLAN(S)	A
	B
	C
	D
	E
	F
	G
	H
	I
	J
	K
	L
	M
	N
	O
	P
	Q
	R
	S
	T
	U
	V
	W
	X
	Y
	Z

TOPIC 5

GWPDC Station 5 Scenarios

It is time for recess and you can't wait to have a good time. Your goal is to have fun. Think of all of the ways you can have fun at recess (indoors and outdoors) and write them down as plans. How many plans can you create?

CLOSING

Review: Classroom & Home Practice

Wrap-up
~5 minutes

Materials

Not Included

- Pencils (1 per student)
- Group Reinforcement Visual
- Each student's *UOT Notebook*

Included

- Classroom Practice 17 & 18
- Home Practice 17 & 18

Instructions

Reinforce…
Sticking to the Plan and following the Code of Conduct
"Remember when we use respectful words with one another we earn tallies, and our tallies get us closer to our Flexibility party."

Students will review the Home Practice and complete the check portion of the Goal, Why, Plan, Do, Check.

1. Hand out the Home Practice sheets. Read the goal aloud. Ask students to think about who will work on their Home Practice (HP) with them. Let students know they will each earn a tally for bringing the completed HP with them next time you meet, and the person who brings in the HP with the most Plan Bs will get extra tallies.
   Tip
   ★ Follow the same procedure every day for reviewing and completing HP (e.g., review HP, monitor all students as they put it in their homework folder, monitor all students as they write it in their homework planner).
2. Guide students to file all worksheets in their *UOT Notebook.*
3. Read the goal for Lessons 17 and 18 aloud to the class. Ask students if they were able to accomplish the goal. Ask students to identify what helped them accomplish the goal.
4. Review the plan. Ask students if they were able to accomplish the plan. Were there steps that we were not able to accomplish? Did we need to revise the plan in any way?
5. Remind students they are working towards a large group prize. Each day you will add their tally marks to a bank. When they reach ____ tallies they will get a group celebration or prize.
   Tip
   ★ During the lesson if you find students sticking to the plan or following the Code of Conduct, remind them what they are working for and reinforce accordingly.
6. Distribute the Classroom Practice handout to all instructors who interact with your students and would benefit from supporting students as they work on their new skills.

Remember to check off this step on the GWPDC!

TOPIC 5

Classroom Practice 17 & 18

A→B

Session Summaries: Today and in our next session, students are practicing using different types of Plan B strategies to use when having problems reaching goals. They are getting this practice by teaming up to play the Goal, Why, Plan, Do, Check Challenge.

What you can do to support your student's learning and generalization:

Over the next couple of weeks, encourage your students to use the strategies below any time they are having trouble meeting their goals, and praise them for trying!

Plan B Strategies

Ask for help	• "Do you need help to get to your goal?" • "This isn't working, who should we ask for help?"
Compromise	• "What if our Plan B is to compromise?" • "We can can change our goal to compromise so we both get part of what we want."
Resist a distractor	• "Can we include this distraction in our plan?" • "What about reaching our goal first, and then we can get distracted?"

TOPIC 5

Home Practice 17 & 18

A→B

Your child participated in the seventeenth session of *Unstuck and On Target!* today. This home practice sheet will count for this session and your child's next session.

Session Summaries: Today and in our next session, your child is practicing using different types of Plan B strategies to use when having problems reaching goals. Your child is getting this practice by playing the Goal, Why, Plan, Do, Check Challenge in group.

What you can try at home:

Over the next couple of weeks, encourage your child to use the strategies below any time they are having trouble getting what they want (meeting their goals), and praise them for trying!

Plan B Strategies

Strategy	Examples
Ask for help	• "Do you need help?" • "This isn't working, who should we ask for help?"
Compromise	• "What if our Plan B is to compromise?" • "We can can change our goal to compromise so we both get part of what we want."
Resist a distractor	• "Can we include this distraction in our plan?" • "What about reaching our goal first, and then we can be distracted after?"

Lesson 19 Event Planning

PURPOSE

Your students have been working diligently to learn how to use GWPDC, Compromise, and create solutions using other UOT strategies. This lesson begins a celebration of their progress and provides a motivating and engaging opportunity to practice using all of their new skills to work together in order to plan an event. This lesson includes one activity.

Materials Required for All Activities

Not Included

- Whiteboard or chart paper
- Dry/wet erase markers
- Tape
- 3 pieces of paper (each labeled with a number 1, 2, or 3)
- Pencils
- Group Reinforcement Visual
- Each student's *UOT Notebook*

Included

- GWPDC for Lesson 19
- Lightning Round Questions
- Visual: Feelings Chain Scenarios
- Classroom Practice 19
- Home Practice 19

INTRODUCTION

Preview: GWPDC & Lightning Round

Review & Game
~5 minutes

Materials

Not Included

- Whiteboard or chart paper and suitable markers
- Tape
- 3 pieces of paper (each labeled with a number 1, 2, or 3)

Included

- GWPDC for Lesson 19
- Lightning Round Questions

Instructions

1. Post the GWPDC on the board before the lesson begins.
2. Review the GWPDC with the group.
3. Complete the Lightning Round activity.

**For a complete set of instructions and tips, refer to the GWPDC and Lightning Round instructions (Topic 1, Lesson 2).*

Reinforce...
Asking for Help
"Great job asking for help. I am giving the group a tally."

G W P D C

Goal: Use our knowledge of GWPDC to plan a great class event.

Why: GWPDC is a tool that can help with many things; one of those things is to plan fun events.

Plan:
1. Lightning Round
2. Plan Class Event
3. Review Home Practice

Do: Follow the plan and earn tallies.

Check: How did it go? Did we accomplish our goal? What was the hardest part about planning the event? What was the easiest part?

Lightning Round Questions

1. When I am Stuck I have ___ choice. (1)
2. When I am Flexible I have ____ choices. (Many)
3. When both people get part of what they want it is called a _____. (Compromise)

Remember to check off this step on the GWPDC!

ACTIVITY 1 *OPTIONAL

Planning a Class Event

Group Activity
~25 minutes

Materials

Not Included

- Whiteboard or chart paper
- Dry/wet erase markers

Included

- Visual: Feelings Chain Scenarios

Instructions

Tips

★ Throughout this acitvity use the Feelings Target and Feelings Chain to help students identify how specific choices and desicions make them, and others in the group, feel.

★ The Planning a Class Event activity is designed to allow students the opportunity to integrate and practice many of their new skills (Compromise, Plan A→B, goal setting, etc.).

★ Before you start the planning process decide what type of events/activities you would feel comfortable allowing in the classroom (length of time, cost). You can help set the tone and shape conversations if you are clear about the parameters.

Event/Activity Ideas (see Troubleshooting section for additional ideas):

- A flexibility party—everything at the party is Flexible
- Make a group snack—trail mix, fruit kabobs
- Watch video clips online—each student selects an appropriate clip to share with the class
- Movie
- Group craft—kites, rockets
- Extra recess
- Scavenger hunt

Alternative to an event:

- Play a game related to UOT
    - Flexibility Freeway Game, etc.

1. Draw a box on the board, inside write the words: *Flexible, Stuck, Compromise, Plan A, Plan B, Goal, Code of Conduct, Feelings Chain.*
2. Write *GWPDC* on the board (leave space for brainstorming).
3. Tell students that they have just about or just earned their group goal and that this time they are in charge of the planning.

   Tip

   ★ Save 10–15 tallies/points so that students can earn the remainging tallies to reach the top of their group goal while they are planning for the event (e.g., earn a tally for Compromising, earn a tally for making a Flexible choice, earn a tally for demonstrating a part of the Code of Conduct).
4. Write the Goal: To plan a fun event to celebrate reaching our group goal.
5. Have students help you fill in the Why.
6. Somewhere on the board record student suggestions. If you have a time limit for the event, share that with the students and write it on the board. Ask students to share their suggestions for the event.
7. Once students have shared their ideas, take a look at the list and as a group begin to shape the ideas into a plan.

Tips

★ Keep a sense of humor. If an idea is outlandish, acknowledge it and provide a light-hearted reason for why it might not work (e.g., if a student suggests an amusement park, reply with "I'd love to go spend the day at the amusement park. I think your reading and math teacher would miss us too much, my car only holds 4 people, and unfortunately I don't have the $1,000 we would need to buy all of the tickets and funnel cakes we'd have to get!").

★ Guide students to their Compromises (e.g., "It sounds like we have 2 really good ideas here. Let's think back to the ways we learned to Compromise. Something new or combine the 2 ideas.")

★ Help students think of a Plan B for their event (e.g., "We will be watching our video on the Internet, what should be our Plan B, be if the Internet is down?" "Having a scavenger hunt outside is a great idea, what should our Plan B be if the weather is bad?").

★ If someone is stuck remind them about their Flexible reputation. If they can think of a way to be Flexible about their idea, there is a good chance their classmates will be Flexible and figure our a way to incorporate his idea.

★ Above all else, keep it simple!

8. As students start to narrow down ideas, record the plan on the board.
9. Fill in the Do—Have the event
10. Ask students to help you generate the Check questions. How will you know if you have accomplished your goal?
11. Hold the event during the following session.

Remember to check off this step on the GWPDC!

CLOSING

Review: Classroom & Home Practice

Wrap-up
~5 minutes

Materials

Not Included

- Pencils (1 per student)
- Group Reinforcement Visual
- Each student's *UOT Notebook*

Included

- Classroom Practice 19
- Home Practice 19

Instructions

Students will review the Home Practice and complete the *check* portion of the Goal, Why, Plan, Do, Check.

1. Hand out the Home Practice sheets. Read the goal aloud. Ask students to think about who will work on their Home Practice (HP) with them. Let students know they will each earn a tally for bringing the completed HP with them next time you meet.
   Tip
   ★ Follow the same procedure every day for reviewing and completing HP (e.g., review HP, monitor all students as they put it in their homework folder, monitor all students as they write it in their homework planner).
2. Guide students to file all worksheets in their *UOT Notebook.*
3. Read the goal for Lesson 19 aloud to the class. Ask students if they were able to accomplish the goal. Ask students to identify what helped them accomplish the goal.
   Tip
   ★ During the first few lessons make sure students are able to accomplish the goal so that they feel a sense of success and develop an understanding of how to earn tallies.
4. Review the plan. Ask students if they were able to accomplish the plan. Were there steps that we were not able to accomplish? Did we need to revise the plan in any way?
   Tip
   ★ Sometimes plans have to change: an unexpected fire drill or a great discussion takes too long and you have to alter the plan. Celebrate these changes and let students know that even though the unexpected happened, they were flexible and made a new plan.
5. Distribute the Classroom Practice handout to all instructors who interact with your students and would benefit from supporting students as they work on their new skills.

TOPIC 5

Classroom Practice 19 & 20

Session Summaries: Your students have been working hard to learn how to set goals, make plans, compromise, and create solutions using *Unstuck and On Target!* strategies. Today's lesson began a celebration of their progress and provided practice using all of their new skills to work together in order to plan a special event for session 20.

What you can do to support your student's learning and generalization:

Whenever you can, work in a discussion with your students about planning an event or an activity. You could talk about historical events, politics, cultural events, or even watch a video in class of a flash mob or someone who planned a special surprise for someone. Ask your students:

- *"What was their **goal**?"*
- *"How many people had to work together to **plan** this event?"*
- *"What would have happened if every person had a different idea?"*
- *"Do you think any of the people planning this event needed to **ask for help**?"*

TOPIC 5

Home Practice 19 & 20

Your child participated in the nineteenth session of *Unstuck and On Target!* today. This home practice sheet will count for this session and your child's next session.

Session Summaries: Your child has been working hard to learn how to set goals, make plans, compromise, and create solutions using *Unstuck and On Target!* strategies. Today's lesson began a celebration of all the group has learned and provided practice using all of their new skills to work together in order to plan a special event for session 20.

What you can try at home:

1. Whenever you can, work in a discussion with your child about planning events. You could talk about events in the news, cultural or sports events, or even talk about a family event or activity.
   - *"What was their **goal**?"*
   - *"How many people had to work together to **plan** this?"*
   - *"What would have happened if every person had a different idea?"*
   - *"Do you think any of the people planning this event needed to **ask for help**?"*
2. Include your child in the planning of an upcoming event. The more practice your child gets in planning, the better he or she will get over time. If you plan and schedule everything for your child, he or she won't get to practice!
   - Try to set up a social event with your child, like meeting a friend in the park or having cousins over to play. Ask your child to help you plan what they will do together before they come, but be sure to talk about Plan Bs!
   - If you'd like to write it down, below is an example:

GOAL: To have fun with my friend.

WHY: So my friend will want to come back another day and I like to be a good friend!

PLAN:

1. Invite my friend over to play
2. Ask my friend what he wants to do (Do what my friend wants to do first because he is the guest)
3. Suggest we build with LEGOs
4. Compromise if we need to
5. Have a snack

DO: Follow the plan (Let's have fun!)

CHECK: How did it go? Did we need a different plan?

TOPIC 5

Lesson 20 Event

PURPOSE

During Topic 5 students have practiced using and creating multiple GWPDCs, developing alternative plans and honing their compromise skills. In Lesson 19 students integrated those skills to plan a class event. Lesson 20 is reserved for the class event.

Materials Required for All Activities

Not Included

- Materials for the class event

TOPIC 5

Topic 5 Progress Report

Student Name: ______________________ Date: ______________________

Teacher Name: ______________________

Over the last few weeks we have covered the following skills and concepts in Topic 5:

Topic 5 is the integration of all of the skills students have learned. Students are provided opportunities to practice the skills and apply them to a real life situation—planning a group event.

- Flexible vs. Stuck
- Goal, Why, Plan, Do, Check
- Plan A → Plan B
- Compromise

Topic 5 Skills	**All of the time**	**Some of the time**	**None of the time**
1. Is able to create a GWPDC in the moment			
2. Is able to create and use a compromise in the moment			
3. Is able to identify a Plan B in the moment			
A success in group:			
Something we will continue to work on:			
Additional Notes:			

X ______________________ (Teacher)

(please detach and returned the signed slip, acknowledging you have received the progress report)

- -

I have received the *Unstuck and On Target!* Progress Report

X ______________________ Date: __________

TOPIC 6

Flexible/Goal-Directed Futures

Unstuck and On Target! presents many new concepts, definitions, scripts, and strategies to help students increase flexibility. Presentation of this material is designed to occur over the better part of a school year. As with any complex curriculum, review is important for the integration and mastery of the material. Students with ASD often have difficulty generalizing new knowledge to novel situations or contexts. To promote generalization, students must first demonstrate competency with the new skills. In the first lesson of this topic, students demonstrate their competency through games. In the second lesson, they plan generalization opportunities for the future.

Lesson 21 Interview (& Optional Game)

PURPOSE

This lesson engages each student in anticipating at least one way in which he or she will apply what has been learned throughout the curriculum. There is one activity and one optional activity in this lesson.

Materials Required for All Activities

Not Included

- Whiteboard
- Markers
- Video camera or smartphone (if making videos)
- Paper to label four corners of the room A, B, C, D
- Pencils
- Group Reinforcement Visual
- Each student's *UOT Notebook*

Included

- GWPDC for Lesson 21
- Handout: Flexible Futures
- Educator Script: Four Corners Questions & Answer Key
- Handout: Graduation Certificate
- Classroom Practice 21
- Home Practice 21

INTRODUCTION

Preview: GWPDC

Review
~3 minutes

Materials

Not Included

- Whiteboard or chart paper and suitable markers

Included

- Goal, Why, Plan, Do, Check (GWPDC) for Lesson 21

Instructions

At the beginning the session, write/post the GWPDC on the board before the lesson begins. Review the GWPDC with the group.

G W P D C	
	Goal: Think about all of the ways I will use my *Unstuck and On Target!* strategies in the future. **Why:** We all use strategies to help us get through the day. Practicing my Unstuck strategies will help me make sure I am ready to use them even when I am not in group. **Plan:** 1. Turn in Home Practice sheets 2. Talk Show 3. Four Corners (optional) **Do:** Follow the plan and earn tallies. **Check:** How did it go?

ACTIVITY 1
Talk Show

Group Activity
~30 minutes

Materials

Not Included

- Video camera or smartphone (if making videos)

Included

- Handout: Flexible Futures

Instructions

1. Explain to students that they will be doing a talk show interview. If you plan to record the interviews on video, let the students know that.
2. Students can create their talk show script by completing Handout: Flexible Futures or by having a one-to-one conversation with you.
3. After the student's script is complete, he or she can pair with another student or with you to film the interview. Even if you do not plan to actually record, it would be helpful to have the students perform their interviews in front of one another.

TOPIC 6

Flexible Futures

Interviewer: You've done an amazing job learning about staying *Unstuck and On Target!*, and I hear that you're graduating today! You've learned so much, and our viewers would love to know more about how what you've learned will help you in the future. I'd like to ask you a couple of questions.

You've learned the definition of *Flexibility* and the definition of *Stuck*. When is a time that you usually get stuck?

Me: ______________________________

____

____

Interviewer: How will what you've learned help you in the future at school and at home?

Me: ______________________________

____

____

Interviewer: You've done a terrific job practicing Plan A and Plan B. I would like to know at least one time when you plan to use it at school and at least one time when you plan to use it at home.

Me: ______________________________

____

____

____

____

Interviewer: When is a time that you think you will use what you've learned about Compromise?

Me: ______________________________

____

Interviewer: What is the number one reason you think being Flexible is good for you?

Me: ______________________________

____

____

Interviewer: I understand that you're working on setting goals. What are you working on now, and what is one thing you plan to work on next?

Me: ______________________________

____

____

____

____

(continued)

Flexible Futures

Interviewer: When do you think Big Deal/Little Deal or Choice/No Choice will help you the most?

Me: ____

Interviewer: How does the Feelings Target help you?

Me: ____

Interviewer: How will being Flexible help you be a better friend?

Me: ____

Interviewer: Which coping skills do you think you will use the most?

Me: ____

Interviewer: Thank you so much for spending time with us. I have one final question for you. What is one thing that you want our audience to know about being Flexible?

Me: ____

Interviewer: Great! Congratulations on becoming *Unstuck and On Target!* (Presents certificate)

ADDITIONAL ACTIVITY *OPTIONAL

Four Corners

Group Activity

~25 minutes

Materials

Not Included

- Paper to label four corners of the room A, B, C, D

Included

- Educator Script: Four Corners Questions & Answer Key

Instructions

It is important to go through the game before introducing it to students and be prepared with the correct answers. You can have students demonstrate Flexibility with their bodies—when they reach the corner they have to try and make their body look like the corresponding corner letter (i.e., in Corner A, you would make your body look like an A).

1. Label each of the corners of your room A, B, C, and D.
2. Tell your students today they will be playing a game called Four Corners to review all of the important information they have learned this year in the group.
3. *Rules of the game:* Students will work as a group to earn as many points as possible. An individual student will be asked a question and given four choices (Choice A, B, C, or D). The student will select an answer and move to that corner of the room.
4. If the student is unsure of the answer, he or she can pick a friend to discuss the answer with and go to the corner of the room together.
5. Each correct answer is awarded 10 points.

TOPIC 6

Four Corners Questions & Answer Key

These people make mistakes.	A. Only teachers B. Only bad friends C. Everyone D. Parents	C. Everyone
You play games, you share secrets, and you sometimes disagree with ____.	A. Your friends B. Your pencil C. Your homework D. Your enemies	A. Your friends
If my Plan A doesn't work, I need ____.	A. To give up B. A Plan B C. To cry D. To quit	B. A Plan B
When I feel disappointed I should ____.	A. Scream B. Hit something C. Cry D. Take a break	D. Take a break
My face can feel hot, my stomach might hurt, and I might clench my teeth and fists when I feel ____.	A. Disappointed B. Tired C. Bored D. Happy	A. Disappointed
When I feel just-right, I am # ____ on the Feelings Target.	A. 5 B. 4 C. 3 D. 1	D. 1
If you and your friend disagree, you have two choices about how you can react. You can be rigid or you can be ____.	A. Flexible B. Angry C. Stuck D. Sad	A. Flexible
Agree to disagree, ask an adult, and decide it is not a Big Deal are all things you can do if you ____.	A. Give up B. Don't care about your friend C. And your friend disagree D. Don't know the answer	C. And your friend disagree
One way to make a Big Deal a Little Deal is to ____.	A. Start screaming B. Quit C. Give up D. Ask for help	D. Ask for help
Being flexible helps me be a good friend because ____.	A. People like to be around flexible people. B. Flexible people have more choices. C. When I am flexible my friends are happy. D. All of the above	D. All of the above

CLOSING

Review: Classroom & Home Practice

Wrap-up
~5 minutes

Materials

Not Included

- Pencils (1 per student)
- Group Reinforcement Visual
- Each student's *UOT Notebook*

Included

- Handout: Graduation Certificate
- Classroom Practice 21
- Home Practice 21

Instructions

Students will review the Home Practice sheets and complete the *check* portion of the Goal, Why, Plan, Do, Check.

1. Add the Flexible Futures handout to the students' *UOT Notebooks*.
2. Hand out the Graduation Certificates to take home with their *UOT Notebooks*. If you are making videos and can send them home to parents, write a note about how you will do that.
3. Ask students if they were able to accomplish the goals of group (to have fun, make friends, learn how to be Flexible, set goals for themselves). Make this a celebratory discussion about how much they've learned.

CONGRATULATIONS!

____

has completed the *Unstuck and On Target!* program.

DATE ________________________

SIGNATURE ________________________

TOPIC 6

Classroom Practice 21

Session Summary: Today was your student's last session of *Unstuck and On Target!* Hopefully, you've noticed big changes in your student's flexibility, planning, and organizing skills and these practice sheets have helped you think about ways to support these skills in all of your students. Thank you for your efforts!

What you can do to support your student's learning and generalization:

Continue to use the vocabulary and concepts that were covered in all of the sessions. Post the list below as a reminder to use these words daily.

Unstuck & On Target!

Flexible	When flexible, more good things happen. • "We can be flexible and make a Plan B." • "I love how you were flexible."
Unstuck	Being stuck feels bad. Getting unstuck feels better. • "I'm getting stuck on ____. How can I get unstuck?" • "Since you got unstuck, now you have more choices."
Plan A → Plan B	The problem is the plan, not the child. Bad plans just need a Plan B. • "What is our Plan B?" • "You always think of great plans."
Compromise	Both people have to be flexible to compromise. • "Let's compromise so we both get some of what we want." • "Something is better than nothing."
Big Deal/Little Deal	Do not tell a child his or her big deal is a little deal. • "How can we **turn** this big deal into a little deal? Let's make a plan."
Choice/No Choice	Remember poor choices are still choices; reserve "No Choice" for taxes, fire drills, etc. • "You have a choice. Let's look at all of your choices."

Goal What and **Why**? → **Plan** How do we do it? → **Do** Try it! → **Check** How did it go?

TOPIC 6

Home Practice 21

Your child participated in the last session of *Unstuck and On Target!* today.

Session Summary: Today was your child's last session of *Unstuck and On Target!* Hopefully, you've noticed big changes in your child's flexibility, planning, and organizing skills and these home practice sheets have helped you think about ways to support your child in using these skills. Thank you for your efforts!

Continue to use the vocabulary and concepts that were covered in all of the sessions. Post the list below as a reminder to use these words daily.

Unstuck & On Target!

Flexible	When flexible, more good things happen. • "We can be flexible and make a Plan B." • "I love how you were flexible."
Unstuck	Being stuck feels bad. Getting unstuck feels better. • "I'm getting stuck on ____. How can I get unstuck?" • "Since you got unstuck, now you have more choices."
Plan A ➔ Plan B	The problem is the plan, not the child. Bad plans just need a Plan B. • "What is our Plan B?" • "You always think of great plans."
Compromise	Both people have to be flexible to compromise. • "Let's compromise so we both get some of what we want." • "Something is better than nothing."
Big Deal/Little Deal	Do not tell a child his or her big deal is a little deal. • "How can we **turn** this big deal into a little deal? Let's make a plan."
Choice/No Choice	Remember poor choices are still choices; reserve "No Choice" for taxes, fire drills, etc. • "You have a choice. Let's look at all of your choices."

Goal What and **Why**? ➔ **Plan** How do we do it? ➔ **Do** Try it! ➔ **Check** How did it go?

TOPIC 6

Topic 6 Progress Report

Student Name: ______________________________ Date: ____________________________________

Teacher Name: ____

Unstuck and On Target Skills	**All of the time**	**Some of the time**	**None of the time**
1. Follows the Code of Conduct			
2. Is able to create a Goal, Why, Plan, Do, Check plan			
3. Is able to explain how s/he feels			
4. Is able to identify how their actions might make others feel			
5. Is able to define/ identify if an item is physically flexible or rigid			
6. Is able to define what it means to be flexible with your mind			
7. Is able to define what it means to be Stuck			
8. Is able to create a Plan A and Plan B before an event or activity			
9. Is able to create a Plan B in the moment (i.e., during an event when Plan A fails)			
10. Is able to define what Compromise means, or provide examples of a Compromise			
11. Is able to come up with a Compromise in a moment of challenge			
12. Using a made-up situation, is able to identify ways to change a Big Deal into a Little Deal			
13. Is able to use strategies to change a Big Deal into a Little Deal in the moment of challenge			
14. Is able to identify something that is a Choice and something that is not a Choice			
15. Is able to identify a strategy to use to help them cope when something Unexpected happens			
16. Is able to identify how it feels to be Stuck			
17. Is able to identify that being Stuck means they don't have choices/ options			
18. Is able to identify that being Flexible means they have choices			
19. Is able to identify the positives of having a Flexible reputation with friends and teachers			
A success in group:			
Something we will continue to work on:			

X ____ (Teacher)

(please detach and returned the signed slip, acknowledging you have received the progress report)

- -

I have received the *Unstuck and On Target!* Progress Report

X ____________________________________ Date:______________

Appendix

HOW EDUCATORS, STUDENTS, AND PARENTS HELPED US WRITE THIS MANUAL

We were first inspired to develop this manual by the work of Mark Ylvisaker and Tim Feeney (Feeney, 2010; Ylvisaker, 2006; Ylvisaker & Feeney, 1998). Working with children with brain injuries, they created key self-regulatory scripts and routines that we have used and modified in the course of developing *Unstuck and On Target*! The "Big Deal/ Little Deal" and "Choice/No Choice" scripts that we introduce in Topic 3 come directly from their work, as do the concepts underlying the "Handling the Unexpected" script. The "Goal, Why, Plan, Do, Check" script described in Topic 1 is also inspired by them, as well as Polatajko and Mandich (2004), who incorporated Goal-Plan-Do-Check in their occupational therapy intervention. In fact, prior to his untimely death, Mark Ylvisaker was a key early member of the *Unstuck and On Target!* team. His guidance and support for this project included many readings of early drafts and conversations regarding the use of self-regulatory scripts and the importance of building internal motivation in children.

Building on the work of Ylvisaker, Feeney, and others, we developed the manual and materials for *Unstuck and On Target!* through a community-based, participatory approach (Brooke et al., 1986; Israel, Schulz, Parker, & Becker, 1998), which involves engagement with community and policy partners, and development and testing of the intervention in collaboration with key community stakeholders, such as teachers, parents, and students (Centers for Disease Control and Prevention, 1999). We also used a bottom-up approach (Sullivan et al., 2005): Instead of developing the intervention in the lab and *then* adapting it to actual settings, we started with the effective techniques that front-line educators were already using to build executive functioning.

Our research team included academic researchers (a clinical and developmental psychologist, and a neuropsychologist), a special educator, two school administrators, an occupational therapist, a parent, and self-advocates. The development and feedback process then proceeded through a series of stages built on the participatory approach which included: observations of master teachers to identify effective strategies; needs assessments and focus groups with teachers, parents and students; and a small trial of *Unstuck and On Target!* followed by modification of the curriculum to address student and educator concerns and recommendations. This participatory process defined the curriculum's structure, delivery, and teaching methods, and ultimately helped us streamline the lessons. The resulting manual describes a curriculum designed for use in a weekly school-based group.

In summary, our approach to developing this intervention was a combination of a participatory process and a theory-driven method based on previously developed executive function interventions and our knowledge of the complex executive function deficits and effective intervention techniques. Because executive function deficits are primarily expressed, and best assessed, in real-world settings, such as classroom, home, and social settings, it was essential that we develop, test, and modify interventions in a real-world setting and that the interventions be administrable by teachers and other school personnel. Thus, we developed our intervention with a participatory model.

DOES *Unstuck and On Target!* WORK?

To date, we have completed two rigorous trials to evaluate the effectiveness of *Unstuck and On Target!* in third- through fifth-grade public elementary school settings. Together they indicate that *Unstuck and On Target!* improves classroom learning and behavior in students with ASD or with ADHD plus flexibility problems when compared to another intervention that was provided with the same "dose" (number of hours) of intervention for students and training for teachers and parents. In both studies, students were randomly assigned to the interventions, and the researchers were blind to intervention type (i.e., they did not know which intervention the students received). Treatment fidelity was generally high, meaning that the school-based staff who taught *Unstuck and On Target!* did a good job of presenting the material in the manual. It is interesting to note that the intervention is robust to imperfect fidelity, as positive outcomes for students were not dependent on high fidelity. The first study (Kenworthy, Anthony, et al., 2014) was funded by the National Institutes of Mental Health, grant number R34MH083053-01A2, the Isadore and Bertha Gudelsky Family Foundation, and the Organization for Autism Research. It compared two groups of students with ASD without intellectual disability who were equivalent in age, sex ratio, race, intelligence, autism symptoms, medication status, and parent education. One group received the *Unstuck and On Target! Research Edition,* intervention and the other group received a social skills intervention (Baker, 2003). Both groups improved, but the average amount of improvement for the *Unstuck and On Target!* group was significantly greater than for the social skills group, as measured by classroom observations of the students' ability to make transitions, follow rules, and be flexible. The *Unstuck and On Target!* group also made more improvement on average than the social skills group on direct child measures requiring problem solving, flexibility, and planning.

We recently finished the second, larger trial using the current version of *Unstuck and On Target!* (funded by Patient-Centered Outcomes Research Institute PCORI-1304-7379). We are preparing the data from this trial for publication in a peer-reviewed journal. Third- through fifth-grade students in low-income schools (in which at least half of the students qualify for free or reduced-cost lunch) with ASD or ADHD plus flexibility problems were randomly assigned to receive *Unstuck and On Target!* or *Parents and Teachers Supporting Students (PATSS). PATSS* is a contingency-behavior management intervention adapted to be accessible/empowering to the students, parents, and teachers (e.g., terminology was adjusted—*antecedent* was changed to *trigger;* students participated in the development of their behavior goals) and to specifically target flexibility and other executive function problems. Once again, we found that students with ASD who received *Unstuck and On Target!* showed more improvement in classroom learning and behavior than those who received the contingency behavior management intervention (PATSS), whereas students with ADHD responded well to both interventions. However, students and their parents reported that they liked *Unstuck and On Target!* more than PATSS. It is important to note that student change was **not** dependent on diagnosis, IQ, age, family income, racial/ethnic background, language spoken in the home, profession of the school staff who ran the groups, amount of knowledge gained by the parents, or any other implementation factor that we measured. This trial confirms 1) that *Unstuck and On Target!* is a potent tool for improving flexibility and other executive functions that support availability for learning in the classroom in students with ASD and 2) also that it is effective beyond ASD—in this case, for children with ADHD.

TROUBLESHOOTING

Below you will find some frequently asked questions and suggestions for solutions to help you while you are implementing the lessons.

Question: How do I manage when students try to take over or disrupt the lessons?

- ***Prevent negativity by maintaining a positive climate in the group lessons.*** This may be the single most powerful message in this book! Just as you teach your students that their behavior has consequences, remember that your mood and behavior have consequences, too. Happiness, sadness, anxiety, and frustration are all contagious. Your actions and mood have a profound effect on the students' actions and moods. Positive feelings from you will create more positive feelings in the student. Negative feelings (expressed in disapproval, yelling, threatening, punishing) from you will increase negative feelings and behaviors in the child. This creates a negative cycle.
- ***Maintain a 5:1 ratio of praise to correction.*** Research shows that praising children or making positive statements at least four times more often than giving commands or reprimands is effective at reducing behavioral problems and improving social skills. Praise should be specific and true (e.g., "I like how you are being flexible about where you sit today" or " "I can see that you are working hard on this project."). It can be a visual sign such as a thumbs up, and it can be directed at the whole group (e.g., "Wow. You guys are doing a great job listening today"). Make sure you are using the reinforcement system frequently.
- ***Use humor to keep the tone of the lessons lighthearted and fun.*** Humor is a powerful tool to keep the tone of lessons positive and fun and it also can help many children when they are getting stuck. Obviously humor is not used at another person's expense, but it can be effective when directed at a situation (e.g., "Oh man! I think we might be breaking a record. Each and every one of us is getting stuck at once!" or "Let's think of some more examples of compromise, if I come to school in my clown suit and red clown nose, and you say you hate clowns, is it a compromise if I take the nose off but leave the suit on?").
- ***Sometimes you can co-opt a negative student by agreeing with him or her.*** For example, if a student doesn't like a game or activity, say, "Yeah, this is kind of lame, how could we change it to make it more fun?" Or if a student complains that he or she is too tired to work today, say "You are right, I feel *completely exhausted* myself, shall we do jumping jacks or a super fast lightning round to wake us up?"
- ***Use visuals.*** Make sure that points for positive behavior are awarded in a visual, systematic way, such as on a chart or with a tangible reward, and counted frequently throughout the day.

Question: How do I keep my students engaged?

- ***Use examples that are relevant to your students to make the lesson content more meaningful.*** We are all inherently more interested in a topic that we care about or when the personal relevance is obvious. We have created lessons with examples and scenarios that we hope would be universally applicable. See if you can think of scenarios or examples from your students' lives it will make the information and strategies inherently more meaningful. For example, if your students are interested in a certain video game or there is a particular movie that they are excited about—weave those characters and themes into your examples. If you know students gravitate towards certain activities or topics during free time or in the lunchroom, integrate those into your examples. Use an example from your own life. Without divulging too much of your personal life, throw in an example from your own life every once in a while. Students are always struck to find out that we have lives outside of the school walls and encouraged to find out we use the strategies in our own lives.
- ***Highlight the "why."*** Throughout this intervention we are explicitly teaching skills that do not necessarily come naturally to students with executive dysfunction. Your students may not immediately see the importance of the skill they are learning to their lives. Make this explicit. Highlight "why" the skill you are teaching is helpful to them.
- ***Build positive momentum by pacing the lesson well, emphasizing the activities your students enjoy most and praising their effort.*** Monitor the pace of the lesson. Keep it moving and be mindful to not lecture. The activities have been designed to be hands on. Throughout the course of the intervention you will find the activities that your students like best, feel free to alter the presentation of an activity to cater to their preferences (e.g., your students may love role plays, or games). Make sure you frequently praise and acknowledge their efforts—we are all more motivated to continue to demonstrate a certain behavior or put forth effort when we see that our efforts are acknowledged.

Question: How do I avoid power struggles?

- ***Model flexibility for the student.*** When a student is getting upset, it is important for you to use your own coping strategies and keep a "clear mind" in order to help him or her. Remember, the student requires your clear and calm cue in order to use a coping strategy. If everyone "loses it," the coping strategies will be forgotten. See the Flexible, Organized and Supportive Educator section of the Introduction to this manual for more ideas.
- ***Use the scripts and coping strategies to back out of a power struggle.*** The process of building the habit of using coping strategies takes persistence and patience. Bring in scripts as needed, discussing key concepts like "flexibility" and creating a Plan A → Plan B. If you have covered compromise and negotiation in Topic 2, use some of those strategies to solve power struggles. You may say to a student, "It seems like we are both having problems with flexibility. Let's both be flexible and meet each other halfway," or "It seems like you might not have a lot of energy to be flexible today, so I can be flexible and do it your way this time."
- ***Don't overload the student with expectations she or he can't meet.*** Be cognizant of demands that might cause the students to become overloaded and shutdown. In those situations, your expectations for what the students should do should match his or her capabilities and skill set. Gradually increase flexibility demands as students become more competent in their skill set. See the Flexible, Organized and Supportive Educator section of the Introduction to this manual for more ideas about priming and other flexibility supports you can use in the classroom.
- ***Let the student make as many choices as possible.*** This does not mean that you turn over control in all situations, but rather that you provide choices within the structure of your agenda for the lesson. For example, "Do you want to hand out these papers or write on the board?"

- ***Provide a buffer from or reduce stimulation and disorder if the student seems overwhelmed.*** Some students are sensitive to noise and shouldn't sit near a noisy doorway or a particularly active, intrusive classmate; others need a set period of downtime at school each day when they don't have to interact with other people. If a student regularly comes to your lessons completely wound up, discuss with the team if he or she needs a break earlier in the day.
- ***When a student's behavior is escalating, talk less and use visuals to communicate.*** Some students respond almost magically well when a request is written as opposed to spoken. Keep a whiteboard handy and experiment with this technique if you have a student who is regularly resisting your requests. If a student is getting stuck on a negative interaction with you or another student consider drawing a quick flowchart to replay a problematic scenario and then rewrite it the way he or she wishes it had gone. Built into these flowcharts is a logical progression that visually demonstrates that the problem scenario did not result in the outcome the child wanted.

Question: How can I get my students to use the *Unstuck* scripts outside of the lessons?

- ***Practice, practice, practice.*** Research tells us that in order for a skill to become automatic or routine we need repeated exposures or practice opportunities. As with any skill your students learn (reading, writing, athletic endeavor, social learning scripts, etc.) the more opportunities they have to practice and try the skill in multiple settings, the more likely they are to be able to use the skills and strategies independently and effectively.
- ***Post visual reminders of the scripts in as many places as possible.*** The most important visual to remind teachers, therapists, parents and others to use the scripts is a list of the scripts.
- ***Make sure all the adults who work the students know the scripts.*** To help students generalize these skills we need to share the scripts and strategies with as many people as possible. If all of the student's therapists, parents, other teachers, etc. that support your students day in and day out are aware and understand the scripts, they can help the students use them and prompt for them when necessary. Throughout the manual we have provided several documents for you to disseminate to those people who can help your students practice using the skills and scripts—we encourage you to customize these documents and make them your own—add information about when and where these scripts have been helpful.
- ***Casting a wide net of support can be as easy as drafting a quick email or document defining the scripts and giving brief examples of how and when to use them.*** Better yet, establish an email chain with the individuals who interact with your students. As you introduce a new script send off a quick email with a description of the script and a brief suggestion for how they can use it. Here is a sample email you could send:

  We just learned about compromise. We think about compromise as a way for everyone to get part of what they want. When the opportunity presents itself, help our guys think about what compromising strategy they'd like to use: each person gets part of what he or she wants, combine ideas, choose a different idea that both people agree on, or take turns.

  Please shoot me an e-mail if you notice or have any experience helping our students come up with a compromise. We will be sure to celebrate it in class!

- ***Let students know you are sharing this information with the people in their world.*** Knowing that others will be supporting them in using these strategies and scripts will offer comfort as they can anticipate a predictable and routine approach to working on those skills that are most difficult for them.

Question: Some of the words/scripts seem to really annoy one of my students. How important is it for me to stick to the scripts?

- ***Don't give up too quickly.*** The scripts and key phrases are an integral component of this intervention. Remember that this is a new skill for your student, and change is not his or her specialty. Keep trying to use the words.
- ***If you decide that the student is truly stuck then consider whether collaborating with him or her to pick a new script might help.*** Students may react negatively to a word or phrase if they have learned to associate it with a negative experience or outcome. For example, a students may become "allergic" to the script "flexible" if it has been used negatively (e.g., "Stop throwing a tantrum, you need to be more flexible!" or "Why can't you just be more flexible, you're making this hard for everyone"). If a student becomes truly allergic to a word or script, choose another word to use in its place that conveys a similar meaning. Be sure that the chosen word or phrase is used frequently and consistently and is shared with others (e.g., other teachers, parents) so they can use it with the student as well.

Question: How do I get through the whole lesson when it seems we always run out of time?

- ***Be proactive in heading off "off-target" conversation by using scripts.*** You can ask the group if it is getting "stuck" on a detail or a little deal.
- ***Delay off-track discussions that are nonetheless important to a group member to the end of the lesson.*** You can write the topic raised by the student on the board and say you will come back to it when you finish the lesson material. If it is something the whole group likes to talk about, you can even use it as a reward for getting through the lesson with 5 minutes to spare.
- ***Post times next to each step of the GWPDC for the day.*** Say that the group has 10 minutes to complete this activity and time them to see if they can get it done on time.
- ***Use your judgment if one part of a lesson is taking longer than expected, but you think it is valuable.*** You can decide to cut another activity out if the students are really getting a lot out of something and you don't want to cut it short. You may have to look ahead to the next couple of lessons to decide what to skip.

Question: My students are finding some of the concepts too hard. How do I help them understand?

- ***Modify lessons to make them accessible to your students.*** Each lesson comes with a Summary and a Goal, which underscore the key components of the intervention. Using this resource as a foundation, it is advisable to modify lessons and activities based on individual skill sets of students. To make the materials relevant to the students, you may want to consider whether students have foundational skills necessary to understand a concept. For example, if a student is having difficulty understanding why it is important to compromise on choosing an activity, check to see whether that student understands that his peers may have a different opinion on what constitutes a fun activity. In this case, you may have to teach this foundational skill and then move forward with the lesson. The following strategies may also be helpful.

- ***Use more visuals.*** Some students, particularly those who have difficulty with language comprehension, benefit greatly from the use of added visuals to illustrate ambiguous concepts. Use pictures, movies, or acting to illustrate concepts and engage students. Having a whiteboard with you on which you can make simple drawings quickly is helpful. For example, if a student doesn't understand the concept of Big Deal, Little Deal you could draw an old fashioned scale of justice type scale and show how Big Deals weigh it down, but Little Deals don't.
- ***Do more role-plays.*** When teaching new concepts, employing the use of role-plays can really get students engaged in learning. Children with executive dysfunction have difficulty translating learned concepts into skills they use on a daily basis. Using role-plays can help children generalize these skills to other settings as well as make abstract concepts more concrete.
- ***Use relevant examples.*** Consider using a student's interests to illustrate concepts. For example, if a student has a particular interest in video games, you might incorporate this interest into developing Plan B scenarios (e.g., "You invite a friend over, but they don't want to play the same video game as you do. How can you be flexible and come up with a Plan B?").

Question: My students are finding the language or concepts too easy or over-simplified. How do I increase the challenge?

- ***Engage the students who find the material easy in mentoring those who do not.*** Usually not all the students in a group find the material easy even if some do. In that case, it is effective to have those who are grasping the concepts quickly teach those who are not. Often different students will find different concepts easy or hard.
- ***If the group as a whole is mastering the concepts quickly you can shorten activities and fill up the time with a focus on generalizing the skills to other settings and increasing independent application of the skills.*** Get the students to come up with 3 times when they will use the skill they have just learned outside of group in the next week. Play games and activities that provide less direct structure to the students and demand more active problem solving on their part.

Question: What do I do if my students don't like an activity?

- ***Assess whether it's too hard and they actually don't understand it.*** See the "My students are finding some concepts too hard" entry above for suggestions if this is the case.
- ***Use your own judgment.*** Just like with the scripts, it may be that your students are averse to a specific activity. You're the teacher, you know them best, feel free to change the activity while keeping the goal of the activity in mind.
- ***Assess whether the problem is a specific activity or a generally negative mindset in the group.*** If your students are objecting to lots of the activities in the curriculum, then see How do I keep my students engaged? and How do I manage when students try to take over or disrupt the lessons? above.

REFERENCES

Baker, J. (2003). *Social skills training for children and adolescents with asperger syndrome and social-communications problems.* Shawnee, KS: Autism Asperger Publishing Co.

Brooke, R.H., Chassin, M.R., Fink, A., Solomon, D.H., Kosecoff, J., & Park, R.E. (1986). A method for the detailed assessment of the appropriateness of medical technologies. *International Journal Technology Assessment in Health Care, 2,* 53–63.

Centers for Disease Control and Prevention. (1999). Framework for program evaluation in public health. *MMWR, 48* (No. RR-11).

Feeney, T.J. (2010). Structured flexibility: The use of context-sensitive self-regulatory scripts to support young persons with acquired brain injury and behavioral difficulties. *Journal of Head Trauma Rehabilitation, 25,* 416–425.

Gilotty, L., Kenworthy, L., Black, D., Wagner, A., & Sirian, L. (2002). Adaptive skills and executive function in Asperger's syndrome and autism. *Child Neuropsychology, 8,* 90–101.

Gioia, G., Isquith, P., Guy, S., & Kenworthy, L. (2015). *Behavior Rating Inventory of Executive Function, Section Edition (BRIEF-2).* Odessa, FL: Psychological Assessment Resources.

Israel, B.A., Schulz, A.J., Parker, E.A., & Becker, A.B. (1998). Review of community-based research: Assessing partnership approaches to improve public health. *Annual Review of Public Health, 19,* 173–202.

Kenworthy, L., Anthony, L.G., Naiman, D.Q., Cannon, L., Wills, M.C., Werner, M.A., . . . Wallace, G.L. (2014). Executive function versus social skills interventions for children on the autism spectrum: An effectiveness trial. *Journal of Child Psychology and Psychiatry.* doi: 10.1111/jcpp.12161

Kenworthy, L., Black, D., Wallace, G., Ahluvalia, T., Wagner, A., & Sirian, L. (2005). Disorganization: The forgotten executive dysfunction in autism spectrum disorders. *Developmental Neuropsychology, 28,* 809–827.

Kenworthy, L.,Yerys, B.E., Anthony, L., & Wallace, G.L. (2008). Understanding executive control in autism spectrum disorders in the lab and in the real world. *Neuropsychology Review, 18,* 320–338.

Kunce, L., & Mesibov, G.B. (1998). Educational approaches to high-functioning autism and Asperger syndrome. In E. Schopler, G.B. Mesibov, & L. Kunce (Eds.), *Asperger syndrome or high-functioning autism?* (p. 231). New York, NY: Plenum Press.

Murphy, D.G.M., Critchley, H.D., Schmitz, N., McAlonan, G., van Amelsvoort, T., Robertson, D., . . . Howlin, P. (2002). Asperger syndrome: A proton magnetic resonance spectroscopy study of brain. *Archives of General Psychiatry,* 59, 885–891.

Polatajko, H., & Mandich, A. (2004). *Enabling occupation in children: The cognitive orientation to daily occupational performance (CO-OP) approach.* Ottawa, ON, Canada: CAOT Publications.

Stein, M.A., Szumowski, E., Blondis, T.A., & Roizen, N.J. (1995), Adaptive skills dysfunction in ADD and ADHD children. Journal of Child Psychology and Psychiatry, 36:663–670

Sullivan, G., Duan, N., Mukherjee, S., Kirchner, J., Perry, D., & Henderson, K. (2005). The role of services researchers in facilitating intervention research. *Psychiatric Services, 56,* 537–542.

Teuber, H.L. (1964). The riddle of frontal lobe function in man. In J.M. Warren & K. Akert (Eds.), *The frontal granular cortex and behavior* (pp. 410–477). New York, NY: McGraw-Hill.

Ylvisaker, M. (2006). *Tutorial: Self-regulation/executive function routines after TBI.* Available on The Brain Injury Association of New York State web site: http://www.projectlearnet.org/tutorials/sr_ef_routines.html

Ylvisaker, M., & Feeney, T.J. (1998). *Collaborative brain injury intervention: Positive everyday routines.* San Diego, CA: Singular Publishing.

Index

Page numbers followed by *t* indicate tables.

Activity
Big Deal / Little Deal Practice, 148–150
Build a Plan A, B, C, 124–125
Cereal, 223–224
Choice / No Choice Practice, 162–164
Code of Conduct, 28–29
Compromise Game, 135–137
Converting Big Deals to Little Deals, 151–152
Coping Choices, 77–78
Coping Skills Investigation, 70–74
Disappointment and Coping, 68–69
Expect the Unexpected Introduction, 170
Flexibility Freeway Game, 188–196
Flexibility Powers, 202–203
As Flexible as Putty, 97–100
Flexible Is Faster, 87
Flexible Reputation, 204–207
Flexible / Stuck Role Play, 110
Goal, Why, Plan, Do, Check (GWPDC) Introduction, 42–43
GWPDC Stations (optional), 234–244
Handling the Unexpected Exploration, 171–175
Mystery Word—Big Deal / Little Deal, 144–147
Mystery Word—Choice / No Choice, 158–161
Mystery Word—Compromise, 131–134
Mystery Word—Flexibility, 93–96
Mystery Word—Plan A / Plan B, 118–122
Mystery Word—Stuck, 106–109
Plan B Strategies, 232–233
Planning a Class Event, 251–252
Rigid Scavenger Hunt, 86
Speed B, 123
Strategy Cards, 75–76
Think Pink—GWPDC, 216–217
Wacky GWPDC, 44–45
What is a Target Goal, 225–226
What to Do When What I Want Is Impossible, 184–187
Who Knows Whom, 30

ADHD, *see* Attention-deficit / hyperactivity disorder
Advantages of Being Flexible lesson
Classroom Practice for, 198
Flexibility Freeway Game activity in, 188–196
Home Practice for, 199
Lightning Round questions for, 183
preview for, 183
purpose of, 182
review for, 197
What to Do When What I Want Is Impossible activity in, 184–187
All About Me handout, 31
As Flexible as Putty activity, 97–100
ASD, *see* Autism spectrum disorder
Attention-deficit / hyperactivity disorder (ADHD), 1, 5, 274–275
Autism Self-Advocacy Network, 4
Autism spectrum disorder (ASD), 1, 259, 274–275

Being Flexible Can Make Good Things Happen lesson
Classroom Practice for, 209
Flexibility Powers activity in, 202–203
Flexible Reputation activity in, 204–207
Home Practice for, 210
Lightning Round questions for, 201
preview for, 201
purpose of, 200
review for, 208
Big Deal / Little Deal, 36, 38
icon for, 17, 36, 38
script for, 36, 38, 115, 116, 273
script practice for, 20
Unstuck and On Target! Dictionary handout for, 147
Big Deal / Little Deal lesson
Big Deal / Little Deal Practice activity in, 148–150
Classroom Practice for, 154
Converting Big Deals to Little Deals activity in, 151–152

Big Deal/Little Deal lesson—*continued*
game cards for, 149–150
handouts for, 145–147, 152
Home Practice for, 155
Lightning Round questions for, 142
Mystery Word—Big Deal/Little Deal activity in, 144–147
preview for, 142
purpose of, 141
review for, 153
Build a Plan A, B, C activity, 124–125
Build a Plan A, B, C handout, 125

Cereal activity, 223–224
Choice/No Choice, 36, 38
icon for, 17, 36, 38
script for, 36, 38, 115, 116, 273
script practice for, 20
Unstuck and On Target! Dictionary handout for, 161
Choice/No Choice lesson
Choice/No Choice Practice activity in, 162–164
Classroom Practice for, 166
game cards for, 163–164
handouts for, 159–161
Home Practice for, 167
Lightning Round questions for, 157
Mystery Word—Choice/No Choice activity in, 158–161
preview for, 157
purpose of, 156
review for, 165
Classroom Practice
for Advantages of Being Flexible lesson, 198
for Being Flexible Can Make Good Things Happen lesson, 209
for Big Deal/Little Deal lesson, 154
for Choice/No Choice lesson, 166
for Compromise lesson, 139
for Emotional Identification lesson, 63
for Event Planning lesson, 254
for Expect the Unexpected lesson, 177
for Flexibility Investigation lesson, 89
for Flexibility lesson, 102
for Get to Know You lesson, 34–36
for Getting Stuck lesson, 112
for Goal, Why, Plan, Do, Check (GWPDC) introduction lesson, 47
for GWPDC Application and Practice lesson, 228
for GWPDC Stations lesson, 247
handout for, 2
for Interview lesson, 269
for Plan A/Plan B lesson, 127
for Setting and Achieving Goals Using GWPDC lesson, 219
for What Can You Do to Feel Better lesson, 80
Coach, social, 8
Code of Conduct, 25
Code of Conduct activity, 28–29
Completion handout, 268
Compromise
icon for, 17, 36, 38
script for, 36, 38
script practice for, 21
self-regulatory script for, 115, 116
Unstuck and On Target! Dictionary handout for, 134
Compromise lesson
Classroom Practice for, 139
Compromise Game activity in, 135–137
game cards for, 137
handouts for, 132–134
Home Practice for, 140
Lightning Round questions for, 130
Mystery Word—Compromise activity in, 131–134
preview for, 130
purpose of, 129
review for, 138
Compromise Station handouts, 238–239
Congratulations handout, 268
Converting Big Deals to Little Deals activity, 151–152
Coping Choices activity, 77–78
Coping Skills Investigation activity, 70–74

Deep Breathing handout, 74
Disappointment and Coping activity, 68–69
Disappointment and Coping handout, 69
Distractor game cards, 241–242
Distractor Game Tracking Sheet, 243

Educator
manual written with help from, 273–274
positive versus negative responses from, 9*t*
supportive, 9–11
Effectiveness, manual, trials in evaluation of, 274–275
Emotional Identification lesson
Classroom Practice for, 63
Feelings Chain activity in, 57–61
Feelings Target activity in, 52–55
Home Practice for, 64
How Does It Make Me Feel activity in, 56
preview for, 50–51
purpose of, 49
review for, 62
Environment, supportive, 7–8
Event lesson, purpose of, 256
Event Planning lesson
Classroom Practice for, 254
Home Practice for, 255
Lightning Round questions for, 250
Planning a Class Event activity in, 251–252
preview for, 250
purpose of, 249
review for, 253
Executive function
definition of, 3–4
examples of, 3–4
Expect the Unexpected
script practice for, 21
self-regulatory script for, 115, 116
Expect the Unexpected lesson
Classroom Practice for, 177
Expect the Unexpected Introduction activity in, 170
game cards for, 174–175

Handling the Unexpected Exploration activity in, 171–175
Home Practice for, 178
Lightning Round questions for, 169
preview for, 169
purpose of, 168
review for, 176

Feelings Chain activity, 57–61
Feelings Target activity, 52–55
Flexibility
definition of, 4
in educator, 9–11
as executive function, 3
icon for, 17, 36, 38
script for, 36, 38
script practice for, 19–20
Unstuck and On Target! Dictionary handout for, 96
see also How to Be Flexible topic; What Is Flexibility topic
Flexibility Freeway Game activity
game board, 190
game cards for, 191–196
game rules, 189
instructions, 188
Flexibility Investigation lesson
Classroom Practice for, 89
Flexible Is Faster activity in, 87
Home Practice for, 90
Lightning Round questions for, 85
preview for, 85
purpose of, 84
review for, 88
Rigid Scavenger Hunt activity in, 86
Flexibility lesson
Classroom Practice for, 102
As Flexible as Putty activity in, 97–100
handouts for, 94–96, 99–100
Home Practice for, 103
Lightning Round questions for, 92
Mystery Word—Flexibility activity in, 93–96
preview for, 92
purpose of, 91
review for, 101
Flexibility Powers activity, 202–203
Flexible Fun handout, 99
Flexible Futures handout, 263–264
Flexible Is Faster activity, 87
Flexible Reputation activity, 204–207
Flexible/Goal-Directed Futures topic
Interview lesson in, 260–270
Progress Report for, 271
summary of, 259
Flexible/Stuck Role Play activity, 110
Foundational Skills topic
background and rationale for, 23–24
criteria for mastery of, 23
Emotional Identification lesson in, 49–64
Get to Know You lesson in, 25–38
Goal, Why, Plan, Do, Check (GWPDC) introduction lesson in, 39–48
Progress Report for, 82
summary of, 23
What Can You Do to Feel Better lesson in, 65–81
Four Corners activity, 265–266
Fun Putty Recipe handout, 100

Game cards
Big Deal/Little Deal, 149–150
Choice/No Choice Practice, 163–164
Compromise, 137
Distractor, 241–242
Handling the Unexpected Exploration, 174–175
Strategy Cards, 75–76
Get to Know You lesson
All About Me handout in, 31
Classroom Practice for, 34–36
Code of Conduct activity in, 28–29
Home Practice for, 37–39
preview for, 26–27
purpose of, 25
review for, 32–33
Who Knows Whom activity in, 30
Getting Stuck lesson
Classroom Practice for, 112
Flexible/Stuck Role Play activity in, 110
handouts for, 107–109
Home Practice for, 113
Lightning Round questions for, 105
Mystery Word—Stuck activity in, 106–109
preview for, 105
purpose of, 104
review for, 111
Goal, Why, Plan, Do, Check (GWPDC), 2
Application and Practice lesson using, 221–229
foundational skills mastery for, 23
icon for, 17, 36, 38
script for, 36, 38
script practice for, 19
Setting and Achieving Goals Using, 214–220
Stations lesson using, 230–248
Goal, Why, Plan, Do, Check (GWPDC) introduction activity, 42–43
Goal, Why, Plan, Do, Check (GWPDC) introduction lesson
Classroom Practice for, 47
Home Practice for, 48
introduction activity in, 42–43
Lightning Round questions for, 41
preview for, 40–41
purpose of, 39
review for, 46
Wacky GWPDC activity in, 44–45
Group goal, example in reinforcement system of, 14
GWPDC, *see* Goal, Why, Plan, Do, Check (GWPDC)
GWPDC Application and Practice lesson
Cereal activity in, 223–224
Classroom Practice for, 228
Home Practice for, 229
Lightning Round questions for, 222
preview for, 222
purpose of, 221
review for, 227
What is a Target Goal activity in, 225–226

GWPDC Stations lesson
- Classroom Practice for, 247
- Distractor game cards in, 241–242
- GWPDC Stations optional activity in, 234–244
- handouts in, 236–244
- Home Practice for, 248
- Lightning Round questions for, 231
- Plan B Strategies activity in, 232–233
- preview for, 231
- purpose of, 230
- review for, 246

Handling the Unexpected Exploration activity
- game board, 173
- game cards for, 174–175
- game rules, 172
- instructions, 171

Handouts
- All About Me, 31
- Big Deal / Little Deal Scale, 152
- Build a Plan A, B, C, 125
- Classroom Practice, 2
- Completion, 268
- Congratulations, 268
- Deep Breathing, 74
- Disappointment and Coping, 69
- Flexible Fun, 99
- Flexible Futures, 263–264
- Fun Putty Recipe, 100
- Home Practice, 2
- How to Feel Just-Right, 71
- Just-Right Strategies Investigation, 72
- My Mission to Get Back to Just-Right, 73
- Mystery Word—Big Deal / Little Deal, 145–146
- Mystery Word—Choice / No Choice, 159–160
- Mystery Word—Compromise, 132–133
- Mystery Word—Flexibility, 94–95
- Mystery Word—Plan A / Plan B, 120–121
- Mystery Word—Stuck, 107–108
- Think Pink—GWPDC, 217
- *Unstuck and On Target!* Dictionary, 96, 109, 122, 134, 147, 161

Home Practice
- for Advantages of Being Flexible lesson, 199
- for Being Flexible Can Make Good Things Happen lesson, 210
- for Big Deal / Little Deal lesson, 155
- for Choice / No Choice lesson, 167
- for Compromise lesson, 140
- for Emotional Identification lesson, 64
- for Event Planning lesson, 255
- for Expect the Unexpected lesson, 178
- for Flexibility Investigation lesson, 90
- for Flexibility lesson, 103
- for Get to Know You lesson, 37–39
- for Getting Stuck lesson, 113
- for Goal, Why, Plan, Do, Check (GWPDC) introduction lesson, 48
- for GWPDC Application and Practice lesson, 229
- for GWPDC Stations lesson, 248
- handout for, 2
- for Interview lesson, 270
- for Plan A / Plan B lesson, 128
- for Setting and Achieving Goals Using GWPDC lesson, 220
- for What Can You Do to Feel Better lesson, 81

How Does It Make Me Feel activity, 56

How to Be Flexible topic
- background and rationale for, 115–116
- Big Deal / Little Deal lesson in, 141–155
- Choice / No Choice lesson in, 156–167
- Compromise lesson in, 129–140
- criteria for mastery of, 115
- Expect the Unexpected lesson in, 168–178
- Plan A / Plan B lesson in, 117–128
- Progress Report for, 179
- summary of, 115

How to Feel Just-Right handout, 71

Icon Glossary, 17, 36, 38

Implementation, prerequisites for successful, 7–11

Inhibition, as executive function, 3

Initiation, as executive function, 3

Interview lesson
- Classroom Practice for, 269
- Four Corners activity in, 265–266
- handouts in, 263–264, 268
- Home Practice for, 270
- preview for, 261
- purpose of, 260
- review for, 267
- Talk Show activity in, 262–264

Just-Right Strategies Investigation handout, 72

Lessons
- Advantages of Being Flexible, 182–199
- Being Flexible Can Make Good Things Happen, 200–210
- Big Deal / Little Deal, 141–155
- Choice / No Choice, 156–167
- Compromise, 129–140
- Emotional Identification, 49–64
- Event, 256
- Event Planning, 249–255
- Expect the Unexpected, 168–178
- Flexibility, 92–103
- Flexibility Investigation, 84–90
- Get to Know You, 25–38
- Getting Stuck, 104–113
- Goal, Why, Plan, Do, Check (GWPDC) Introduction, 39–48
- GWPDC Application and Practice, 221–229
- GWPDC Stations, 230–248
- Interview, 260–270
- Plan A / Plan B, 117–128
- Setting and Achieving Goals Using GWPDC, 214–220

troubleshooting running out of time for, 278
troubleshooting students disrupting, 275
troubleshooting using scripts outside of, 277–278
What Can You Do to Feel Better, 65–81

Memory, as executive function, 4
My Mission to Get Back to Just-Right handout, 73
Mystery Word—Big Deal / Little Deal activity, 144–147
Mystery Word—Big Deal / Little Deal handout, 145–146
Mystery Word—Choice / No Choice activity, 158–161
Mystery Word—Choice / No Choice handout, 159–160
Mystery Word—Compromise activity, 131–134
Mystery Word—Compromise handout, 132–133
Mystery Word—Flexibility activity, 93–96
Mystery Word—Flexibility handout, 94–95
Mystery Word—Plan A / Plan B activity, 118–122
Mystery Word—Plan A / Plan B handout, 120–121
Mystery Word—Stuck activity, 106–109
Mystery Word—Stuck handout, 107–108

Organization
definition of, 5
as executive function, 4
school team's role in, 9–11

Plan A / Plan B
icon for, 17, 36, 38
script for, 36, 38, 115, 116
script practice for, 20
Unstuck and On Target! Dictionary handout for, 122
Plan A / Plan B lesson
Build a Plan A, B, C activity in, 124–125
Classroom Practice for, 127
handouts for, 119–122, 125
Home Practice for, 128
Lightning Round questions for, 118
Mystery Word—Plan A / Plan B activity in, 118–122
preview for, 118
purpose of, 117
review for, 126
Speed B activity in, 123
Plan B Strategies activity, 232–233
Planning
definition of, 5
as executive function, 4
goal-directed, 6*t*
Planning a Class Event activity, 251–252

Reinforcement system
group goal example in, 14
system construct in, 13–14
troubleshooting in, 14–16
visuals in, 14–16
Research, manual written with help from, 273–274
Rigid Scavenger Hunt activity, 86

Safe person, 8
School team, supportive, 7–8
Script practice
for Big Deal / Little Deal, 20
for compromise, 21
for flexibility, 19–20
for Goal, Why, Plan, Do, Check (GWPDC), 19
for Plan A / Plan B, 20
for target goal, 21
Self-awareness and self-advocacy skills, 7
Self-monitoring, as executive function, 4
Self-regulatory scripts
Big Deal / Little Deal, 115, 116
Choice / No Choice, 115, 116
Compromise, 115, 116
development of, 273
Expect the Unexpected, 115, 116
Plan A / Plan B, 115, 116
Setting and Achieving Goals Using GWPDC lesson
Classroom Practice for, 219
handout in, 217
Home Practice for, 220
Lightning Round questions for, 215
preview for, 215
purpose of, 214
review for, 218
Think Pink—GWPDC activity in, 216–217
Speed B activity, 123
Strategy Cards activity, 75–76
Stuck
icon for, 17, 36, 38
script for, 36, 38
script practice for, 20
Unstuck and On Target! Dictionary handout for, 109
Support
from educator, 9–11
environmental features for, 7–8
from school team, 7–8
System construct, 13–14

Talk Show activity, 262–264
Target Goal
icon for, 17, 36, 38
script for, 36, 38
script practice for, 21
Think Pink—GWPDC
activity, 216–217
handout, 217
Troubleshooting
concepts too easy, 279
concepts too hard, 278–279
keep students engaged, 276
motivating students to behave, 14–15
power struggle avoidance, 276–277
reinforcing prize selection, 15
rewards as bribe, 16
running out of time for lesson, 278
students disrupt lessons, 275
students don't like activity, 279

Troubleshooting—*continued*
using scripts outside of lessons, 277–278
words/scripts annoy student, 278

Unstuck and On Target! Dictionary handout
Big Deal/Little Deal, 147
Choice/No Choice, 161
Compromise, 134
Flexibility, 96
Plan A/Plan B, 122
Stuck, 109

Wacky GWPDC activity, 44–45
What Can You Do to Feel Better lesson
Classroom Practice for, 80
Coping Choices activity in, 77–78
Coping Skills Investigation activity in, 70–74
Disappointment and Coping activity in, 68–69
handouts for, 69, 71–74
Home Practice for, 81
Lightning Round questions for, 67
purpose of, 65
review for, 66–67, 79
Strategy Cards activity in, 75–76
What is a Target Goal activity, 225–226
What Is Flexibility topic
background and rationale for, 83
criteria for mastery of, 83
Flexibility Investigation lesson in, 84–90
Flexibility lesson in, 92–103
Getting Stuck lesson in, 104–113
Progress Report for, 114
summary of, 83
What to Do When What I Want Is Impossible activity, 184–187
Who Knows Whom activity, 30
Why Be Flexible topic
Advantages of Being Flexible lesson in, 182–199
background and rationale for, 181
Being Flexible Can Make Good Things Happen lesson in, 200–210
criteria for mastery of, 181
Progress Report for, 211
summary of, 181

Your Goals topic
background and rationale for, 213
criteria for mastery of, 213
Event lesson in, 256
Event Planning lesson in, 249–255
GWPDC Application and Practice lesson in, 221–229
GWPDC Stations lesson in, 230–248
Progress Report for, 257
Setting and Achieving Goals Using GWPDC lesson in, 214–220
summary of, 213